DESIGNS of our time

beazley
the **designs of the year**
DESIGN
MUSEUM

foreword

This book was published to celebrate the ten-year anniversary of *Designs of the Year* at the Design Museum. Starting in 2008, the exhibition is an annual review of the most innovative, relevant and thought-provoking projects in contemporary design.

The process starts with the vigilance of international designers, curators and critics who are alert to new developments in both their area of expertise and their region of the world. Their nominations are sent to the Design Museum, together with their reasons for why their chosen project deserves to be awarded. The shortlisted, nominated designs are then presented in an exhibition at the museum and, finally, to an independent jury who decide the year's winners. A design can win in its category – architecture, digital, fashion, graphics, product and transport – or it can win the overall award.

Over the past ten years, 840 projects have been selected by 205 nominators: 135 projects in architecture, 117 in digital, 92 in fashion, 145 in graphics, 276 in product and 76 in transport. This book brings this remarkable collection of designs together in one place.

The Design Museum is proud to partner with Beazley and greatly appreciates their support of *Beazley Designs of the Year*.

introduction

The idea that mundane objects can be the starting point for drawing wider conclusions has a long history. It's an attitude that is hinted at in Ernesto Rogers' suggestion that the architect needed to operate at the scale of the spoon as well as the city. The writer Phil Patton, for example, had written a 7000-word essay on the nature of the plastic lids from disposable coffee cups.
'Rolled out of polystyrene sheets, carefully crimped for strength, folded and lapped to fit snugly, scored and sculpted to provide flaps that come loose and look so we can sip on the go, these little discs are coinage of our sped-up society, airy wheels that are also testimony to the way we Americans differ from the rest of the world.' [1]
And then consider Reyner Banham, who, in three carefully crafted sentences, wrote the following about clipboards:
'Tread softly if you carry a big stick, but tread how you like if you carry a clipboard because no one dare question your authority. Few portable artefacts pack such symbolic power as this piece of plank with a bulldog clip at its top. Sceptre, sword and crozier may lose their way but the man with the clipboard commands instant respect.' [2]
While design is no longer marked out exclusively by objects, the digital explosion of the past decade can be understood using a similar approach. What can we make of the world of the present day, as represented by the hundreds of objects of all kinds, from architectural landmarks to refugee shelters, from websites to rehydration kits, which grace the pages of this book? The nominated designs for the *Designs of the Year* exhibition, now in its tenth year, were selected by the Design Museum and its collaborators, an international network of spotters in every field of design. While these projects were selected for their innovative contributions to design, seeing them together in this book conveys how the pace of change is radically accelerating.

It was Buckminster Fuller who once suggested that 'the best way to predict the future is to design it'. Steve Jobs certainly followed his advice when he marshalled all the resources of the not-yet-all-conquering Apple to produce the first iPhone in 2007. Jobs knew that he was offering the world more than a somewhat eccentric re-imagining of a mobile phone that many of us at first assumed it to be. Rather than following the path of established phone makers who were making ever smaller mobiles, Apple made one that was considerably larger than the norm, and had almost no physical buttons. In product design terms, it was a handbrake turn.

During the launch of the iPhone, Jobs teased his audience by suggesting that he was combining three different products into one: 'a widescreen iPod with touch controls, a revolutionary mobile phone and a breakthrough internet communications device'. That seemed like a slightly dubious multiplicity of attributes. A Swiss army penknife is equipped with scissors, magnifying glass and corkscrew, but you wouldn't necessarily use one to open a bottle of Chateau Margaux. But for once, for the iPhone, multiplicity was everything.

1 Phil Patton, *Top This and Other Parables of Design: Selected Writings by Phil Patton* (New York: Cooper Hewitt, 2016).

2 Reyner Banham, *A Critic Writes: Selected Essays by Reyner Banham*, eds. Mary Banham, Sutherland Lyall, Cedric Price and Paul Barker (Oakland: University of California Press, 1996).

Not many could have guessed that the iPhone was going to make Uber possible, a corporation which has utterly transformed the nature of public transport. Nobody predicted the rise of Airbnb, now a giant that has transformed tourism and the hotel industry. These are two developments that are blamed for a range of negative outcomes: everything from destroying jobs to undermining neighbourhoods. However, they are also credited with making daily life considerably more convenient for those who are able to use the services that they offer. For that matter, the smartphone can be seen as transforming politics: think about the digital lynch mob that is Twitter. And think about the way in which some of us now conduct our emotional lives, which have been transformed through dating apps downloaded to our mobile devices.

So if an object, which can fit comfortably into a pocket, can do all this in half a generation, where will we be in another ten years' time, given the accelerating pace of change?

As we know, there are billionaires in California who are planning on living to be 1,000 years old. Some of the same people are working on getting to Mars, with privately funded budget rockets using as many off-the-shelf components as possible. And like-minded algorithmic oligarchs are already buying presidential elections with their fortunes and their careful mining of data. Elon Musk, who is involved with the Martian adventure, is also aiming to overturn the conventional wisdoms about building, powering and marketing cars, up to and including printing them.

Designers work in the context of emerging technologies. For instance, the designer is the ringmaster for the various forms of artificial intelligence that will change our homes and our cities. Artificial intelligence that may kill off our love affair with cars. When a car drives itself, why would we measure our status or virility through it? As in so many areas, the middle is being squeezed out of existence. The future of furniture, for example, might well be defined by IKEA at one end, and by limited edition pieces at the other. For the automotive industry, the two poles could be the Google car, and a Ferrari.

Change is not just about the move, say, from the radicalism of the Memphis years in the 1980s to the cult of the ordinary as expressed by Jasper Morrison or Naoto Fukasawa. For example, the very idea of the designer as individual author – in the manner of Philippe Starck – is no longer something that a new generation of designers who prefer to work collaboratively are interested in. Of course it is a mood which may change again. But we are in a time when the invisible world of code that shapes digital design is not always easily associated with the work of a single individual. The idea of the socially responsible as a driving force for design is now impossible to ignore.

Design is a discipline that maintains its relevance by constantly changing its parameters. It is about the material as well as the digital, the social as well as the technical, the cultural as well as the commercial. In the midst of the gales of change, design's key responsibility is to underpin those human values that are always with us and by which we define ourselves.

DEYAN SUDJIC
Director, the Design Museum

architecture

Nembro Library
NEMBRO, ITALY

Designed by Laura Andreini, Marco Casamonti, Silvia Fabi,
Massimiliano Giberti, Gianna Parisse and Giovanni Polazzi
of Archea Associati for Nembro Municipality
NOMINATED BY FRANCESCA FERGUSON

Nordpark Railway Stations
INNSBRUCK, AUSTRIA

Designed by Zaha Hadid Architects for INKB (Innsbrucker Nordkettenbahnen GmbH) Public Private Partnership

NOMINATED BY HELEN EVENDEN

Chocolate Museum
TOLUCA, MEXICO

Designed by Michel Rojkind of Rojkind Arquitectos for Nestlé
NOMINATED BY FRANCESCA FERGUSON

The main stadium for the 2008 Olympic Games
BEIJING, CHINA

Designed by Herzog & de Meuron for National Stadium Co. Ltd, Beijing
NOMINATED BY DEYAN SUDJIC

category winner

Fahle House
TALLINN, ESTONIA

Designed by Raivo Kotov and Andrus Koesaar of KOKO Architects
for Koger & Partners
NOMINATED BY FRANCESCA FERGUSON

New Museum
NEW YORK, USA

Designed by Kazuo Sejima and Ryue Nishizawa
of SANAA for the New Museum
NOMINATED BY LUCY BULLIVANT, VICKY RICHARDSON AND TERENCE RILEY

BMW WELT
MUNICH, GERMANY

Designed by Coop Himmelb(l)au for BMW AG
NOMINATED BY TERENCE RILEY

East Beach Cafe
LITTLEHAMPTON, ENGLAND

Designed by Heatherwick Studio for Jane Wood at Brownfield Catering
NOMINATED BY FRANCESCA FERGUSON AND WAYNE HEMINGWAY

Hongluo Clubhouse
BEIJING, CHINA

Designed by MAD Architects and Ma Yansong
NOMINATED BY OU NING

Casa Levene Single Family House
SAN LORENZO DEL ESCORIAL, MADRID, SPAIN

Designed by Eduardo Arroyo of NO.MAD Arquitectos for Mr Richard Levene
NOMINATED BY OLE BOUMAN

Stephen Lawrence Centre
LEWISHAM, UK

Designed by Adjaye Associates for the Stephen Lawrence Charitable Trust
NOMINATED BY LUCY BULLIVANT

Castleford Bridge
CASTLEFORD, UK

Designed by McDowell + Benedetti for Wakefield Metropolitan District Council
NOMINATED BY LUCY BULLIVANT

CaixaForum
MADRID, SPAIN

Designed by Herzog & de Meuron for Obra Social Fundación 'LaCaixa' and Caixa d'Estalvis i Pensions de Barcelona; associate architects: Mateu i Bausells Arquitectura
NOMINATED BY CATHERINE INCE

Accordia Housing
CAMBRIDGE, UK

Designed by Feilden Clegg Bradley Studios, MaccreanorLavington
and Alison Brooks Architects for Countryside Properties (Accordia) Ltd
NOMINATED BY CATHERINE INCE

10x10 Low Cost Housing Project
CAPE TOWN, SOUTH AFRICA

Designed by Design Indaba for Interactive Africa/Design Indaba;
sponsored by PG Bison/Pennypinchers
NOMINATED BY PATRICK BURGOYNE

Westminster Academy
LONDON, UK

Designed by Allford Hall Monoghan Morris for Westminster Academy,
Department for Children, Schools and Families (DCSF),
Westminster City Council and Exilarch Foundation; sponsor:
Exilarch Foundation, David Dangoor; graphic designer: Studio Myerscough;
services, structure and landscape: BDP; quantity surveyor: Davis Langdon;
main contractor: Galliford Try; project manager: Capita Symonds
NOMINATED BY WAYNE HEMINGWAY

Spadina WaveDeck
TORONTO, CANADA

Designed by West 8 Urban Design & Landscape Architecture
and DTAH for Waterfront Toronto
NOMINATED BY LUCY BULLIVANT

Bubbletecture H
SAYO-CHO, HYÕGO PREFECTURE, JAPAN

Designed by Shuhei Endo Architects
NOMINATED BY FRANCESCA FERGUSON

Linked Hybrid
BEIJING, CHINA

Designed by Steven Holl Architects for Modern Green Development Co.
NOMINATED BY OU NING

KAIT Workshop

KANAGAWA INSTITUTE OF TECHNOLOGY, KANAGAWA-KU, YOKOHAMA, JAPAN

Designed by junya.ishigami+associates for Kanagawa Institute
of Technology; structural engineers: Konishi; technical engineers:
Kankyo Engineering; general contractors: Kajima Corporation
and Takasago Thermal Engineering Co.
NOMINATED BY FLAVIO ALBANESE

Eight Inscribed Houses and Three Courtyards
CANARY ISLANDS, SPAIN

Designed by Romera y Ruiz Arquitectos for Canary Islands Housing Institute
NOMINATED BY FRANCESCA FERGUSON

Norwegian National Opera and Ballet
OSLO, NORWAY

Designed by Snøhetta for Ministry of Church and Cultural Affairs;
integrated art by artists: Kristian Blystad, Kalle Grude, Jorunn Sannes
NOMINATED BY HENRIETTA THOMPSON

category winner

Sergio Cardell Plaza tram stop

ALICANTE, SPAIN

Designed by Subarquitectura for Ferrocarrils de la Generalitat Valenciana (FGV); structural design: Subarquitectura; contractor: ECISA + COMSA

NOMINATED BY CATHERINE INCE

Museum of Contemporary Art Denver
DENVER, USA

Designed by Adjaye Associates for Museum of Contemporary Art Denver;
architect of record: Davis Partnership
NOMINATED BY JULIE V. IOVINE

Hutong Bubble 32
BEIJING, CHINA

Designed by Ma Yansong and Dang Qun of MAD Architects; design team:
Dai Pu, Yu Kui, Stefanie Helga Paul, He Wei and Shen Jianghai
NOMINATED BY FRANCESCA FERGUSON

Neues Museum
BERLIN, GERMANY

Designed by David Chipperfield Architects and Julian Harrap Architects
for Stiftung Preußischer Kulturbesitz
NOMINATED BY CATHERINE INCE AND ELLIS WOODMAN

The High Line
NEW YORK, USA

Designed by James Corner Field Operations, Diller Scofidio + Renfro
and Piet Oudolf for the City of New York and Friends of the High Line
NOMINATED BY PAOLA ANTONELLI, LUCY BULLIVANT,
PATRICK BURGOYNE AND FRANCESCA FERGUSON

TEA Tenerife Espacio de las Artes
SANTA CRUZ DE TENERIFE, CANARY ISLANDS, SPAIN

Designed by Herzog & de Meuron for Cabildo Insular de Tenerife;
partner architect: Virgilio Gutiérrez Herreros
NOMINATED BY FLAVIO ALBANESE

Raven Row
LONDON, UK

Designed by 6a Architects for Raven Row
NOMINATED BY CAROLINE ROUX

Porchdog House Prototype
MISSISSIPPI, USA

Designed by Marlon Blackwell Architect; sponsored by
Architecture for Humanity for Biloxi Model Homes
NOMINATED BY CAMERON SINCLAIR

British Embassy, Warsaw

WARSAW, POLAND

Designed by Tony Fretton Architects for the Foreign & Commonwealth Office
NOMINATED BY ELLIS WOODMAN

MAXXI: National Museum of the XXI Century Arts
ROME, ITALY

Designed by Zaha Hadid and Patrik Schumacher with project architect
Gianluca Racana of Zaha Hadid Architects for the Italian Ministry of Culture
and Fondazione MAXXI
NOMINATED BY JONATHAN GLANCEY

Brandhorst Museum
MUNICH, GERMANY

Designed by Matthias Sauerbruch, Louisa Hutton and
Juan Lucas Young of Sauerbruch Hutton for Freistaat Bayern
and Staatliches Hochbauamt München
NOMINATED BY MAX RISSELADA AND RUTH UR

Monterrey housing
MONTERREY, MEXICO

Designed by ELEMENTAL SA for Instituto de la Vivienda
de Nuevo León (IVNL)
NOMINATED BY CATHERINE INCE

category winner

YoulHwaDang Book Hall
PAJU BOOK CITY, SOUTH KOREA

Designed by Florian Beigel of Architecture Research Unit with
Choi JongHoon of Network in Architecture
NOMINATED BY ELLIS WOODMAN

Melbourne Recital Centre and MTC Southbank Theatre
MELBOURNE, AUSTRALIA

Designed by ARM Architecture for Major Projects Victoria
and University of Melbourne
NOMINATED BY WAYNE HEMINGWAY

Ningbo History Museum
NINGBO, CHINA

Designed by Wang Shu and Lu Wenyu of Amateur Architecture Studio
with the design team Song Shuhua, Jiang Weihua and Chen Lichao
NOMINATED BY FLAVIO ALBANESE

Balancing Barn
SUFFOLK, UK

Designed by MVRDV for Living Architecture; co-architect Mole Architects
NOMINATED BY SAM HECHT

Stonebridge Hillside Hub
LONDON, UK

Designed by Edward Cullinan Architects for Hyde Housing Association
and Hillside Action Trust
NOMINATED BY WAYNE HEMINGWAY

1111 Lincoln Road
MIAMI BEACH, USA

Designed by Herzog & de Meuron; envisioned by Robert Wennett
NOMINATED BY RAYMUND RYAN

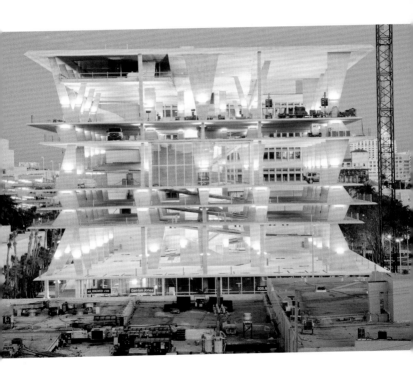

Tape Installations
VARIOUS LOCATIONS

Designed by Numen/For Use
NOMINATED BY THOMAS GEISLER

Nottingham Contemporary
NOTTINGHAM, UK

Designed by Caruso St John Architects for Nottingham City Council
NOMINATED BY RAYMUND RYAN

Ladakh Commonwealth Peace Pavilion and Classroom Initiative
LADAKH, TIBET

Designed by Sergio Palleroni of BaSiC Initiative
NOMINATED BY CYNTHIA SMITH

Open Air Library

MAGDEBURG, GERMANY

Designed by KARO Architekten for Landeshaupstadt Magdeburg;
participation process: Architektur+Netzwerk
NOMINATED BY HUIB VAN DER WERF

category winner

University of Oxford: Department of Earth Sciences
OXFORD, UK

Designed by WilkinsonEyre Architects for the University of Oxford
NOMINATED BY JAMES DYSON

A Forest for a Moon Dazzler
GUANACASTE, COSTA RICA

Designed by Studio Saxe for Helen Saxe
NOMINATED BY LUCY BULLIVANT

Void House
BRUSSELS, BELGIUM

Designed by Gon Zifroni in collaboration with Pom Archi
NOMINATED BY HUIB VAN DER WERF

Burj Khalifa
DUBAI, UNITED ARAB EMIRATES

Designed by Skidmore, Owings and Merrill LLP (SOM)
for Emaar Properties PJSC
NOMINATED BY GUY NORDENSON

UK Pavilion Shanghai Expo 2010
SHANGHAI, CHINA

Designed by Heatherwick Studio for the Foreign & Commonwealth Office,
United Kingdom
NOMINATED BY PAOLA ANTONELLI AND SHANE WALTER

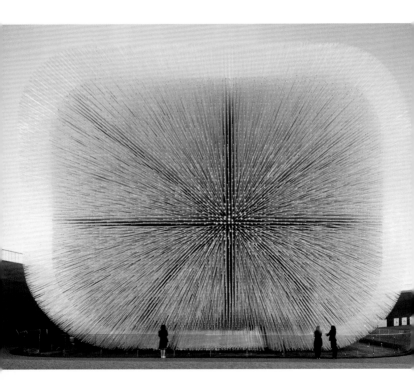

Concrete Canvas Shelters
VARIOUS LOCATIONS

Designed by Peter Brewin, William Crawford and Phillip Greer
of Concrete Canvas
NOMINATED BY HUIB VAN DER WERF

VitraHaus
WEIL AM RHINE, GERMANY

Designed by Herzog & de Meuron for Vitra Verwaltungs GmbH
NOMINATED BY DAVID ROWAN

Media-TIC Building
BARCELONA, SPAIN

Designed by Enric Ruiz-Geli of Cloud 9 for Consortium of the
Zona Franca and 22@Barcelona
NOMINATED BY LUCY BULLIVANT

The Hepworth Wakefield
WAKEFIELD, UK

Designed by David Chipperfield Architects for Wakefield Council
NOMINATED BY ANTONY GORMLEY

National Park of Mali Buildings

BAMAKO, MALI

Designed by Kéré Architecture for Aga Khan Development Network (AKDN)
and Aga Khan Trust for Culture (AKTC)
NOMINATED BY DAVID ADJAYE AND LUCY BULLIVANT

Moses Bridge, Fort de Roovere
HALSTEREN, NETHERLANDS

Designed by RO&AD Architecten for the Municipality of Bergen op Zoom
NOMINATED BY ANTOINETTE KLAWER

The Iron Market
PORT-AU-PRINCE, HAITI

Designed by John McAslan + Partners for Institut de Sauvegarde
de Patrimoine National and Digicel
NOMINATED BY RAYMUND RYAN

Maggie's Centre Gartnavel
GLASGOW, UK

Designed by OMA for Maggie Keswick Jenck's Cancer Caring Centres
NOMINATED BY LUCY BULLIVANT

Care Home
HUISE-ZINGEM, BELGIUM

Designed by Sergison Bates architects for Home Vijvens
NOMINATED BY IAN CARTLIDGE

Folly for a Flyover
LONDON, UK

Designed by Assemble; project supported by CREATE Festival,
Barbican Art Gallery and Muf Architecture/Art
NOMINATED BY PETE COLLARD

Guangzhou Opera House
GUANGZHOU, CHINA

Designed by Zaha Hadid Architects for Guangzhou Municipal Government
NOMINATED BY JONATHAN GLANCEY

Spaceport America
NEW MEXICO, USA

Designed by Foster + Partners London in collaboration with
SMPC Architects for New Mexico Spaceport Authority (NMSA)
NOMINATED BY LUCY BULLIVANT

London 2012 Velodrome
LONDON, UK

Designed by Hopkins Architects with Expedition Engineering
and BDSP Partnership for the Olympic Development Authority
NOMINATED BY SEBASTIAN CONRAN

category winner

Butaro Hospital
BURERA, RWANDA

Designed by MASS Design Group Boston for Rwanda Ministry
of Health and Partners In Health

NOMINATED BY LAURA BOSSI AND LUCY BULLIVANT

Youth Factory
MÉRIDA, SPAIN

Designed by Selgas Cano Arquitectura for the Junta de Extremadura
NOMINATED BY RAYMUND RYAN

Book Mountain
SPIJKENISSE, NETHERLANDS

Designed by MVRDV for Gemeente Spijkenisse
NOMINATED BY CATHERINE INCE

The Library Building

LONDON, UK

Designed by Studio Egret West; developed by Cathedral Group
and United House in partnership with London Borough of Lambeth
NOMINATED BY LYNDA RELPH-KNIGHT

The Shard
LONDON, UK

Designed by Renzo Piano Building Workshop for Sellar Property Group
NOMINATED BY TIM ABRAHAMS AND LUCY BULLIVANT

Tour Bois le Prêtre Tower
PARIS, FRANCE

Designed by Frédéric Druot, Anne Lacaton and Jean Philippe Vassal
for Paris Habitat
NOMINATED BY JUSTIN MCGUIRK

category winner

IKEA Disobedients
NEW YORK, USA

Designed by Andrés Jaque Arquitectos and Office for Political Innovation
NOMINATED BY BEATRICE GALILEE

Home-for-All
RIKUZENTAKATA, JAPAN

Designed by Akihisa Hirata, Sou Fujimoto, Kumiko Inui
and Toyo Ito; photographer: Naoya Hatakeyama;
exhibited at 2012 Venice Architecture Biennale
NOMINATED BY JOHANNA AGERMAN ROSS

Daikanyama T-Site
TOKYO, JAPAN

Designed by Klein Dytham Architecture for Tsutaya
NOMINATED BY LUCY BULLIVANT

Franklin D. Roosevelt Four Freedoms Park

NEW YORK, USA

Designed by Louis I Kahn
NOMINATED BY TONY CHAMBERS

Metropolitan Arts Centre (MAC)

BELFAST, UK

Designed by Hackett Hall McKnight Architects for Belfast City Council
NOMINATED BY RAYMUND RYAN

2013

Kukje Gallery
SEOUL, SOUTH KOREA

Designed by SO-IL for Kukje Gallery
NOMINATED BY ARIC CHEN

Superkilen

COPENHAGEN, DENMARK

Designed by BIG (Bjarke Ingels Group), TOPOTEK 1 and Superflex
for Copenhagen Municipality and Realdania
NOMINATED BY LUCY BULLIVANT

Astley Castle
WARWICKSHIRE, UK

Designed by Witherford Watson Mann Architects for the Landmark Trust
NOMINATED BY KATE GOODWIN

Galaxy SOHO
BEIJING, CHINA

Designed by Zaha Hadid Architects for SOHO China
NOMINATED BY SHELL XU

Museum of Contemporary Art (MOCA) Cleveland
CLEVELAND, USA

Designed by Farshid Moussavi Architecture
NOMINATED BY RAYMUND RYAN AND ZOË RYAN

Museum of Innocence

ISTANBUL, TURKEY

Designed by Orhan Pamuk with Ihsan Bilgin and Cem Yücel;
with Carlotta Werner and Johanna Sunder-Plassmann of
Sunder-Plassman Architekten
NOMINATED BY JOHANNA AGERMAN ROSS

A Room for London
LONDON, UK

Designed by David Kohn Architects; in collaboration with Fiona Banner;
for Living Architecture and Artangel with the Southbank Centre
NOMINATED BY ELIAS REDSTONE

Thalia Theatre

LISBON, PORTUGAL

Designed by Gonçalo Byrne Arquitectos and Barbas Lopes Arquitectos
for Portuguese Ministry of Education and Science
NOMINATED BY TIM ABRAHAMS

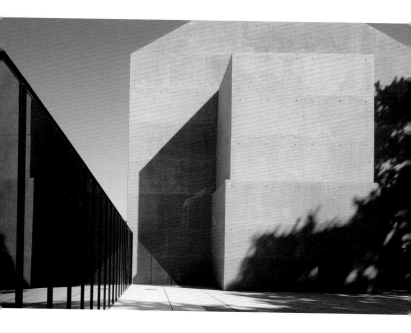

Museo Jumex
MEXICO CITY, MEXICO

Designed by David Chipperfield Architects for Eugenio Lopez
NOMINATED BY JOSE CASTILLO

Marsan Mediatheque
MONT-DE-MARSAN, FRANCE

Designed by archi5 for the Communauté d'agglomération du Marsan
NOMINATED BY LUCY BULLIVANT

Child Chemo House
OSAKA, JAPAN

Designed by Yui Tezuka of Tezuka Architects for Child Chemo House
NOMINATED BY RAYMUND RYAN

FRAC Nord-Pas de Calais
DUNKIRK, FRANCE

Designed by Anne Lacaton and Jean Philippe Vassal of Lacaton & Vassal
for Communauté Urbaine de Dunkerque
NOMINATED BY LUCY BULLIVANT

Makoko Floating School
LAGOS, NIGERIA

Designed by Kunlé Adeyemi of NLÉ
NOMINATED BY CATHERINE INCE AND RAYMUND RYAN

Heydar Aliyev Centre

BAKU, AZERBAIJAN

Designed by Zaha Hadid Architects for the Republic of Azerbaijan
NOMINATED BY JOSEPH GIOVANNINI

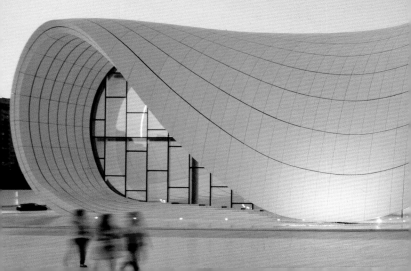

St Moritz Church interior renovation
AUGSBURG, GERMANY

Designed by John Pawson for Moritzkirche
NOMINATED BY ALAIN DE BOTTON

The New Crematorium at the Woodland Cemetery
STOCKHOLM, SWEDEN

Designed by Johan Celsing Arkitektkontor for the
Stockholm Cemetery Committee
NOMINATED BY NOEMÍ BLAGER

Praça das Artes Performing Arts Centre
SÃO PAULO, BRAZIL

Designed by Brasil Arquitetura for the Municipal Department of Culture
NOMINATED BY CATHERINE INCE

La Tallera
CUERNAVACA, MEXICO

Designed by Frida Escobedo for Sala de Arte Publico Siqueiros
NOMINATED BY BEATRICE GALILEE

Paul Smith shop facade
LONDON, UK

Designed by 6a Architects for Sir Paul Smith, Nicola Koller and Nicholas Chandor
NOMINATED BY KATE GOODWIN

Newhall Be Housing Scheme
HARLOW, UK

Designed by Alison Brooks Architects for Linden Homes
NOMINATED BY NOEMÍ BLAGER

Les Turbulences, FRAC Centre
ORLÉANS, FRANCE

Designed by Jakob + MacFarlane for Région Centre
NOMINATED BY RAYMUND RYAN

La Última Esperanza – The Last Hope
MANABÍ, ECUADOR

Designed by Al Borde for the Puerto Cabuyal community
NOMINATED BY NOEMÍ BLAGER

House for Trees
HO CHI MINH CITY, VIETNAM

Designed by Vo Trong Nghia Architects
NOMINATED BY RAYMUND RYAN

Desert Courtyard House
ARIZONA, USA

Designed by Wendell Burnette Architects
NOMINATED BY ELIAS REDSTONE

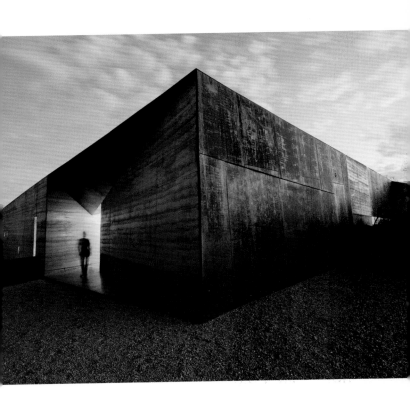

Fondation Louis Vuitton
PARIS, FRANCE

Designed by Gehry Partners with Studios Architecture
for Fondation Louis Vuitton
NOMINATED BY MARIE-ANGE BRAYER

Markthal Rotterdam
ROTTERDAM, NETHERLANDS

Designed by MVRDV; mural by Arno Coenen and Iris Roskam
NOMINATED BY WAYNE HEMINGWAY, RAYMUND RYAN AND JEROEN VAN ERP

One Central Park
SYDNEY, AUSTRALIA

Designed by Ateliers Jean Nouvel for Frasers Property and Sekisui House
NOMINATED BY BERNARD MCCOY

Forfatterhuset Kindergarten
COPENHAGEN, DENMARK

Designed by COBE for the City of Copenhagen
NOMINATED BY KATE GOODWIN

Arena do Morro
NATAL, BRAZIL

Designed by Herzog & de Meuron for Ameropa Foundation,
Centro Sócio-Pastoral Nossa Senhora da Conceição
NOMINATED BY RAYMUND RYAN

Philharmonic Hall
SZCZECIN, POLAND

Designed by Fabrizio Barozzi and Alberto Veiga of Barozzi / Veiga
NOMINATED BY GRZEGORZ PIATEK

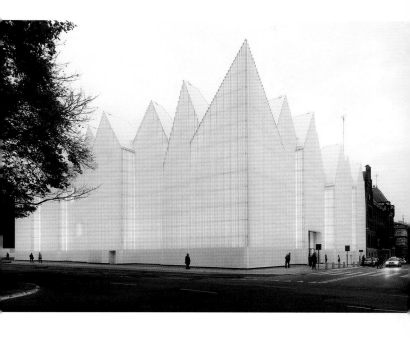

2015

Saw Swee Hock Student Centre
LONDON, UK

Designed by O'Donnell + Tuomey for the London School of Economics
NOMINATED BY ALEX MILTON AND TIM ABRAHAMS

Garden School
BEIJING, CHINA

Designed by OPEN Architecture for the Changyang Government
NOMINATED BY ARIC CHEN

Waterbank Campus
ENDANA, KENYA

Designed by PITCHAfrica for the Annenberg Foundation
NOMINATED BY LUCY BULLIVANT

2015

UC Innovation Center
SANTIAGO, CHILE

Designed by ELEMENTAL for Grupo Angelini
NOMINATED BY NATHALIE WEADICK

category winner

Sancaklar Mosque
ISTANBUL, TURKEY

Designed by Emre Arolat Architects for Sancaklar Foundation
NOMINATED BY TEVFIK BALCIOĞLU

Long Museum West Bund

SHANGHAI, CHINA

Designed by Atelier Deshaus for Shanghai Xuhui Waterfront Development, Investment & Construction Co. Ltd
NOMINATED BY KATE GOODWIN

Granby Workshop
LIVERPOOL, UK

Designed by Assemble with Granby Four Streets Community Land Trust (CLT)
NOMINATED BY CATHERINE INCE AND CATHARINE ROSSI

Fondazione Prada

MILAN, ITALY

Designed by OMA; led by Rem Koolhaas and Chris van Duijn;
with Federico Pompignoli; for Fondazione Prada

NOMINATED BY TIM ABRAHAMS, TONY CHAMBERS,
KATE GOODWIN AND VICKY RICHARDSON

Sustainable Housing
MEXICO

Designed by Tatiana Bilbao Estudio for Financiera Sustentable
NOMINATED BY RAYMUND RYAN

Nida House
NAVIDAD, CHILE

Designed by Mauricio Pezo and Sofia von Ellrichshausen with Diego Perez
for Carlos Atala
NOMINATED BY NOEMÍ BLAGER

The Green
LONDON, UK

Designed by AOC for Southwark Council
NOMINATED BY PETE COLLARD

Dreamland Margate
MARGATE, UK

Designed by HemingwayDesign with Guy Holloway and Ray Hole Architects;
advertising agency: M&C Saatchi
NOMINATED BY JEREMY MYERSON

Better Shelter

VARIOUS LOCATIONS

Designed by Johan Karlsson, Dennis Kanter, Christian Gustafsson, John van Leer and Tim de Haas in partnership with IKEA Foundation and UNHCR

NOMINATED BY DANIEL CHARNY AND BERNARD MCCOY

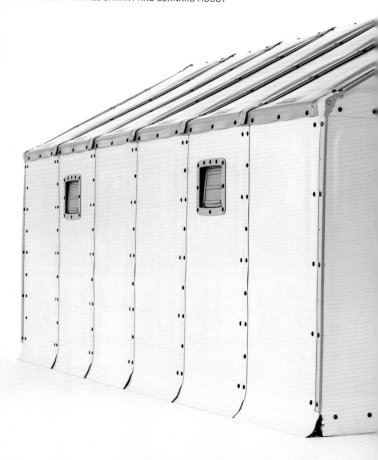

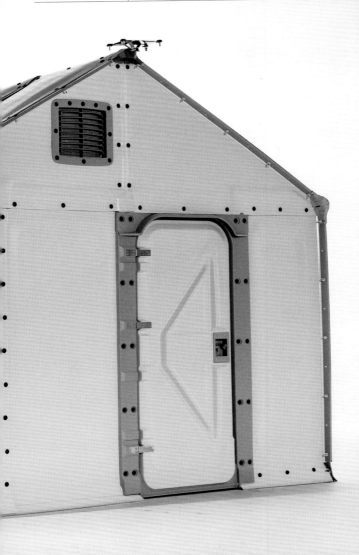

SL11024
LOS ANGELES, USA

Designed by Lorcan O'Herlihy for Phoenix Property Company
NOMINATED BY LUCY BULLIVANT

Arena for Learning
LIMA, PERU

Designed by Grafton Architects for the Universidad
de Ingeniería y Tecnología (UTEC)
NOMINATED BY ALEX MILTON AND RAYMUND RYAN

Harbin Opera House
HARBIN, CHINA

Designed by MAD Architects; led by Ma Yansong, Dang Qun and
Yosuke Hayano; for Harbin Songbei Investment and Development Group
NOMINATED BY ARIC CHEN

VIA 57 West
NEW YORK, USA

Designed by BIG (Bjarke Ingels Group) for the Durst Organization
NOMINATED BY RAYMUND RYAN

Tate Modern Blavatnik Building

LONDON, UK

Designed by Herzog & de Meuron for Tate
NOMINATED BY ROWAN MOORE

Design That Saves Lives
BANGLADESH

Designed by Arup Ireland; led by Rory McGowan, George Faller and
Aidan Madden; for Inditex, the Bangladesh Accord for Fire & Building Safety
and the International Labour Organisation
NOMINATED BY ALEX MILTON

Lycée Schorge Secondary School
KOUDOUGOU, BURKINA FASO

Designed by Kéré Architecture
NOMINATED BY PAPA OMOTAYO

Hegnhuset, Memorial and Learning Centre
UTØYA, NORWAY

Designed by Blakstad Haffner Arkitekter
NOMINATED BY TIM ABRAHAMS

Fondaco dei Tedeschi
VENICE, ITALY

Designed by OMA
NOMINATED BY JOHANNA AGERMAN ROSS

Warka Water
ETHIOPIA

Designed by Arturo Vittori
NOMINATED BY JANE WITHERS

Weltstadt – Refugees' Memories and Futures as Models
BERLIN, GERMANY

Designed by Schlesische27 International Youth, Arts and Culture Center
in collaboration with Raumlaborberlin and the SRH Hochschule der
Populären Künste (hdpk)
NOMINATED BY JANA SCHOLZE

Sala Beckett Theatre and International Drama Centre
BARCELONA, SPAIN

Designed by Flores Prats Arquitectes for Sala Beckett with
Institut de Cultura de Barcelona and Generalitat de Catalunya
NOMINATED BY KATE GOODWIN

Croft Lodge Studio
LEOMINSTER, UK

Designed by Kate Darby Architects and David Connor Design
NOMINATED BY KATE GOODWIN

The Environmental Enhancement of the Five Dragons Temple
RUICHENG, CHINA

Designed by Urbanus
NOMINATED BY ARIC CHEN

Port House
ANTWERP, BELGIUM

Designed by Zaha Hadid and Patrik Schumacher
of Zaha Hadid Architects for Antwerp Port Authority
NOMINATED BY JONATHAN GLANCEY

digital

Rapid Liquid Printing
USA/UK

Designed by Self-Assembly Lab at Massachusetts Institute
of Technology (MIT), Christophe Guberan and Steelcase

fashion

Nike Pro Hijab
USA

Designed by Rachel Henry, Baron Brandt, Megan Saalfeld
and Brogan Terrell for Nike

graphics

**'Fractured Lands', The New York Times Magazine,
14 August 2016**
USA

Editor-in-chief: Jake Silverstein; design director: Gail Bichler;
art director: Matt Willey

product

AIR-INK
INDIA

Designed by Graviky Labs

transport

Scewo
SWITZERLAND

Designed by Thomas Gemperle, Adrien Weber, Naomi Stieger,
Stella Mühlhaus, Bernhard Winter and Pascal Buholzer at the
Swiss Federal Institute of Technology

overall winner

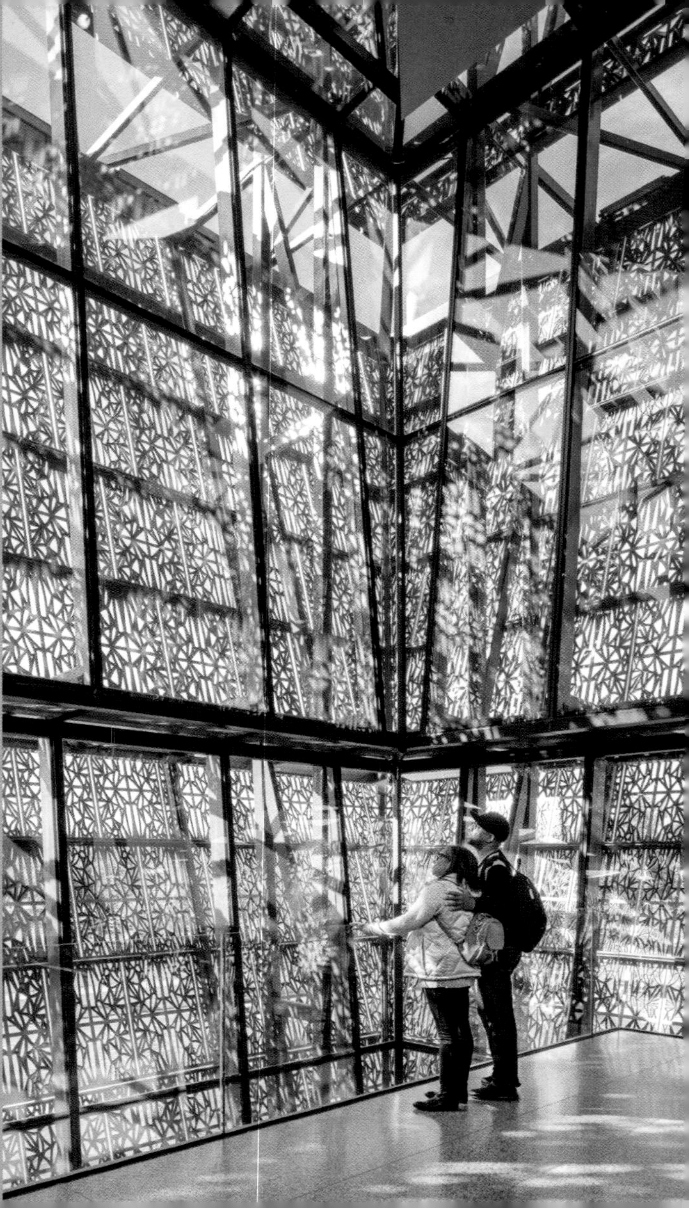

Smithsonian National Museum of African American History and Culture
WASHINGTON DC, USA

Designed by Adjaye Associates, The Freelon Group, Davis Brody Bond,
SmithGroupJJR for the Smithsonian Institution
NOMINATED BY ABRAHAM THOMAS

Wind and Rain Bridge
PEITIAN, CHINA

Designed by Donn Holohan with students from the University of Hong Kong
and Peitian community craftsmen
NOMINATED BY NATHALIE WEADICK

Mrs Fan's Plug-In House
BEIJING, CHINA

Designed by People's Architecture Office
NOMINATED BY BEATRICE LEANZA

The Calais Builds Project

CALAIS, FRANCE

Designed by Gráinne Hassett with migrants living in the Calais Jungle
and students of architecture from the University of Limerick
NOMINATED BY NATHALIE WEADICK

digital

Volume
UK

Conceived and created by United Visual Artists with audio composed by Onepointsix; originally commissioned by the Victoria and Albert Museum and Sony Playstation; originally installed in the Victoria and Albert's John Madejski Garden from November 2006 to January 2007

NOMINATED BY LAUREN PARKER, HANNAH REDLER AND SHANE WALTER

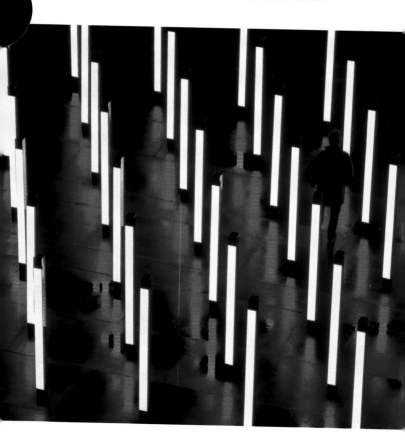

The Replenishing Body kiosk
UK

Concept and interactive design by Ross Phillips for SHOWstudio; editorial and creative directors: Penny Martin and Paul Hetherington; editorial assistant: Andrew Gow; production: Ada Yan Tsuen; project designer: Paul Bruty; technical development by Dorian Moore; design assistants: Joe Baglow and Sinem Erkas; photographic assistants: Phil Taylor and Anna Gudbrandottir; thanks: Shine Communications and Evian
NOMINATED BY DEE HALLIGAN

FixMyStreet
UK

Designed by mySociety
NOMINATED BY MATT JONES

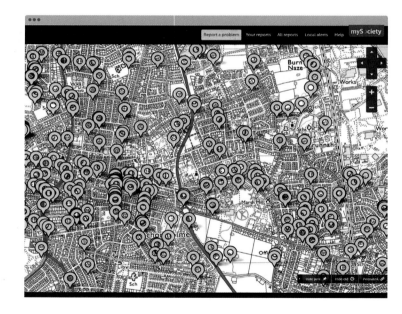

Sharkrunners
USA

Designed by Area/Code
NOMINATED BY MATT JONES

Le Sacre du Printemps
AUSTRIA

Conceived and art directed by Klaus Obermaier with Ars Electronica Futurelab; featuring Julia Mach; for the Brucknerhaus Linz and the Ars Electronica Festival
NOMINATED BY ROSS PHILLIPS

Trulia Hindsight
USA

Designed by Stamen Design
NOMINATED BY MATT JONES

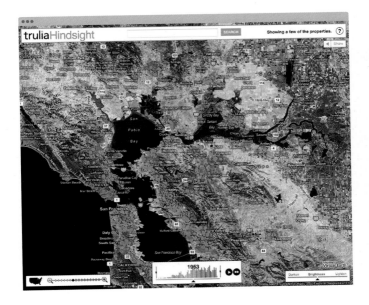

Private View exhibition for Trussardi, Palazzo Trussardi Alla Scala
UK

Designed by Paul Cocksedge Studio
NOMINATED BY MORITZ WALDEMEYER

Burble London
UK

Designed by Umbrellium with Seth Garlock and Rolf Pixley
NOMINATED BY LOUISE SHANNON AND SHANE WALTER

TED website
UK/USA

Designed by Method
NOMINATED BY DEE HALLIGAN

Unlimited
UK

Website designed by Poke for Orange; creative director/partner: Nik Roope;
art director: Julie Barnes; flash developer and animator: Caroline Butterworth;
project lead: Alex Light. flash developer and technical lead: Dereck McKenna;
project manager: Karen Slade; design director: Nicky Gibson; illustrator
and animator: Rex Crowle; developer: Andrew Knott; Orange: Daniel Bye,
Alex Snape and Spencer McHugh
NOMINATED BY ROSS PHILLIPS

'Terminal 5 is Working'
UK

Designed by Bartle Bogle Hegarty for British Airways, Heathrow, Terminal 5
NOMINATED BY MATT JONES

**YESTERDAY
AT T5
AVERAGE TIME
THROUGH
CHECK-IN WAS
8.3 MINS**
This picture was taken at
9.11am yesterday and shows
Manjeeta Pawar and her
daughter in Departures.
8.3 minutes was the average
time the 838 customers we
asked told us it took them
to pass through Check-in
yesterday, between 6am and
2pm. We had to stop at 2pm
so we could make this ad.
ba.com/t5

BRITISH AIRWAYS
Terminal 5 is working
Try it for yourself

Appeel
GERMANY

Designed by Frédéric Eyl, Gunnar Green, Willy Sengewald,
Richard The of TheGreenEyl
NOMINATED BY ANDY CAMERON AND ROSS PHILLIPS

'House of Cards' music video
UK

Directed by James Frost of Zoo Films for Radiohead
NOMINATED BY PATRICK BURGOYNE

Kinetic Sculpture – The Shapes of Things to Come
GERMANY

Designed by ART+COM for the BMW Museum
NOMINATED BY ANDY CAMERON

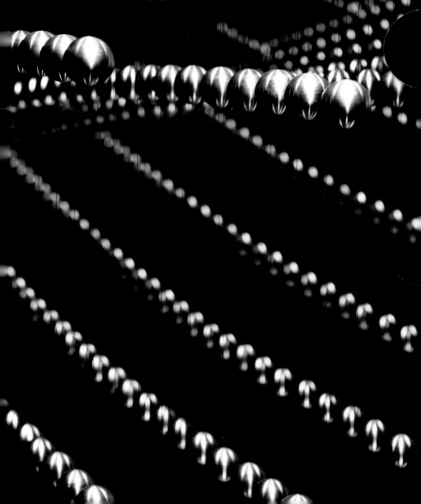

'Integral' interactive music video
UK

Designed by Rumpus Room for the Pet Shop Boys
NOMINATED BY DEE HALLIGAN

Fid.Gen Barcodes
UK

Designed by Karsten Schmidt of Post-Spectacular
NOMINATED BY MATT JONES

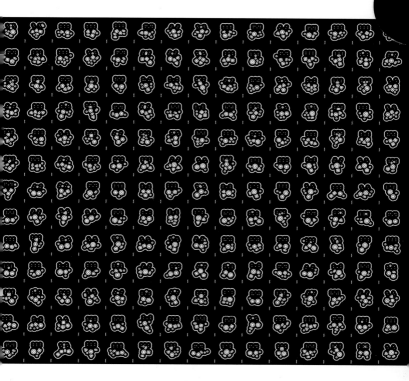

LittleBigPlanet

UK

Developed by Media Molecule; published by Sony Computer
Entertainment Europe

NOMINATED BY MATT JONES

This Happened events series
UK

Curated by Chris O'Shea (Pixelsumo), Joel Gethin Lewis
and Andreas Müller (Nanika)
NOMINATED BY DURRELL BISHOP

Dinner Table Game
UK

Designed by Luckybite; commissioned by The Science Of... for the exhibition
Science of Survival at the Science Museum; graphic design by Marcia Mihotich;
sound design by Dominic Robson
NOMINATED BY DEE HALLIGAN

Make: magazine
UK

Published by Maker Medi
NOMINATED BY MORITZ WALDEMEYER

category winner

vol. 06

Make:
technology on your time

Throw
Me!
page 116

ROBOTS!

Build this pair of electronic insects and more

» Rodent-
Powered
Nightlight

» Floating
Tower
Sculpture

» Bug Sucker

54

76

88

100

O'REILLY makezine.com

Cloud

UK

Designed by Conny Freyer, Sebastien Noel and Eva Rucki of Troika for
a British Airways Commission for Terminal 5, Heathrow; curated by Artwise;
manufactured by Mike Smith Studio; controls by Pharos Architectural Controls;
installation by Alternative Access Ltd

NOMINATED BY DEE HALLIGAN

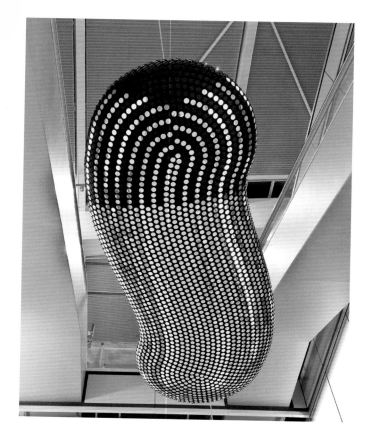

Digital by Design
UK

Written and designed by Conny Freyer, Sebastien Noel and Eva Rucki
of Troika; published by Thames & Hudson
NOMINATED BY DURRELL BISHOP

Absolut Quartet
USA

Designed by Jeff Lieberman and Dan Paluska for Absolut Visionaries;
copyright and sponsorship: Absolut V+S
NOMINATED BY LOUISE SHANNON

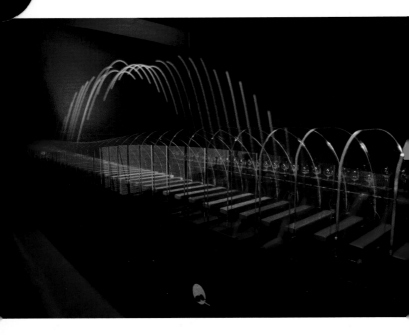

L-E-D-LED-L-ED
JAPAN

Designed by Dilight
NOMINATED BY HANNAH REDLER

Graffiti Taxonomy: Paris

FRANCE

Concept and design by Evan Roth

NOMINATED BY SHANE WALTER

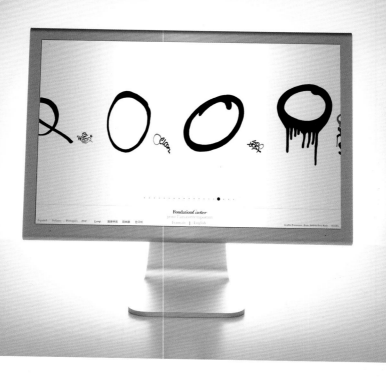

2010

The EyeWriter
USA

Developed by members of Free Art and Technology (FAT), openFrameworks, Graffiti Research Lab, the Ebeling Group and Tony Quan (Tempt1)
NOMINATED BY SHANE WALTER

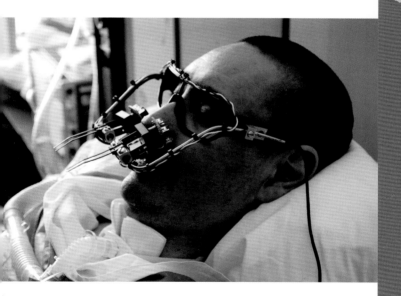

Bloom
UK

Designed by Brian Eno and Peter Chilvers
NOMINATED BY QUENTIN NEWARK

openFrameworks

USA

Developed by Zach Lieberman, Theodore Watson, Arturo Castro
and the OF community

NOMINATED BY MORITZ WALDEMEYER

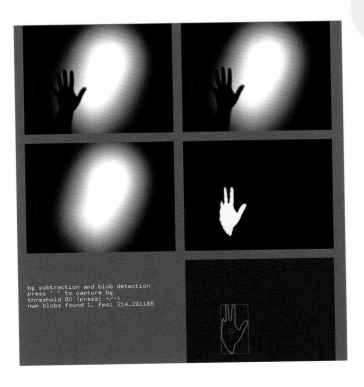

BBC iPlayer

UK

Designed by the BBC

NOMINATED BY SIMON ESTERSON

Pachube

UK

Developed by Usman Haque, Sam Mulube and Christopher Burman
NOMINATED BY MATT JONES

Amazon Kindle DX
USA

Designed by Amazon
NOMINATED BY MATT JONES

YCN Library
UK

Designed by Young Creative Network; interior by Klassnik Corporation;
identity by Eat Sleep Work/Play; window by Jiggery Pokery
NOMINATED BY JEREMY LESLIE

Panda Eyes
UK

Designed by Jason Bruges Studio for WWF
NOMINATED BY ROSS PHILLIPS

The Incidental
ITALY/UK

Concept and creative direction by Daniel Charny of From Now On;
commissioned and produced by the British Council, Arts & Architecture;
project development and design: BERG and Åbäke; the design team
included: Jérôme Rigaud of Bannocks&Hill
NOMINATED BY DEE HALLIGAN

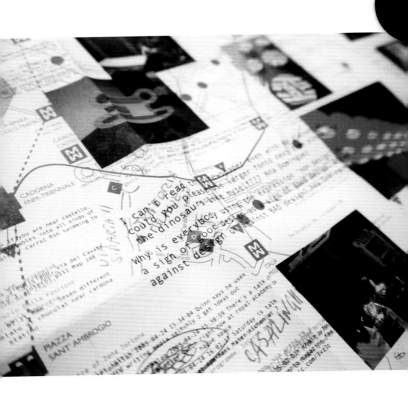

onedotzero_adventures in motion festival identity
UK

Designed by no space Wieden+Kennedy and Karsten Schmidt of
PostSpectacular; creative directors: Tony Davidson, w+k London
and Shane RJ Walter of onedotzero; creative team: David Bruno,
Tom Seymour, Karen Jane of Eze Blaine and Sermad Buni of W+K
NOMINATED BY DANIEL BROWN

Paint
UK

Designed by Greyworld for Nokia
NOMINATED BY DALJIT SINGH

The Johnny Cash Project
USA

Designed by Chris Milk, Aaron Koblin, Radical Media, Rick Rubin
and the Cash Estate
NOMINATED BY SHANE WALTER

The Elements iPad app
USA

Designed by Touch Press; written by Theodore Gray
NOMINATED BY PATRICK BURGOYNE

Rock Band 3
USA

Designed by Harmonix Music Systems
NOMINATED BY ROSS PHILLIPS

Reactable Mobile
SPAIN

Designed by Reactable Systems
NOMINATED BY DEE HALLIGAN

Wallpaper* Custom Covers
UK

Art director: Meirion Pritchard; interaction design and programming by Kin;
content by Anthony Burrill, Hort, James Joyce, Nigel Robinson and Kam Tang
NOMINATED BY PATRICK BURGOYNE AND SHANE WALTER

Flipboard
USA

Designed by Mike McCue and Evan Doll
NOMINATED BY PATRICK BURGOYNE AND JEREMY LESLIE

Angry Birds
FINLAND

Designed by Rovio Mobile
NOMINATED BY MATT JONES

Wired Magazine iPad app
USA

Designed by Scott Dadich, Jeremy Clark and Condé Nast Digital
NOMINATED BY SIMON ESTERSON

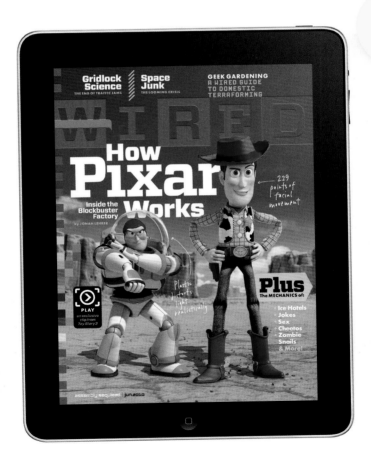

E.chromi: Living Colour from Bacteria

UK

Designed by Alexandra Daisy Ginsberg and James King in collaboration with the University of Cambridge iGEM 2009 team

NOMINATED BY PAOLA ANTONELLI

CellScope
USA

Designed by Daniel Fletcher and the Cellscope Team; animations by
Aardman Animations; animation commissioned by Wieden+Kennedy
for Nokia
NOMINATED BY DAVID KESTER

Mimosa
UK

Designed by Jason Bruges Studio for Philips
NOMINATED BY SARAH WEIR

2011

Guardian Eyewitness iPad app
UK

Designed by Andy Brockie, Alastair Dent, Jonathan Moore,
Martin Redington and Roger Tooth of the Guardian Technology Team
NOMINATED BY SIMON ESTERSON

Speed of Light
UK

Designed by United Visual Artists for Virgin Media
NOMINATED BY PATRICK BURGOYNE

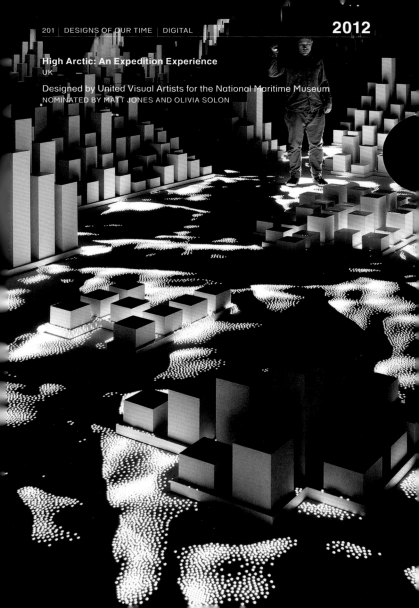

High Arctic: An Expedition Experience
UK

Designed by United Visual Artists for the National Maritime Museum
NOMINATED BY MATT JONES AND OLIVIA SOLON

Guardian iPad edition
UK

Designed by Guardian News and Media in consultation with Mark Porter
NOMINATED BY MATT JONES

The Stanley Parable
USA/UK

Written and created by Davey Wreden; narrated by Kevan Brighting;
additional map design by Lyle Millar
NOMINATED BY ROSS PHILLIPS

Musicity
UK

Conceived by Nick Luscombe and Simon Jordan;
designed and programmed by Jump Studios
NOMINATED BY VICKY RICHARDSON

category winner

Microsoft Kinect for Xbox 360 and Kinect SDK
UK/USA

Designed by Microsoft Games Studios, Microsoft Research and Xbox
NOMINATED BY MATT JONES

Suwappu
UK

Design concept by Dentsu in consultation with BERG
NOMINATED BY OLIVIA SOLON

Homeplus Virtual Store
SOUTH KOREA

Designed by Homeplus
NOMINATED BY WAYNE HEMINGWAY

BBC Homepage Version 4
UK

Designed by BBC
NOMINATED BY JEREMY LESLIE

2012

Beck's The Green Box Project
UK/NEW ZEALAND

Designed by Mother London, Jason Bruges Studio and Motim Technologies
for Anheuser-Busch InBev
NOMINATED BY AL COX AND REUBEN HALPER

Letter to Jane
USA

Designed by Tim Moore
NOMINATED BY JEREMY LESLIE

Face Substitution
USA

Designed by Arturo Castro and Kyle McDonald;
FaceTracker Library by Jason Saragih
NOMINATED BY LOUISE SHANNON

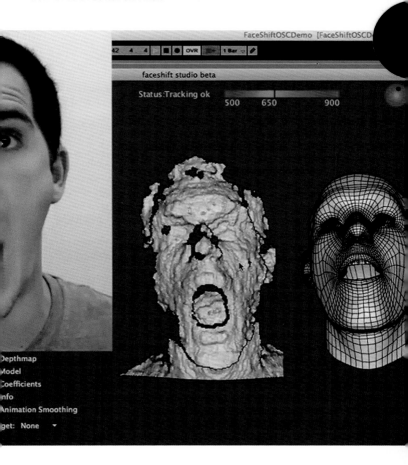

City Tracking Part 2

USA

Designed by Stamen Design
NOMINATED BY ZOË RYAN

English Hedgerow augmented reality plate
UK

Designed by Jason Jameson, James Hall and Rhys Griffin of Unanico Group
with Andrew Tanner Design and Royal Winton
NOMINATED BY PATRICK MYLES

Free Universal Construction Kit
USA

Designed by Free Art and Technology Lab (FAT) and Sy-Lab
NOMINATED BY CONNY FREYER

A Superstitious Fund
UK

Designed by Shing Tat Chung
NOMINATED BY PAOLA ANTONELLI AND JANA SCHOLZE

Rain Room

UK

Designed by Random International; exhibited at the Barbican's Curve Gallery

NOMINATED BY ALEX BEC, SEBASTIAN CONRAN,
WAYNE HEMINGWAY AND OLIVIA SOLON

Candles in the Wind lighting installation
UK

Designed by Moritz Waldemeyer for Ingo Maurer
NOMINATED BY PAOLA ANTONELLI

Wind Map
USA

Designed by Martin Wattenberg and Fernanda B Viégas
NOMINATED BY PAOLA ANTONELLI

Chirp app
UK

Designed by Patrick Bergel and Anthony Steed for Animal Systems
NOMINATED BY NICOLAS ROOPE

Zombies, Run! app
UK

Designed by Six to Start and Naomi Alderman
NOMINATED BY ONKAR KULAR

Digital Postcards and Postcard Player
UK

Designed by Uniform
NOMINATED BY JANE WITHERS

Raspberry Pi
UK

Designed by Raspberry Pi Foundation
NOMINATED BY WAYNE HEMINGWAY AND EVONNE MACKENZIE

Windows Phone 8 operating system
USA

Designed by Microsoft
NOMINATED BY PATRICK BURGOYNE

GOV.UK website
UK

Designed by Government Digital Service
NOMINATED BY JOCELYN BAILEY, PATRICK BURGOYNE AND BEATRICE GALILEE

Dashilar app
JAPAN

Designed by Nippon Design Center, Inc.
NOMINATED BY CAROLINE ROUX

Light Field Camera
USA

Designed by Lytro
NOMINATED BY SEBASTIAN CONRAN

Oculus Rift Virtual Reality Development Kit
USA

Designed by OculusVR Inc.
NOMINATED BY MATT WEBB

Touch Board
UK

Designed by Bare Conductive
NOMINATED BY THOMAS GEISLER

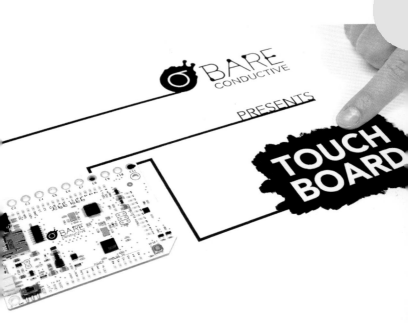

Sidekick Creatives crowdfunding service
UK

Designed by Sidekick Creatives
NOMINATED BY CATHARINE ROSSI

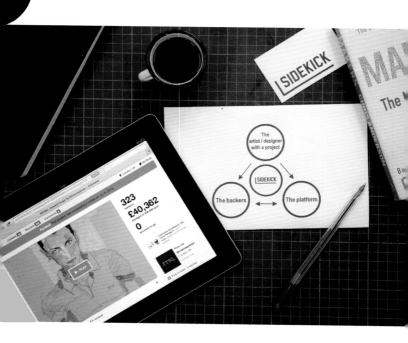

Public Lab Foldable Mini-Spectrometer

USA

Designed by Public Lab contributors; released under the
CERN Open Hardware Licence

NOMINATED BY JON ROGERS

AeroSee crowdsourced search-and-rescue drone
UK

Designed by Paul Egglestone, Darren Ansell and Dan Etherington
NOMINATED BY JON ROGERS

PEEK (Portable Eye Examination Kit)
UK

Designed by PeekVision
NOMINATED BY DANIEL CHARNY

Lego Calendar
UK

Designed by Vitamins Design
NOMINATED BY JOCELYN BAILEY

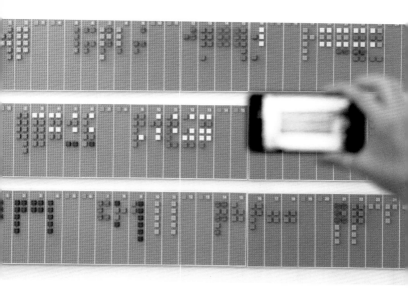

Dumb Ways to Die
AUSTRALIA

Designed by McCann Australia for Metro Trains
NOMINATED BY WAYNE HEMINGWAY

Citymapper app
UK

Designed by Azmat Yusuf, Gilbert Wedam, Joe Hughes,
Nicholas Skehin and Emil Vaughan
NOMINATED BY MATT WEBB

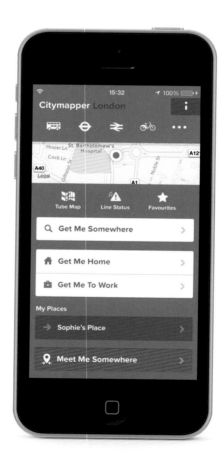

Hello Lamp Post
UK

Designed by PAN Studio in collaboration with Tom Armitage
and Gyorgyi Galik; produced by Watershed Arts
NOMINATED BY MATT WEBB

Générations Game
FRANCE

Designed by Kevin Lesur, Brice Roy, Franck Weber
of One Life Remains with Arthur Schmitt
NOMINATED BY PAOLA ANTONELLI

The Walls Have Eyes

UK

Designed by BBC Research and Development for Mozilla Festival 2014
NOMINATED BY JON ROGERS

The Refugee Project
USA

Designed by Ekene Ijeoma and Hyperakt for the UN High Commissioner
for Refugees (UNHCR)
NOMINATED BY FREDERICO DUARTE

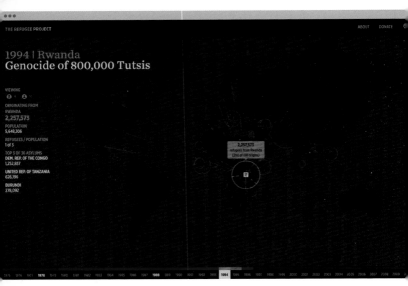

2015

The Ocean Cleanup
NETHERLANDS

Designed by Erwin Zwart; CEO and founder: Boyan Slat;
lead engineer: Jan de Sonneville
NOMINATED BY JOCELYN BAILEY

Monument Valley
UK

Designed by Ken Wong with artist David Fernández Huerte and programmers
Manesh and Van Le of ustwogames
NOMINATED BY BEN TERRETT AND NICOLAS ROOPE

MegaFaces
UK

Designed by Asif Khan for MegaFon
NOMINATED BY KATE GOODWIN AND MORITZ WALDEMEYER

Disclosed
UK

Designed by Marion Ferrec with Kate Wakely
NOMINATED BY JOCELYN BAILEY

Of Instruments and Archetypes
BELGIUM/NETHERLANDS/UK

Designed by Unfold with Penny Webb and Jesse Kirschner
NOMINATED BY CATHARINE ROSSI

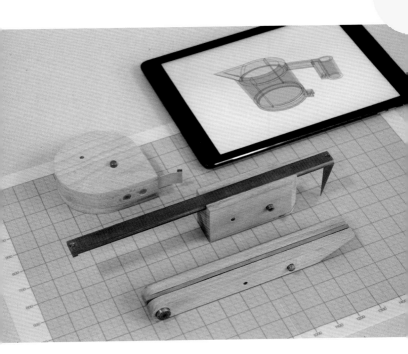

Responsive Street Furniture

UK

Designed by Ross Atkin Associates and Jonathan Scott at Marshalls

NOMINATED BY JEREMY MYERSON

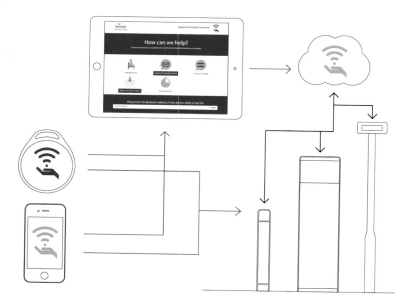

No Man's Sky

UK

Designed by Hello Games

NOMINATED BY JONATHAN SMITH

2015

Shadowing
UK

Designed by Jonathan Chomko and Matthew Rosier for Watershed Arts
NOMINATED BY SEBASTIAN CONRAN

Refugee Republic
NETHERLANDS

Designed by Jan Rothuizen, Martijn van Tol, Dirk Jan Visser,
Aart Jan van der Linden and Yaniv Wolf
NOMINATED BY JEROEN VAN ERP

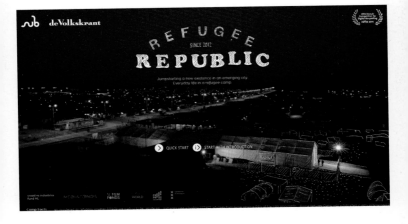

MTV Martin Luther King Day
UK

Concept by Richard Turley for MTV
NOMINATED BY BEN TERRETT

Phonvert

JAPAN

Designed by Tomo Kihara, Keisuke Shiro, Kosuke Takahashi,
Toshinari Takahashi and Nagomu Sugimoto
NOMINATED BY JON ROGERS

SH:24

UK

Designed by a team led by founding directors Gillian Holdsworth,
Chris Howroyd and Mollie Courtenay

NOMINATED BY MAT HUNTER

2016

OpenSurgery
UK/JAPAN

Designed by Frank Kolkman with the Design Interactions department
of the Royal College of Art and the Kyoto Institute for Technology
NOMINATED BY NOAM TORAN

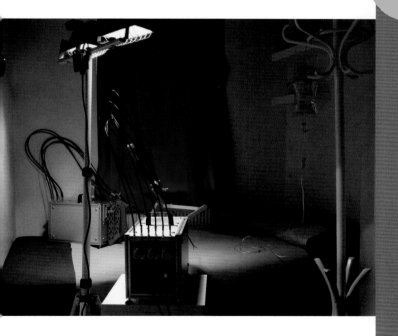

In the Eyes of the Animal
UK

Designed by Marshmallow Laser Feast for Abandon Normal Devices
and Forestry; commissioned by England's Forest Art Works
NOMINATED BY SHANE WALTER

This War of Mine
POLAND

Designed by Przemysław Marszał and Michał Drozdowski of 11 bit studios
NOMINATED BY PAOLA ANTONELLI

Unmade
UK

Co-founded by Ben Alun-Jones, Hal Watts and Kirsty Emery
NOMINATED BY DANIEL CHARNY AND MATT WEBB

Precious Plastic
NETHERLANDS

Designed by Dave Hakkens
NOMINATED BY LIZ FARRELLY

Casa Jasmina Turin
ITALY

Designed by Lorenzo Romagnoli and Alessandro Squatrito
with curators Bruce Sterling and Massimo Banzi
NOMINATED BY JON ROGERS

Moth Generator
USA

Designed by Katie Rose Pipkin and Loren Schmidt
NOMINATED BY MATT WEBB

the abrupt moth
gricomma silisila

morbid-catoptria mountain
dipsis unemen

Pokémon GO
USA

Designed by Niantic
NOMINATED BY ABRAHAM THOMAS

Professional women emoji

USA

Designed by Agustin Fonts, Rachel Been, Mark Davis,
Nicole Bleuel and Chang Yang
NOMINATED BY ALEX BEC

Premier League on-air branding
UK

Designed by DixonBaxi
NOMINATED BY ABRAHAM THOMAS

Google Noto
USA

Designed by Adobe, Google and Monotype
NOMINATED BY CATHERINE FLOOD

Meet Graham: The Only Person Designed to Survive on Our Roads
AUSTRALIA

Designed by Patricia Piccinini in collaboration with Dr Christian Kenfield,
Dr David Logan and Clemenger BBDO for Transport Accident Commission
NOMINATED BY MANDI KEIGHRAN

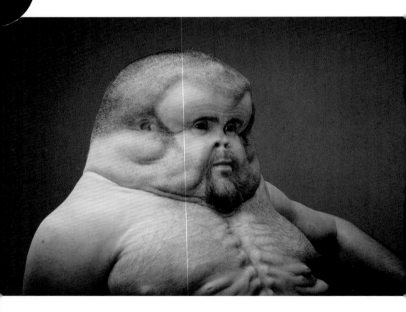

Refugee Text
DENMARK

Designed by Kåre MS Solvåg, Caroline Arvidsson and Ciarán Duffy
NOMINATED BY SIMONA MASCHI

Saydnaya: Inside a Syrian Torture Prison
UK

Designed by Forensic Architecture and Amnesty International
NOMINATED BY KAREN VERSCHOOREN

Rapid Liquid Printing
USA/UK

Designed by Self-Assembly Lab at Massachusetts Institute of Technology (MIT),
Christophe Guberan and Steelcase
NOMINATED BY LIBBY SELLERS

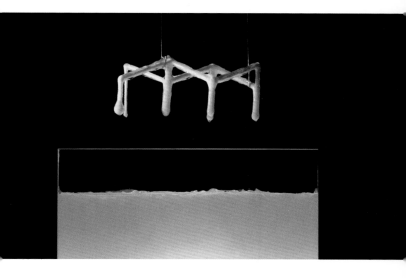

OTHR
USA

Designed by Joe Doucet, Dean Di Simone and Evan Clabots
NOMINATED BY STEVEN LEARNER

Pierre Chareau: Modern Architecture and Design
USA

Designed by Diller Scofidio + Renfro
NOMINATED BY FELIX BURRICHTER

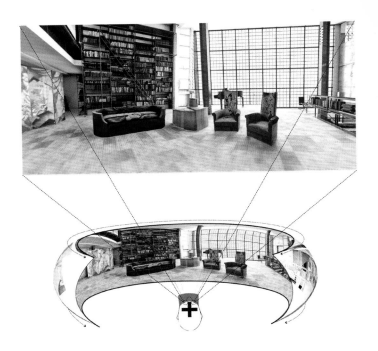

fashion

Illuminati II/Noir Collection 2007
DENMARK

Designed by Peter Ingerswen
NOMINATED BY CLAIRE WILCOX

Danielle Scutt Spring/Summer 2007
UK

Designed by Danielle Scutt
NOMINATED BY CLAIRE WILCOX

Jil Sander Spring/Summer 2008
ITALY

Designed by Raf Simons
NOMINATED BY ISSEY MIYAKE

Issey Miyake Spring/Summer 2008
JAPAN

Designed by Dai Fujiwara
NOMINATED BY ISSEY MIYAKE

Dior Haute Couture Spring/Summer 2007
FRANCE

Designed by John Galliano
NOMINATED BY COLIN MCDOWELL

Giles Deacon Spring/Summer 2008
UK

Designed by Giles Deacon
NOMINATED BY NICK KNIGHT

Ronaldo Fraga Autumn/Winter 2007/2008
BRAZIL

Designed by Ronaldo Fraga
NOMINATED BY EMILY CAMPBELL

Yves Saint Laurent Downtown Tote
FRANCE

Designed by Yves Saint Laurent
NOMINATED BY PAULA REED

Osman Yousefzada Autumn/Winter 2007/2008
UK

Designed by Osman Yousefzada
'NOMINATED BY CLAIRE WILCOX

Ma Ke Wuyong (Useless) collection 2007
CHINA

Designed by Ma Ke
NOMINATED BY OU NING

Arena Homme+ cover shoot Summer/Autumn 2007, issue no. 27
UK

Photography and styling by Nick Knight and Simon Foxton; commissioned by
editor-in-chief Jo-Ann Furniss of Arena Homme+
NOMINATED BY PENNY MARTIN

2008

Hussein Chalayan Airborne, Autumn/Winter 2007/2008
UK

Designed by Hussein Chalayan; sponsored by Swarowski,
Turquality and Han Nefkens of H&F/Fashion on the Edge Projects
NOMINATED BY COLIN MCDOWELL

Pierre Hardy Fashion Accessories Spring/Summer 2008
ITALY

Designed by Pierre Hardy
NOMINATED BY PENNY MARTIN AND PAULA REED

UNIQLO Cashmere Project with Pantone
LONDON

Designed by UNIQLO
NOMINATED BY PAULA REED

Prada Spring/Summer 2009
ITALY

Designed by Miuccia Prada
NOMINATED BY COLIN MCDOWELL

Maison Martin Margiela Spring/Summer 2009,
Twentieth Anniversary Collection
FRANCE

Designed by Martin Margiela
NOMINATED BY PENNY MARTIN

Basso & Brooke Spring/Summer 2009
UK

Designed by Bruno Basso and Christopher Brooke
NOMINATED BY COLIN MCDOWELL

The Thoughtful Dresser
UK

Created by Linda Grant
NOMINATED BY RUTH UR

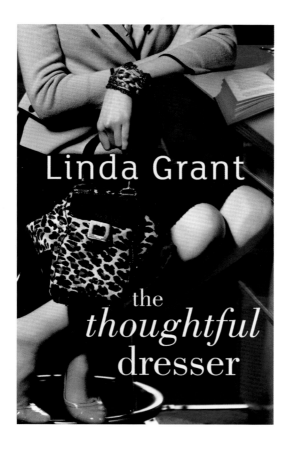

Duckie Brown Spring/Summer 2009
USA

Designed by Stephen Cox and Daniel Silver of Duckie Brown
NOMINATED BY SONNET STANFILL

'A Black Issue', July 2008
ITALY

Designed by Vogue Italia; published by Condé Nast
NOMINATED BY PENNY MARTIN AND ALISON MOLONEY

Louise Goldin Spring/Summer 2009
UK

Designed by Louise Goldin
NOMINATED BY SONNET STANFILL

Lanvin Spring/Summer 2009
FRANCE

Designed by Alber Elbaz
NOMINATED BY COLIN MCDOWELL

Trembled Blossoms
ITALY

Designed by James Lima for Miuccia Prada
NOMINATED BY PENNY MARTIN

The House of Viktor&Rolf retrospective
UK

Exhibition designed by Siebe Tettero; concept by Viktor&Rolf;
curator: Jane Alison; assistant curator: Ariella Yedgar
NOMINATED BY ALISON MOLONEY

Wonderland
UK

Designed by Helen Storey with Tony Ryan; film by Nick Knight
NOMINATED BY PENNY MARTIN

Christopher Kane Spring/Summer 2009
UK

Designed by Christopher Kane
NOMINATED BY ZOË RYAN

Comme des Garçons Autumn/Winter 2009/2010
JAPAN

Designed by Rei Kawakubo
NOMINATED BY SARAH MOWER

Alexander McQueen Spring/Summer 2010 and Spring/Summer 2010 'Plato's Atlantis' catwalk presentation

UK

Designed by Alexander McQueen; catwalk presentation by
Alexander McQueen, Nick Knight, Raquel Zimmerman and Ruth Hogben
NOMINATED BY SONNET STANFILL

Boudicca Spring/Summer 2010 'Real Girl' Lookbook
UK

Designed by Zowie Broach and Brian Kirkby for Boudicca
NOMINATED BY SARAH MOWER

Beth Ditto at Evans
UK

Designed by Beth Ditto and Lisa Marie Peacock
NOMINATED BY BRONWYN COSGRAVE

Balmain Jacket
FRANCE

Designed by Christophe Decarnin
NOMINATED BY DYLAN JONES

Goggle Jacket '989–'009
UK

Designed by Aitor Throup for C.P. Company
NOMINATED BY SARAH MOWER

Hats: An Anthology by Stephen Jones
UK

Curated by Stephen Jones and Oriole Cullen for the Victoria & Albert Museum; exhibition design by Michael Howells; exhibition graphics by Lawrence Mynot
NOMINATED BY BRONWYN COSGRAVE

Madeleine Vionnet, puriste de la mode exhibition
FRANCE

Curated by Pamela Golbin for Musée de la mode et du textile; designed by Andrée Putman
NOMINATED BY COLIN MCDOWELL

Accessoires et objets, témoignages de vies de femmes à Paris 1940–1944
FRANCE

Curated by Christine Levisse-Touzé, Fabienne Falluel and Marie-Laure Gutton;
designed by Jean-Jacques Raynaud; graphics by CL Design; for Ville de Paris
by Paris-Musées; realised with Musée Galliera; shown at Mémorial du Maréchal
Leclerc de Hauteclocque et de la Libération de Paris-Musée Jean Moulin
NOMINATED BY SONNET STANFILL

Comme des Garçons Trading Museum
JAPAN

Designed and conceived by Rei Kawakubo
NOMINATED BY ALISON MOLONEY

Lanvin Spring/Summer 2011
FRANCE

Designed by Alber Elbaz
NOMINATED BY PAULA REED

Ohne Titel Spring/Summer 2011
USA

Designed by Flora Gill and Alexa Adams
NOMINATED BY PAOLA ANTONELLI

Melonia Shoe
SWEDEN

Designed by Naim Josefi and Souzan Youssouf
NOMINATED BY ED ANNINK

Gareth Pugh Spring/Summer 2011
UK

Designed by Gareth Pugh
NOMINATED BY SONNET STANFILL

Organic Jewellery Collection
BRAZIL

Designed by Flavia Amadeu
NOMINATED BY ADÉLIA BORGES

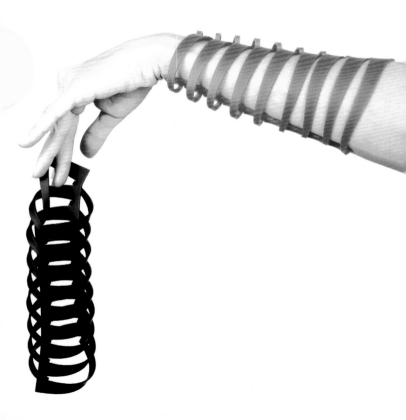

category winner

UNIQLO + J Autumn/Winter 2010/2011
JAPAN

Designed by Jil Sander for UNIQLO
NOMINATED BY PAULA REED

Tess Giberson Spring/Summer 2011, Shift
USA

Designed by Tess Giberson
NOMINATED BY SONNET STANFILL

Margaret Howell Plus Shirt
UK

Designed by Kenneth Grange and Margaret Howell
NOMINATED BY JAMES DYSON

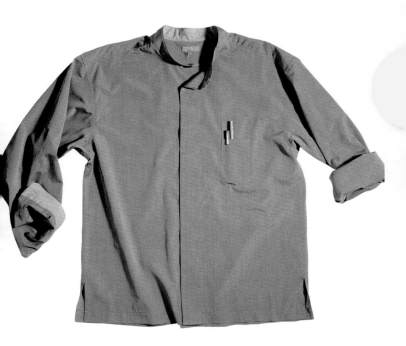

Film for Gareth Pugh Spring/Summer 2012
UK

Directed by Ruth Hogben
NOMINATED BY KAAT DEBO

Alexander McQueen: Savage Beauty

USA

Curated by Andrew Bolton with Harold Koda for the Costume Institute
at the Metropolitan Museum of Art; creative direction by Sam Gainsbury;
production design by Joseph Bennett; head masks by Guido

NOMINATED BY KAAT DEBO AND ALISON MOLONEY

Céline Crombie
FRANCE

Designed by Phoebe Philo for Céline
NOMINATED BY SARAH MOWER

132.5
JAPAN

Designed by Miyake Design Studio; design director: Issey Miyake;
textile engineer: Manabu Kikuchi; pattern engineer: Sachiko Yamamoto
NOMINATED BY VICKY RICHARDSON

Vivienne Westwood Ethical Fashion Africa collection
UK

Designed by Vivienne Westwood
NOMINATED BY ALISON MOLONEY

Suno Spring/Summer 2011
USA

Designed by Suno
NOMINATED BY HETTIE JUDAH

Mary Katrantzou Autumn/Winter 2011/2012
UK

Designed by Mary Katrantzou
NOMINATED BY BRONWYN COSGRAVE AND SARAH MOWER

The Duchess of Cambridge's wedding dress
UK

Designed by Sarah Burton of Alexander McQueen
NOMINATED BY SARAH MOWER

Melissa and Gaetano Pesce boot and flip flop
USA

Designed by Gaetano Pesce; manufactured by Melissa
NOMINATED BY ADÉLIA BORGES

Late Night Chameleon Café
UK

Store design by Gary Card; creative director: John Skelton of LN-CC;
brand director: Dan Mitchell of LN-CC
NOMINATED BY BRONWYN COSGRAVE

Oratory cycling jacket
UK

Designed by Will Carleysmith of Brompton Bicycle Ltd
NOMINATED BY GARETH WYN DAVIES

Craig Green Autumn/Winter 2012/2013 collection
UK

Designed by Craig Green
NOMINATED BY PETER JENSEN

I Want Muscle
UK

Directed by Elisha Smith-Leverock; produced by Creature of London
and KnockKnock with Stamp London
NOMINATED BY ALISON MOLONEY

Louis Vuitton Summer 2012 collection
JAPAN

Designed by Yayoi Kusama
NOMINATED BY TONY CHAMBERS AND ALISON MOLONEY

Giles Deacon Autumn/Winter 2012/2013 collection
UK

Designed by Giles Deacon
NOMINATED BY SONNET STANFILL

Prada Spring/Summer 2012 ready-to-wear collection
ITALY

Designed by Miuccia Prada
NOMINATED BY SONNET STANFILL

Anna Karenina Costumes
UK

Designed by Jacqueline Durran
NOMINATED BY CHRISTOPHER BREWARD

Diana Vreeland: The Eye has to Travel
USA

Directed by Lisa Immordino Vreeland
NOMINATED BY BRONWYN COSGRAVE

Proenza Schouler Autumn/Winter 2012/2013 collection
USA

Designed by Lazaro Hernandez and Jack McCollough
NOMINATED BY SONNET STANFILL

Comme des Garçons Autumn/Winter 2012/2013 ready-to-wear collection
JAPAN

Designed by Rei Kawakubo
NOMINATED BY WENDY DAGWORTHY

Rick Owens Spring/Summer 2014 collection presentation
USA

Designed by Rick Owens
NOMINATED BY HETTIE JUDAH

Prada Spring/Summer 2014 collection
ITALY

Designed by Miuccia Prada
NOMINATED BY PETER JENSEN

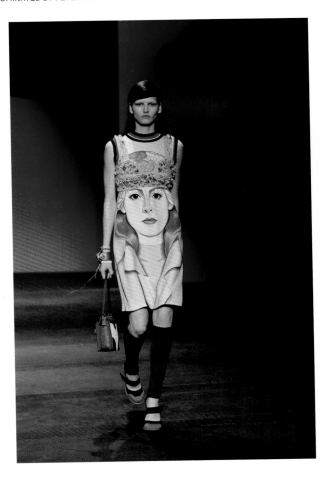

DAS Autumn/Winter 2013/2014 collection
UNITED ARAB EMIRATES

Designed by Reem and Hind Beljafla
NOMINATED BY BRONWYN COSGRAVE

A Magazine curated by Stephen Jones
UK

Designed by Stephen Jones and edited by Dan Thawley
NOMINATED BY HETTIE JUDAH

The Hinterland of Ronaldo Fraga
BRAZIL

Designed by Ronaldo Fraga
NOMINATED BY ADÉLIA BORGES

Totemic Collection
UK

Designed by Sadie Williams
NOMINATED BY PETER JENSEN

Dior ready-to-wear Spring/Summer 2013 collection
FRANCE

Designed by Raf Simons
NOMINATED BY ALISON MOLONEY

Tracey Neuls Geek reflective bike shoes
UK

Designed by Tracey Neuls; rubber sole manufactured by Bolflex
NOMINATED BY VICKY RICHARDSON

BACK Spring/Summer 2015 collection
SWEDEN

Designed by Ann-Sofie Back
NOMINATED BY PETER JENSEN

category winner

Thomas Tait Autumn/Winter 2013/2014
UK

Designed by Thomas Tait
NOMINATED BY HETTIE JUDAH

Satu Maaranen Spring/Summer 2015 collection, Geometry of Futufolk
FINLAND

Designed by Satu Maaranen
NOMINATED BY SUVI SALONIEMI

Fausto Puglisi Autumn/Winter 2014/2015 collection
ITALY

Designed by Fausto Puglisi
NOMINATED BY SONNET STANFILL

Rodarte Autumn/Winter 2014/2015, collection finale
USA

Designed by Kate and Laura Mulleavy
NOMINATED BY BRONWYN COSGRAVE

Raf Simons/Sterling Ruby Autumn/Winter 2014/2015
BELGIUM/USA

Designed by Raf Simons and Sterling Ruby
NOMINATED BY HETTIE JUDAH

J.W. Anderson Spring/Summer 2015 women's catwalk show
UK

Designed by Jonathan Anderson; collection stylist:
Benjamin Bruno; millinery by Noel Stewart
NOMINATED BY PETER JENSEN

Archivist – Three Faces, Archive Chalayan
UK

Founded by Jane Howard and Michael Harrison; edited by Dal Chodha;
photographs by Axel Hoedt
NOMINATED BY SHAUN COLE

Chromat Autumn/Winter 2015/2016, Lumina Collection
USA

Designed by Chromat with Intel
NOMINATED BY PAOLA ANTONELLI

Agi and Sam Autumn/Winter 2015/2016, The Coolman Collection
UK

Designed by Agi Mdumulla and Sam Cotton with screen printing
by Faye McNulty; manufactured by Unlimited Fashion
NOMINATED BY SHAUN COLE

Richard Malone Spring/Summer 2016
UK

Designed and manufactured by Richard Malone
NOMINATED BY ALEX MILTON

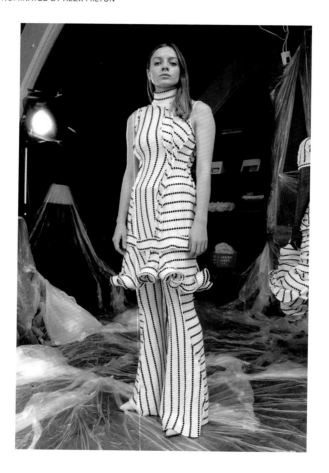

2016

Kids vs Fashion
SPAIN

Directed by Yolanda Domínguez
NOMINATED BY ALEX BEC

Yakampot Autumn/Winter 2015/2016 Colección 7
MEXICO

Creative director: Francisco Cancino; coordinator and fashion consultant:
Lara Gustavo García Villa; art director: Ernesto Moncada
NOMINATED BY RENATA BECERRIL

Craig Green Spring/Summer 2015
UK

Designed by Craig Green
NOMINATED BY SHAUN COLE AND HETTIE JUDAH

Nike Pro Hijab
USA

Designed by Rachel Henry, Baron Brandt, Megan Saalfeld and Brogan Terrell for Nike
NOMINATED BY WAYNE HEMINGWAY

Ecoalf
SPAIN

Designed by Ecoalf
NOMINATED BY SAM BARON

Pussyhat Project
USA

Designed by Krista Suh, Jayna Zweiman, Kat Coyle and Aurora Lady
NOMINATED BY LIBBY SELLERS

Levi's Commuter trucker jacket with Google Jacquard
USA

Designed by Google with Levi's
NOMINATED BY PAMELA GOLBIN

'The Rite of Spring/Summer/Autumn/Winter' New Object Research
UK

Designed by Aitor Throup
NOMINATED BY DIANE PERNET

Life of Pablo pop-up store
USA

Designed by Kanye West and Mat Vlasic for Bravado
NOMINATED BY BEN TERRETT

KNOCKE
KNACKE
KNICKE

MARRIAGE IS AN INSTIT
...AND THAT'S WHERE A COUPLE F

DO YOU KNOW THAT FIVE OUT OF
THREE PEOPLE CAN'T DO FRACTIONS?

I'VE HAD MY POTENTIAL SPOTTED
I CAN GET IT OUT WITH A TISSUE, I THINK.

I FELL IN LOVE WITH A LADY CONTORTIONIST
BUT SHE TURNED THE OTHER CHEEK

A LOT OF PEOPLE SAY:
DO YOU BELIEVE IN REINCARNATION?
I DON'T SEE THE POINT
IN COMING BACK AS
A TIN OF MILK.

LEONARD TOOK SOME PHOTOS
HE'S GOT A BIG POLAROID!
OOH, THEY CAN BE PAINFUL.

WE'VE GOT ARTISTS FROM ALL
CORNERS OF THE LABOUR EXCHANGE
WE'VE GOT A FUNNY LADY FROM BELGIUM
ANN TWERP
WE'VE GOT A SEXY RUSSIAN LADY
EVA VESTOFT
AND WE'VE GOT THE FAMOUS LION TAMER
CLAUD BOTTOM

WOULD YOU LIKE A MOONLIGHT DIP
YOU'LL HAVE TO WARM YOUR HAN

HOW TICKLED I AM
UNDER THE CIRCUMSTANCES
HAVE YOU EVER BEEN
TICKLED UNDER
THE CIRCUMSTANCES
MISSUS?

KING SOLOMON HAD A THOUSAND WIVES.
HE SERENADED THEM DAILY.
WHAT'S THE GOOD OF A THOUSAND WIVES
WHEN YOU'VE ONLY GOT ONE UKULELE?

I THOUGHT, I'D BETTER PUT A ROOF ON THIS LAVAT

I HAD THE
HARDEST JOB IN
THE CHIP SHOP
I PUT THE DAMP
SALT IN THE
CRUETS

DISCUMKNOCKERA
PLUMPTIOUS
TATTIFILA

TO ME IS THIS WORLD IS A WO
I'M THE LUCKIEST HUMAN IN
I'VE GOT NO SILVER AND I
BUT I'VE GOT HAPPINE
HAPPINESS TO ME IS
A SUNSET FADING ON A
A BIG OLD HEAVEN FULL
WHEN I'M IN THE ARMS

OH, HAPPINESS, HAPPINESS, THE GR
I THANK THE LORD THAT
WITH MORE THAN MY S

HAPPINESS IS A F
TURNING ITS FACE TO
I SEE IT IN THE SUNSHINE
HAPPINESS, HAPPIN
A WISE OLD MAN T
HAPPINESS IS A
WHEN YOU GO TO MEAS
DON'T COUNT MONE

MY GRANDAD USED TO GO TO
THE DIARY AND JOAN CLUB
I DON'T KNOW WHAT HE DID
BUT HE GOT THREE NOTCHES
ON HIS WALKING STICK.

graphics

Helvetica
USA

Realised and directed by Gary Hustwit
NOMINATED BY PATRICK BURGOYNE

Monograph December Issue '07
UK

Concept and text by Daniel Mason; designed by Creative Review;
art directors: Nathan Gale and Paul Pensom; designed by James Melaugh;
photography by Will Thom; edited by Patrick Burgoyne;
published by Creative Review
NOMINATED BY M/M (PARIS)

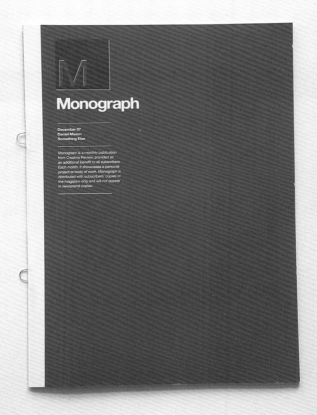

Prada Prototypes auction website
NETHERLANDS

Designed by AMO
NOMINATED BY EMILY KING

Museum für Gestaltung exhibition posters
SWITZERLAND

Designed by various designers for the Museum für Gestaltung Zürich
NOMINATED BY PATRICK BURGOYNE

magCulture Website
UK

Designed and edited by Jeremy Leslie
NOMINATED BY SIMON ESTERSON

The magCulture shop is open in London...
Mon–Fri 11am–7pm, Sat 12–5pm

...and also online
Over 400 magazines available worldwide

Studio **Journal** Shop

MAGCULTURE
We love magazines

Events About Contact

Magazine of the week: **mono.kultur #43**

Event: **The Modern Magazine 2017**

Out now: **Positive News #90**

Audio: **magCulture Meets Racquet**

11.07.17

New York, 13 July:
presents 'Politics.
Media. Design,' a 1
about how we mig
deal with fake new
and the new media
landscape.

London, 18 July: S
are gathering some
last year's Stack
Awards winners to
inspire entries for
years Awards. A gr
lineup.

Read *Vestoj*'s inter
that caused a sensa
around the change
Bristish *Vogue*.

03.07.17

London, this Weds,
July, as Wimbledon
opens, magCulture
Meets Racquet.

Congratulations to

Greta typeface family
NETHERLANDS

Designed by Peter Bilak of Typotheque
NOMINATED BY SIMON ESTERSON

Soir

GRETA GRANDE BOLD

Opinión

GRETA GRANDE MEDIUM

Periódico

GRETA GRANDE REGULAR

Independent

GRETA GRANDE LIGHT

Metropolitano

GRETA GRANDE LIGHT ITALIC

The Grand Tour

UK

Designed and art directed by the Partners for the National Gallery

NOMINATED BY PATRICK BURGOYNE

**BUTT BOOK: The best of the first 5 years of BUTT magazine –
Adventures in 21st century gay subculture**
NETHERLANDS

Designed by Jop van Bennekom
NOMINATED BY EMILY KING

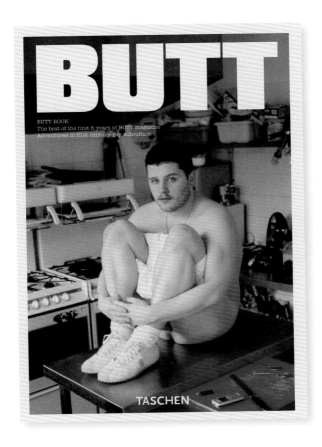

Clean City Law
BRAZIL

Initiative by São Paulo Municipality; photographs by Tony de Marco
NOMINATED BY RICK POYNOR AND PATRICK BURGOYNE

'Silently' music video
USA

Designed and art directed by Mike Mills
NOMINATED BY EMILY KING

He whispers into her ear and kisses her forehead.

Nassim typeface
AUSTRIA

Designed by Titus Nemeth
NOMINATED BY EMILY KING

Scientific Journal 3.0

أَجِيدُوا اَلْخَطَّ فَإِنَّهُ حِلْيَةُ كُتُبِكُمْ

Réchauffement Climatique

فرهنگ و هنر

Educational Books

اَلْعُلُومُ الطَّبِيعِيَّةِ

PRÄDIKAT: PÄDAGOGISCH WERTVOLL!

Penguin Classics Deluxe Edition
USA

Designed by various artists for Penguin Group USA
NOMINATED BY RICK POYNOR

Performa '07: Performa Art Biennial identity and graphics
USA

Designed by A Practice for Everyday Life (APFEL)
NOMINATED BY NINA DUE

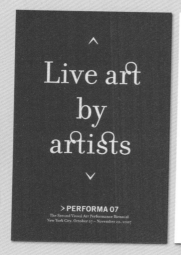

'adidas Originals' footwear catalogue
CHINA

Designed by MEWE Design Alliance and Guang Yu
NOMINATED BY OU NING

Selfridges wayfinding and signage

UK

Designed by Cartlidge Levene; commissioned by Selfridges & Co; installation by Endpoint; manufactured by Alternative Plastics
NOMINATED BY MORAG MYERSCOUGH

Kate Moss identity
UK

Designed by Peter Saville and Paul Barnes
NOMINATED BY PATRICK BURGOYNE

kate moss

Swiss National Bank banknotes
SWITZERLAND

Designed by Manuela Pfrunder
NOMINATED BY EMILY KING

Varoom! The Illustration Report
USA/NORWAY

Designed and art directed by Non-Format for the
AOI (Association of Illustrators)
NOMINATED BY SIMON ESTERSON AND RICK POYNOR

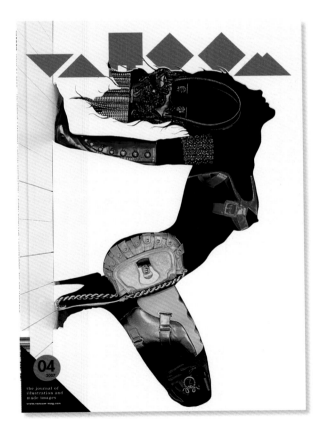

Your House

GERMANY

Concept and art direction by Olafur Eliasson; realised by
Michael Heimann and Claudia Baulesch; produced by Kremo;
commissioned by Museum of Modern Art

NOMINATED BY EMILY KING

This Is Not A Brothel... sticker
UK

Designed by Peter Saville; commissioned by Mother
NOMINATED BY PATRICK BURGOYNE

THIS IS NOT A BROTHEL
THERE ARE NO PROSTITUTES
AT THIS ADDRESS

Unrest
UK

Exhibition by Jonathan Ellery at the Wapping Project
NOMINATED BY QUENTIN NEWARK

Letman
NETHERLANDS

Typography and design by Job Wouters
NOMINATED BY QUENTIN NEWARK

Project Vitra
SWITZERLAND

Concept, design, layout and production by Cornel Windlin;
edited by Cornel Windlin and Rolf Fehlbaum; published by Birkhäuser
NOMINATED BY TONY BROOK

Aesop retail stores and branding
AUSTRALIA

Designed by Aesop with March Studio
NOMINATED BY FLEUR WATSON

Designing Design
JAPAN

Designed by Kenya Hara; published by Lars Müller Publishing
NOMINATED BY ELLEN LUPTON

Is Not Magazine: Issue Eleven – All That Glitters Is/Not Gold
AUSTRALIA

Designed by Stuart Geddes with Mel Campbell, Natasha Ludowyk,
Penny Modra and Jeremy Wortsman of Chase & Galley
NOMINATED BY FLEUR WATSON

Big Brother logo
UK

Designed by Daniel Eatock for Channel 4
NOMINATED BY QUENTIN NEWARK

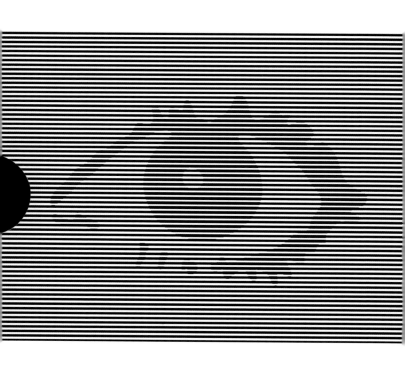

The Social Innovation Lab for Kent (SILK)
UK

Designed by Engine Service Design for Kent County Council
NOMINATED BY DANIEL CHARNY

Barack Obama Poster
USA

Designed by Shepard Fairey for Artists for Obama
NOMINATED BY PATRICK BURGOYNE

All the Time in the World
UK

Designed by Conny Freyer, Sebastien Noel and Eva Rucki of Troika;
manufactured by Elumin8; commissioned by British Airways for Terminal 5;
curated by Artwise
NOMINATED BY PATRICK BURGOYNE

Statistical Representation of the Economic Situation
UK

Designed by the *Guardian* design team, led by Michael Robinson
NOMINATED BY SIMON ESTERSON

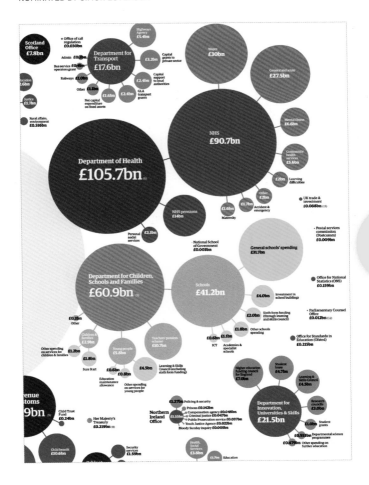

Baghdad Calling
NETHERLANDS

Designed by Mevis & Van Deursen; published by Episode Publishers
NOMINATED BY TONY BROOK

Martin Kippenberger: The Problem Perspective exhibition catalogue
USA

Designed by Lorraine Wild
NOMINATED BY EMILY KING

Barack Obama official election campaign logo
USA

Designed by Sender LLC and mo/de; creative director: Sol Sender;
designers: Amanda Gentry and Andy Keene of Sender LLC;
project managers: Steve Juras and Colin Carter of mo/de
NOMINATED BY ZOË RYAN

OASE 74 – Journal for Architecture: Invention
NETHERLANDS

Designed by Karel Martens and Enrico Bravi of Workplaats Typografie;
published by Eelco van Welie of NAi Publishers;
production: Barbera van Kooij of NAi Publishers
NOMINATED BY TONY BROOK

Jan Bons: A Designer's Freedom
NETHERLANDS

Designed by Lex Reitsma; published by De Buitenkant
NOMINATED BY SIMON ESTERSON

Cafe of Equivalent$

UK

Designed by kennardphillipps
NOMINATED BY ANGHARAD LEWIS

It's Nice That
UK

Edited by Will Hudson and Alex Bec; designed by It's Nice That
in collaboration with Joseph Burrin
NOMINATED BY SIMON ESTERSON

The Happy Hypocrite
UK

Designed by A Practice for Everyday Life (APFEL); edited by Maria Fusco;
published by Book Works
NOMINATED BY RICK POYNOR

The New Yorker cover, 2 November 2009
USA

Designed by Chris Ware
NOMINATED BY PATRICK BURGOYNE

032c magazine
GERMANY

Art direction by Mike Meiré
NOMINATED BY JEREMY LESLIE

Altermodern: Tate Triennial catalogue and poster design
UK

Designed by M/M (Paris)
NOMINATED BY RICK POYNER

The Newspaper Club
UK

Created by Ben Terrett, Russell Davies and Tom Taylor; supported by 4iP
NOMINATED BY SIMON ESTERSON AND JEREMY LESLIE

category winner

Russian Criminal Tattoo Encyclopaedia Volume III
UK

Designed and published by FUEL Design and Publishing
NOMINATED BY QUENTIN NEWARK

Voltaic: Songs from the Volta Tour
FRANCE

Designed by M/M (Paris) for Björk and released by One Little Indian
NOMINATED BY ZOË RYAN

War Memorial

UK

Designed by Harry Pearce at Pentagram for the Science Museum
NOMINATED BY PATRICK BURGOYNE

Yes
UK

Designed by Mark Farrow, Gary Stillwell and Sabine Fasching of Farrow
for Pet Shop Boys and the Vinyl Factory
NOMINATED BY PATRICK BURGOYNE

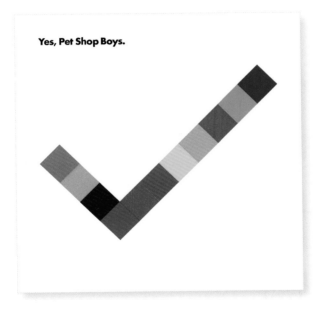

Corporate Diversity: Swiss Graphic Design and Advertising by Geigy 1940–1970
SWITZERLAND

Designed by NORM; edited by Andres Janser and Barbara Junod; published by Lars Müller Publishers and Museum für Gestaltung Zürich
NOMINATED BY TONY BROOK

Trillion Dollar Campaign
ZIMBABWE

Designed by TBWA\Hunt Lascaris for The Zimbabwean;
art directors: Shelley Smoler and Nadja Lossgott;
copywriters: Raphael Basckin and Nicholas Hulley
NOMINATED BY PATRICK BURGOYNE

The Indian Type Foundry
INDIA

Designed by Peter Bil'ak and Satya Rajpurohit
NOMINATED BY PATRICK BURGOYNE

Daily Visual Column for de Volkskrant
NETHERLANDS

Concept and design by De Designpolitie, Herman van Bostelen
and Lesley Moore of Gorilla
NOMINATED BY ANGHARAD LEWIS

Typographic Trees, Crawley Library
UK

Designed by Gordon Young and why not associates
NOMINATED BY DAVID KESTER

PIG 05049
NETHERLANDS

Written and designed by Christien Meindertsma and Julie Joliat
NOMINATED BY PAOLA ANTONELLI

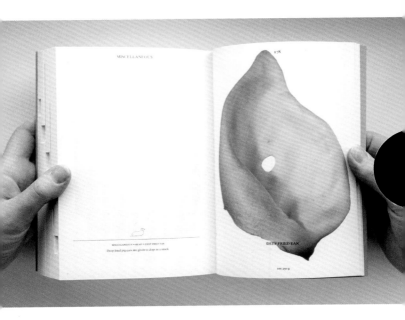

The Life and Opinions of Tristram Shandy, Gentleman
UK

Designed by A Practice For Everyday Life (APFEL); written by Laurence Sterne; published by Visual Editions
NOMINATED BY SIMON ESTERSON AND WILL HUDSON

Four Corners Familiars series
UK

Designed by John Morgan Studio and collaborators
NOMINATED BY CATHERINE INCE

Irma Boom: Biography in Books
NETHERLANDS

Designed by Irma Boom and published by Grafische Cultuurstichting
NOMINATED BY PAOLA ANTONELLI

Unit Editions
UK

Designed by Tony Brook and Adrian Shaughnessy
NOMINATED BY JEREMY LESLIE

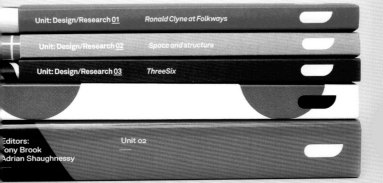

A Love Letter for You
USA

Designed by Stephen Powers, Icy, Mural Arts Philadelphia
and the Pew Center for Arts & Heritage
NOMINATED BY ALEX BEC

Homemade is Best
SWEDEN

Designed by Forsman & Bodenfors for IKEA
NOMINATED BY DAVID KESTER

category winner

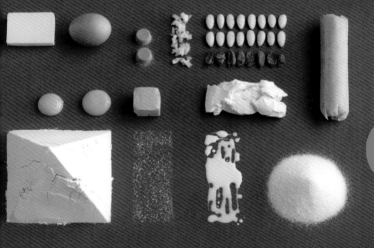

I Wonder
CANADA

Designed by Marian Bantjes and published by Thames & Hudson
NOMINATED BY SIMON ESTERSON

were meant for display, announcements in honour of an occasion afforded all the graphic pomp and circumstance befitting the historic event.

In the Jewish tradition, the act of honouring things related to God through beauty and adornment is called *hiddur mitzvah*. *Hiddur* means to make beautiful, and is a commandment or good deed. In this case, it is considered a good deed for one to take the time and effort to make or buy more beautiful ceremonial objects. The Jewish *ketubah* is a marriage document, a declaration of vows, a contract – and originally a pre-nuptial agreement – which is often displayed in the home as a reminder of the promises made between the couple. These, too, are often beautifully illuminated. Examples from the 17th century show elaborately designed and decorated *ketubot*, but even the *ketubah* is now available online as a pre-printed template (a choice that can't help but strike me as boding ill for the marriage).

In fact, most commemorative certificates are now mass-produced templates, sometimes still embellished with hand calligraphy for the honouree's name, but increasingly typeset, often in a blackletter typeface: the last nod to something from another time, and the layman's idea of 'fancy'. It seems that over the last two centuries, the time invested in the creation of documents slowly decreased, from the decline of highly elaborate penmanship, to the rise of templated engraving to haphazardly designed laser printouts.

For documents of true monetary value, fine detail, complexity, and intricate ornament served as an anticounterfeiting device, as it required a rare person of

great skill to duplicate the design and printing. In this way, stocks and bonds were also finely and beautifully engraved. As anti-counterfeiting measures have changed with the advancement of technology, and the use of computers has released the need of paper documents for proof of ownership, the ornamentation on most things – except money – has declined or disappeared altogether. Contemporary stock certificates still have a modicum of (templated) detailed bordering, but can't compare to those from before the 1970s. On cheques, stamps and credit cards, the formal complexity has been replaced with the casual and everyday: Those things that were once carefully designed and engraved with a minutiae of detail are now slapped up with pictures of kittens and sunsets beneath a slather of corporate logos. Credit cards are visual nightmares, and finding one that I can bear to look at on a daily basis is nearly impossible. They look neither valuable nor honourable to me, but rather like cheap, sentimental postcards or stills from swirling website advertisements.

For the past few years I have taken a series of small commissions from *Maclean's* magazine to create illustrations for their back page, which is always devoted to an obituary. The *Maclean's* obituaries are chosen not so much for the importance of the deceased, as for the significant details of the life in relation to the death. They are frequently poignant in the touching simplicity of the person and the tragic, often ironic end. The assignment is to draw a frame for the photo of the deceased, but to give the style or content of the frame some meaning to

Coalition of the Willing
AUSTRALIA

Directed and produced by Knife Party; written by Tim Rayner;
voiceover artist: Colin Tierney
NOMINATED BY SHANE WALTER

London College of Communication, Power of Ten Summer Show '10
UK

Designed by Studio Myerscough
NOMINATED BY IAN CARTLIDGE

Design Criminals edible catalogue
AUSTRIA

Designed by Andreas Pohancenik
NOMINATED BY THOMAS GEISLER

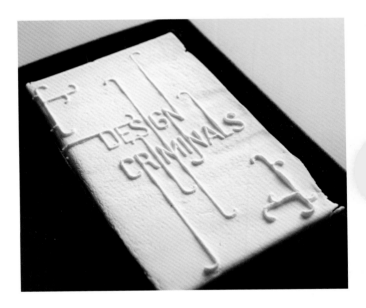

AA Files
UK

Designed and art directed by John Morgan Studio; edited by Tom Weaver; published by the Architectural Association
NOMINATED BY QUENTIN NEWARK

Photo-Lettering
USA

Designed by House Industries
NOMINATED BY SIMON ESTERSON

GF Smith 10,000 Digital Paintings campaign
UK

Designed by SEA Design; digital art by FIELD
NOMINATED BY SIMON ESTERSON

Beauty is in the Street: A Visual Record of the May '68 Paris Uprising
UK/USA/FRANCE

Cover designed by John Morgan Studio; book interior designed by
Pierre Le Hors; edited by Johan Kugelberg and Philippe Vermès;
published by Four Corners Books
NOMINATED BY ALEX BEC

Join Us cover artwork and video
USA

Designed for They Might Be Giants by Office of Paul Sahre; video production
by John Flansburgh and Paul Sahre; directed by Paul Sahre and Joe Hollier
NOMINATED BY TONY BROOK

The Comedy Carpet Blackpool

UK

Designed by Gordon Young with why not associates
NOMINATED BY PATRICK BURGOYNE AND MICHA WEIDMANN

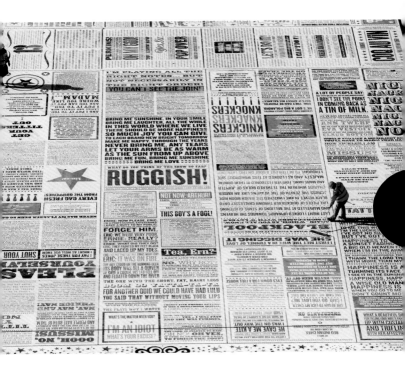

One Thousand Cranes for Japan
UK

Concept by Anomaly and UNIT9, using illustration agencies Breed, CIA, Blink Art, Dutch Uncle, Jelly and Picasso Pictures
NOMINATED BY PATRICK MYLES

Matthew Hilton identity and website
UK

Designed by Spin with photography by Matthew Hilton
NOMINATED BY IAN CARTLIDGE

What Design Can Do
NETHERLANDS

Designed by De Designpolitie
NOMINATED BY ADÉLIA BORGES

Cut it Out
UK

Designed by Noma Bar and partnered by Outline Editions
NOMINATED BY PATRICK MYLES

Bloomberg Businessweek

USA

Creative director: Richard Turley of Bloomberg Businessweek;
director of photography: David Carthas; design director: Cynthia Hoffman;
art director: Robert Vargas; graphics director: Jennifer Daniel
NOMINATED BY SIMON ESTERSON AND JEREMY LESLIE

Your Browser Sent a Request that this Server Could Not Understand
NETHERLANDS

Illustration by Koen Taselaar
NOMINATED BY FABIENNE VAN BEEK

Self Service
FRANCE

Published by Petronio Associates; editor-in-chief: Ezra Petronio;
fashion director: Suzanne Koller; managing editor: Claire Thomson-Jonville;
art director: Zachary Ohlman; senior designer: Xavier Encinas
NOMINATED BY TONY BROOK

Arizona Muse photographed by Alasdair McLellan

Nokia Pure
UK

Designed by Dalton Maag for Nokia
NOMINATED BY MICHA WEIDMANN

Stockmann Packaging
FINLAND

Designed by Kokoro & Moi for Stockmann
NOMINATED BY TONY BROOK

Dekho: Conversations on Design in India
INDIA

Designed, written and published by Codesign
NOMINATED BY AANCHAL SODHANI

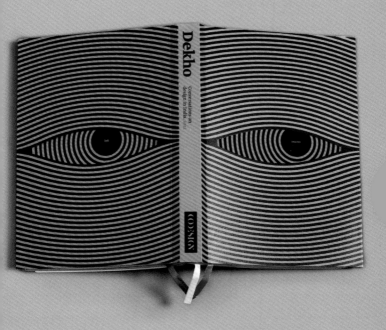

Austria Solar 2011 annual report
GERMANY

Designed by Serviceplan Group
NOMINATED BY EVONNE MACKENZIE

Zumtobel 2011/12 annual report
UK

Designed by Brighten the Corners; art direction by Anish Kapoor
NOMINATED BY ALEX BEC AND PATRICK MYLES

Bauhaus: Art as Life exhibition identity
UK

Designed by A Practice for Everyday Life (APFEL)
for the Barbican Art Gallery
NOMINATED BY TEAL TRIGGS

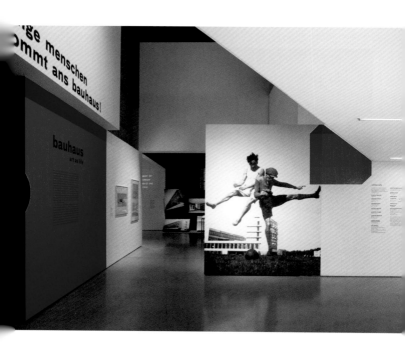

Kapow!
UK

Designed by Studio Frith and written by Adam Thirlwell
NOMINATED BY CATHERINE INCE

Doclisboa '12 identity
PORTUGAL

Designed by Pedro Nora
NOMINATED BY FREDERICO DUARTE

Rijksmuseum identity
NETHERLANDS

Designed by Irma Boom; typeface by Paul van der Laan of Bold Monday
NOMINATED BY FABIENNE VAN BEEK

Strelka institute identity
UK

Designed by OK-RM (Oliver Knight and Rory McGrath)
NOMINATED BY PATRICK MYLES AND TEAL TRIGGS

Organic
UK

Designed by Kapitza
NOMINATED BY LIZ FARRELLY

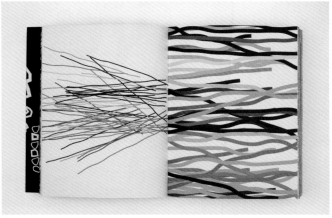

The Occupied Times of London
UK

Designed by Lazaros Kakoulidis and Tzortzis Rallis
NOMINATED BY PATRICK BURGOYNE, FREDERICO DUARTE AND TEAL TRIGGS

category winner

Venice Architecture Biennale identity
UK

Designed by John Morgan Studio
NOMINATED BY SARA DE BONDT AND SIMON ESTERSON

Made in L.A.: Work by Colby Poster Printing Co.
UK

Curated by Anthony Burrill and exhibited at KK Outlet
NOMINATED BY SARA DE BONDT

The Gentlewoman Magazine, Issue #6
NETHERLANDS

Designed by Studio Veronica Ditting and Jop van Bennekom;
cover image by Terry Richardson
NOMINATED BY JEREMY LESLIE

Australian cigarette packaging
AUSTRALIA

Commissioned by the Australian Government
Department of Health and Ageing
NOMINATED BY MANDI KEIGHRAN

Ralph Ellison series
USA

Designed by Cardon Webb
NOMINATED BY SARA DE BONDT

Grand-Central
SWITZERLAND

Designed by ECAL (École cantonale d'art de Lausanne) and Thibault Brevet
NOMINATED BY TONY BROOK

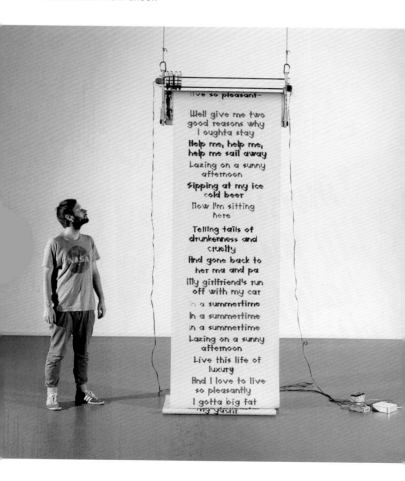

Drone Shadows
UK

Designed by James Bridle
NOMINATED BY PAOLA ANTONELLI

Serpentine Galleries identity
UK

Designed by Brian Boylan of Wolf Olins and Marina Willer
with Daniel Weil of Pentagram
NOMINATED BY SIMON ESTERSON AND TEAL TRIGGS

FRAC Provence-Alpes-Côte-d'Azur identity and signage
FRANCE

Designed by Jean-Marie Courant, Marie Proyart with Olivier Vadrot
and Alaric Garnier
NOMINATED BY FREDERICO DUARTE

2	**centre de documentation** documentation centre	→
	terrasse urbaine sidewalk terrace	→
1	**plateau exposition 2** stage exhibition 2	↙
	plateau multimédia multimedia stage	↙
	terrasse intérieure courtyard patio	↙
0	**accueil** reception area	↙
	restaurant restaurant	↙
-1	**plateau exposition 1** stage exhibition 1	↙

Escuyer identity
BELGIUM

Designed by Modern Practice
NOMINATED BY TONY BROOK

Works That Work: A Magazine of Unexpected Creativity
NETHERLANDS

Designed by Atelier Carvalho Bernau; editor-in-chief and publisher: Peter Bil'ak
NOMINATED BY SIMON ESTERSON AND TEAL TRIGGS

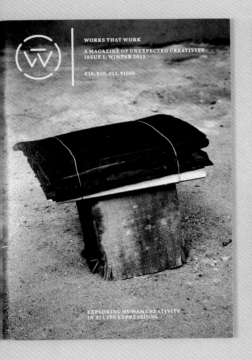

Chineasy
UK

Designed by ShaoLan Hsueh with illustrations by Noma Bar
NOMINATED BY TONY CHAMBERS

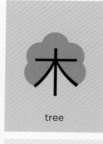

fire

tree

sun

moon

person

mouth

door

mountain

water

roof

king

woman

M to M of M/M (Paris)
UK

Designed by Graphic Thought Facility and written by Emily King
NOMINATED BY ZOË RYAN

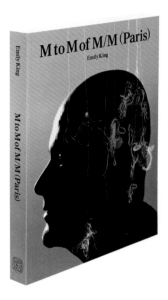

Whitney Museum of American Art identity
NETHERLANDS/USA

Designed by Experimental Jetset and the Whitney Museum design team
NOMINATED BY MICHA WEIDMANN

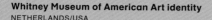

Art Directors Annual: 91
SWEDEN

Designed by Rami Niemi
NOMINATED BY ALEX BEC

Building Stories
USA

Designed and written by Chris Ware
NOMINATED BY SIMON ESTERSON

Castledown Primary School type family
UK

Designed by Anthony Sheret, Edd Harrington and Rupert Dunk
NOMINATED BY LIZ FARRELLY

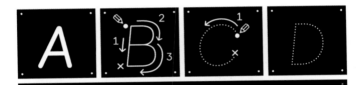

Castledown allows schools *flexibility* of use via both proportional and *cursive* cuts of the same *typeface*.

The Gourmand

UK

Editing and art direction by David Lane and Marina Tweed

NOMINATED BY SIMON ESTERSON

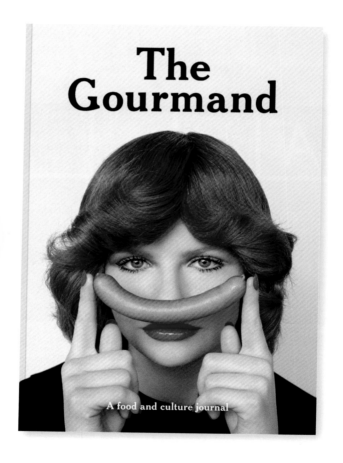

Modern Design Review
UK

Edited by Laura Houseley and designed by Graphic Thought Facility
NOMINATED BY MASON WELLS

Jurriaan Schrofer (1926–1990)
NETHERLANDS

Written by Frederike Huygen; designed by Jaap van Triest and Karel Martens; published by Astrid Vorstermans at Valiz
NOMINATED BY SIMON ESTERSON

Banknote design for Norges Bank
NORWAY

Designed by Metric Design, T Tønnessen and Snøhetta Design
for Norges Bank
NOMINATED BY MICHA WEIDMANN

MIT Media Lab identity
USA

Designed by Michael Bierut and Aron Fay of Pentagram for the
Massachusetts Institute of Technology (MIT)
NOMINATED BY LIZ FARRELLY

WIRED custom typeface
UK

Designed by Sawdust for WIRED magazine
NOMINATED BY BERNARD MCCOY

Designing for the Sixth Extinction
UK

Designed by Alexandra Daisy Ginsberg for the Science Gallery, Dublin
NOMINATED BY FRITH KERR

The Way of the Shovel: Art as Archaeology
FRANCE/USA

Designed by Romain André and Michael Savona for
the Museum of Contemporary Art Chicago
NOMINATED BY TIM PARSONS

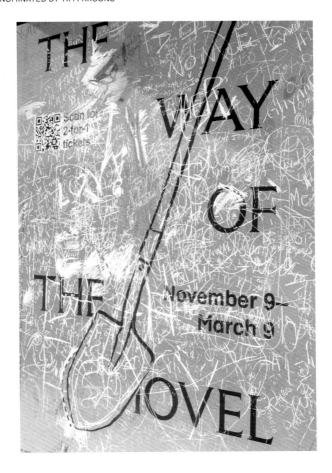

Kenzopedia
FRANCE

Designed by Toni Halonen for Kenzo Paris
NOMINATED BY SUVI SALONIEMI

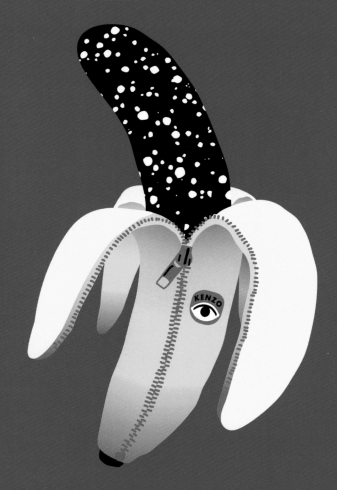

Riposte magazine
UK

Founded and edited by Danielle Pender; creative director: Shaz Madani
NOMINATED BY SIMON ESTERSON

100 Years of Swiss Graphic Design
SWITZERLAND

Designed by NORM and published by Lars Müller
NOMINATED BY MASON WELLS

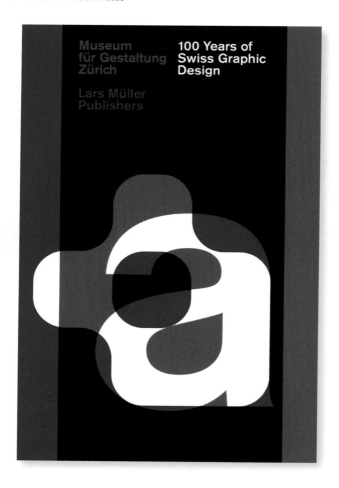

Franchise Animated
NETHERLANDS

Project initiated by Jeroen Krielaars of Animography;
type design by Derek Weathersby
NOMINATED BY LIZ FARRELLY

No.5 Culture Chanel
NETHERLANDS

Designed by Irma Boom for Chanel
NOMINATED BY JEROEN VAN ERP

Inglorious Fruits and Vegetables
FRANCE

Designed by Marcel for Intermarché
NOMINATED BY ALEX BEC AND MAX FRASER

Glasgow International 2014 identity
UK

Designed by Kellenberger–White for Festival Director Sarah McCrory
NOMINATED BY VICKY RICHARDSON

P98a Paper
GERMANY

Designed by Susanna Dulkinys, Erik Spiekermann and Ferdinand Ulrich
NOMINATED BY LIZ FARRELLY

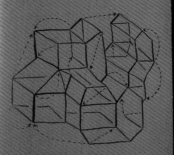

Cuyperspassage tile mural
NETHERLANDS

Designed by Irma Boom for Benthem Crouwel Architects;
manufactured by Royal Tichelaar Makkum
NOMINATED BY JEROEN VAN ERP

Shot on iPhone: World Gallery
USA

Designed by Duncan Milner at TBWA/Media Arts Lab for Apple
NOMINATED BY MICHA WEIDMANN

Bottom Ash Observatory

NETHERLANDS

Designed by Christien Meindertsma; photographs by Mathijs Labadie; published by Thomas Eyck

NOMINATED BY ZOË RYAN

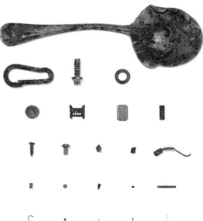

category winner

UK

Designed by Jonathan Barnbrook of Barnbrook for David Bowie
and Sony Entertainment Inc.
NOMINATED BY SHANE WALTER

The Norwegian Landscape passport design
NORWAY

Designed by Benjamin Stenmarck, Lars Håvard Dahlstrøm,
Øystein Haugseth and Gørill Kvamme of Neue Design Studio
NOMINATED BY WAYNE HEMINGWAY

We Listen
UK

Designed by MullenLowe; photographs by Nadav Kander;
for Network Rail and Samaritans
NOMINATED BY WAYNE HEMINGWAY

First Aid Kit for Refugees & NGOs
AUSTRIA

Designed by Erwin K. Bauer, Anne Hofmann, Dasha Zaichanka,
Katharina Hölzl and Miriam S. Koller at Buero Bauer
NOMINATED BY THOMAS GEISLER

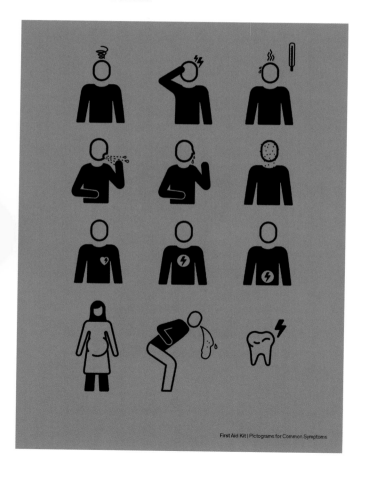

First Aid Kit | Pictograms for Common Symptoms

Channel 4 rebrand
UK

Designed by DBLG; led by creative director Steven Qua and by Neville Brody
of Brody Associates for 4Creative; idents directed by Jonathan Glazer for
A+/Academy Films
NOMINATED BY ADRIAN SHAUGHNESSY

Hello Ruby
FINLAND

Designed by Linda Liukas with Jemina Lehmuskoski
NOMINATED BY SUVI SALONIEMI

Dear Data
USA/EUROPE

Designed by Giorgia Lupi and Stefanie Posavec
NOMINATED BY PAOLA ANTONELLI

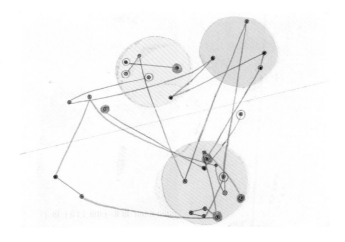

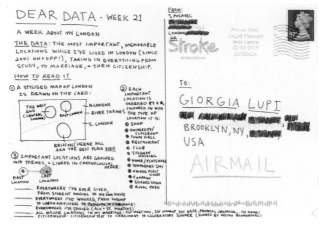

Almadía Books cover design
MEXICO

Designed by Alejandro Magallanes for Almadía Books
NOMINATED BY FELIPE TABORDA

GRUPA protest posters and placards
MALAYSIA

Designed by Grafik Rebel Untuk Protes & Aktivisme (GRUPA)
NOMINATED BY FREDERICO DUARTE

Dikke Van Dale Dutch language dictionary
NETHERLANDS

Designed by Studio Joost Grootens for Van Dale Publishers
NOMINATED BY MICHA WEIDMANN

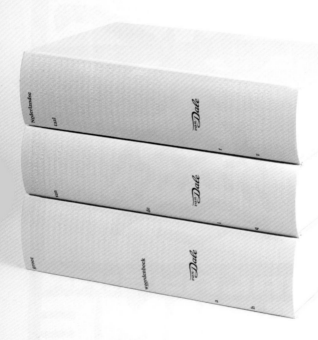

'Fractured Lands', The New York Times Magazine, 14 August 2016
USA

Editor-in-chief: Jake Silverstein; design director: Gail Bichler;
art director: Matt Willey
NOMINATED BY SIMON ESTERSON

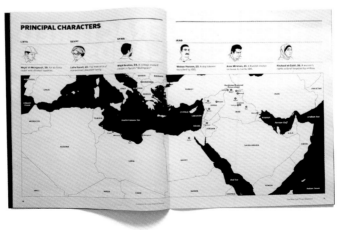

Pro-EU Anti-Brexit Poster Campaign (Vote Remain 23 June), 2016
UK

Designed by Wolfgang Tillmans for Between Bridges
NOMINATED BY CATHARINE ROSSI

The Refugee Nation Flag
INTERNATIONAL

Designed by Yara Said with The Refugee Nation for Amnesty International
NOMINATED BY DAVID KESTER

Finding Her

JAPAN

Designed by IC4DESIGN with DDB Dubai for UN Women Egypt

NOMINATED BY ANNIINA KOIVU

Wales nation brand
UK

Designed by Smörgåsbord
NOMINATED BY WILL HUDSON

Ibiza Mykonos Jeremy Corbyn (Political Posters)
UK

Designed by Michael Oswell
NOMINATED BY BEN TERRETT

Your Flat Will Continue To Deteriorate And Its Rent Increase.

You Will Be Intimidated By Vandalism And Petty Crime. The Bus Service Will Get Worse.

There Will Be More Traffic And Noise Pollution And An Increased Risk Of Getting Knocked Down Crossing The Road.

There Will Be More Drunks Pissing In The Street When You Look Out Of Your Window And More Children Taking Drugs On The Stairs When You Come Home At Night.

Your Job Will Be At Risk And Subjected To Interference. Your Income Will Decrease. You Will Drink More And Less Well. You Will Be Ill More Often. You Will Die Sooner, And Also Fuck You.

Real Review
UK

Editor-in-chief: Jack Self; creative directors:
Oliver Knight and Rory McGrath of OK-RM
NOMINATED BY ALEX MILTON

N.A.A.F.I
MEXICO

Designed by Alberto Bustamante a.k.a. Mexican Jihad
NOMINATED BY JOSÉ ESPARZA CHONG CUY

Unit Editions
UK

Designed by Tony Brook, Adrian Shaughnessy and Patricia Finegan
NOMINATED BY QUENTIN NEWARK

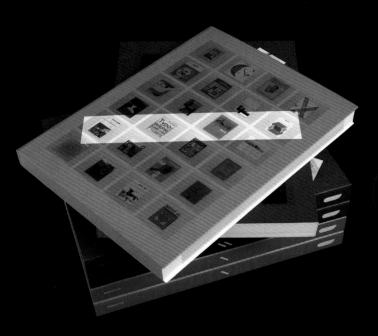

ME & EU

UK

Designed by Nathan Smith and Sam T. Smith of GBH London
NOMINATED BY MICHA WEIDMANN

Protest Banner Lending Library

USA

Designed by Aram Han Sifuentes in collaboration with
Verónica Casado Hernández, Ishita Dharap and Tabitha Anne Kunkes
NOMINATED BY CATHERINE FLOOD

Reykjavik Art Museum visual identity
USA

Designed by karlssonwilker inc. for Listasafn Reykjavíkur
(Reykjavik Art Museum)
NOMINATED BY SARAH ARCHER

product

Nobody chair

BELGIUM

Designed by Komplot for HAY

NOMINATED BY MARCUS FAIRS

Neo-Country Furniture
NETHERLANDS

Design by Ineke Hans for Cappellini
NOMINATED BY PENNY SPARKE

Anglepoise Fifty table light
UK

Designed by Anthony Dickens for Anglepoise
NOMINATED BY DANIEL CHARNY

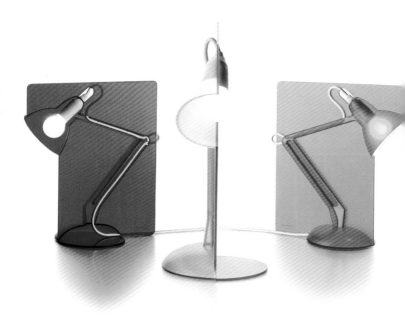

Facett Sofa and Chairs
FRANCE

Design by Ronan and Erwan Bouroullec for Ligne Roset
NOMINATED BY ZEEV ARAM

3W LED torch
JAPAN

Designed by Yohei Kuwano for MUJI
NOMINATED BY SAM HECHT

Panna Chair
JAPAN

Designed by Tokujin Yoshioka Design for Moroso
NOMINATED BY FRANCESCA PICCHI

Make/Shift shelving
GERMANY

Designed by Peter Marigold for Movisi
NOMINATED BY ZEEV ARAM

2008

100 Chairs in 100 Days
UK

Designed and manufactured by Martino Gamper
NOMINATED BY NADINE JARVIS

INFOBAR 2 mobile phone

JAPAN

Designed by Naoto Fukasawa for KDDI Corporation

NOMINATED BY SAM HECHT

Bambu Table and Chairs
FINLAND

Designed by Artek Studio
NOMINATED BY DEYAN SUDJIC

Electronic Calculator S

JAPAN

Designed by Naoto Fukasawa Design for PLUS MINUS ZERO CO., LTD
NOMINATED BY ANTHONY DUNNE

Mayuhana lamp series
JAPAN

Designed by Toyo Ito for Yamagiwa
NOMINATED BY STEFANO CASCIANI

One Laptop Per Child
USA

Designed by Yves Béhar of fuseproject for OLPC and Quanta Computer Inc.
NOMINATED BY TONY CHAMBERS

Smithfield hanging lights
UK

Designed by Jasper Morrison for Flos
NOMINATED BY DEYAN SUDJIC

Sketch Furniture
SWEDEN

Designed by FRONT
NOMINATED BY NADINE JARVIS

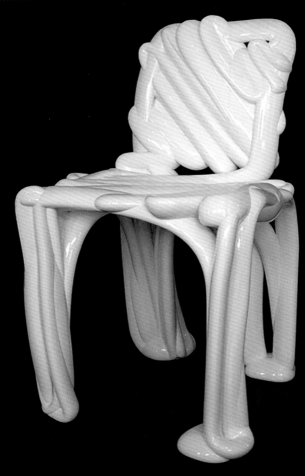

Eva Solo Bin

DENMARK

Designed by Tools Design for Eva Solo A/S
NOMINATED BY DANIEL CHARNY

Moore Armchair
FRANCE

Designed by Philippe Starck for Driade
NOMINATED BY PENNY SPARKE

MEDIA SKIN mobile phone
JAPAN

Designed by Tokujin Yoshioka for KDDI CORPORATION
NOMINATED BY DEYAN SUDJIC

El Ultimo Grito en La Casa Encendida: 100m bench installation
SPAIN

Designed and built by El Ultimo Grito for La Casa Encendida
NOMINATED BY DANIEL CHARNY

Muon four-way loudspeakers
UK

Designed by Ross Lovegrove; concept by KEF
NOMINATED BY DEYAN SUDJIC

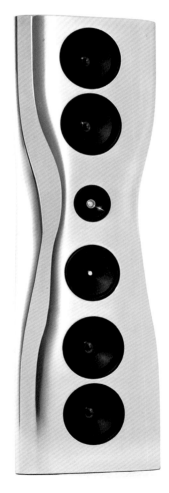

iPhone
USA

Designed by Jonathan Ive for Apple Inc.
NOMINATED BY ANTHONY DUNNE, SAM HECHT, MATT JONES AND LYNDA RELPH-KNIGHT

XL X-Beam Ratcheting Wrench
USA

Designed by Richard Macor of Proprietary Technologies Inc. for Gear Wrench
NOMINATED BY SAM HECHT

Saturn coat stand
UK

Designed by Barber & Osgerby for ClassiCon
NOMINATED BY PHILIP GARNER

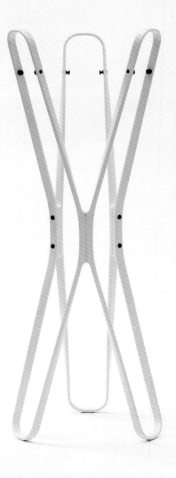

Tab Lamp prototype with reflector
UK

Designed by Barber & Osgerby for Flos
NOMINATED BY DEYAN SUDJIC

Wind Up Radio
JAPAN

Designed by Yohei Kuwano for MUJI
NOMINATED BY DEYAN SUDJIC

Piggyback table
UK

Designed by Heatherwick Studio for Magis
NOMINATED BY DEYAN SUDJIC

TransPlastic Series
BRAZIL

Designed by Fernando and Humberto Campana
NOMINATED BY AMBRA MEDDA

Samsung Refrigerator J-Series
UK

Designed by Jasper Morrison for Samsung
NOMINATED BY FRANCESCA PICCHI

PizzaKobra table lamp
UK

Designed by Ron Arad for iGuzzini
NOMINATED BY DEYAN SUDJIC

Tenori-On digital musical instrument
JAPAN

Designed by Toshio Iwai and produced by Yu Nishibori of Yamaha

NOMINATED BY ANTHONY DUNNE, EMMA QUINN,
MORITZ WALDEMEYER AND SHANE WALTER

Ten Key Calculator
JAPAN

Designed by Ippei Matsumoto/Industrial Facility for IDEA International Japan
NOMINATED BY ANTHONY DUNNE

Volant armchair
ITALY

Designed by Patricia Urquiola for Moroso
NOMINATED BY PENNY SPARKE

Wavy Chair
UK

Designed by Ron Arad for Moroso
NOMINATED BY DEYAN SUDJIC

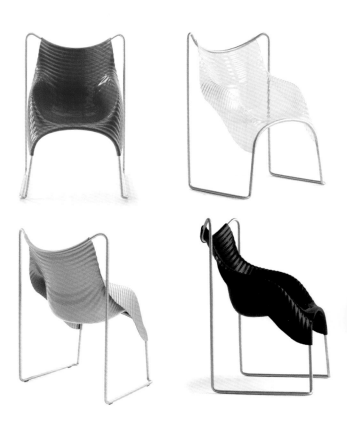

Nintendo Wii
JAPAN

Designed and produced by Nintendo
NOMINATED BY ANTHONY DUNNE

Jar Tops
NETHERLANDS

Designed by Jorre van Ast for Royal VKB
NOMINATED BY SAM HECHT

Stack chest of drawers
UK

Designed by Raw Edges and Shay Alkalay for Established & Sons Ltd
NOMINATED BY DANIEL CHARNY

Lover's Chair from the Evolution Series
SPAIN

Designed by Nacho Carbonell
NOMINATED BY ALEXANDRA CUNNINGHAM

Composite bench system
SPAIN

Designed by El Ultimo Grito
NOMINATED BY DANIEL CHARNY

Fig Leaf wardrobe
UK

Designed by Studio Tord Boontje for Meta
NOMINATED BY EMILY CAMPBELL

CLEAN
FRANCE

Designed by Vincent Baranger, Anthony Lebossé, Claire Renard,
Jean-Sebastien Blanc of 5.5 designstudio; in partnership with
Cyril Delage of Enkidoo
NOMINATED BY IAN JOHNSTON

HomeHero fire extinguisher
USA

Designed by Peter Arnell for Home Depot
NOMINATED BY SAM HECHT

Ipogeo Tasklight
ITALY

Designed by Joe Wentworth for Artemide
NOMINATED BY RUTH UR

Cabbage Chair
JAPAN

Designed by Nendo for XXIst Century Man
at 21_21 Design Sight, Tokyo, Japan
NOMINATED BY HENRIETTA THOMPSON

Surface Table
UK

Designed by Terence Woodgate and John Barnard for Established & Sons Ltd
NOMINATED BY SHERIDAN COAKLEY

The MacGuffin Library
UK

Designed by Onkar Kular and Noam Toran for Somerset House
NOMINATED BY ANTHONY DUNNE

Pixel Clock
FRANCE

Designed by François Azembourg for Ligne Roset
NOMINATED BY IAN JOHNSTON

2009

MYTO chair
ITALY

Designed by Konstantin Grcic and manufactured by Plank
NOMINATED BY FRANCESCA PICCHI, VICKY RICHARDSON,
ZOË RYAN AND EMILIA TERRAGNI

Armadillo vest with face mask
NORWAY

Designed by Leif Verdu-Isachsen, Marianne Støren Berg,
Mads Hadler of Kode Design; in partnership with Norsk Folkehjelp,
Rofi Industrier; for Design without Borders (DwB)
NOMINATED BY ANNA THORUD HAMMER

WorKit office system
SWITZERLAND

Designed by Arik Levy for Vitra
NOMINATED BY MARTINO GAMPER

Stitch Chair
ITALY

Designed by Adam Goodrum for Cappellini
NOMINATED BY BRIAN PARKES AND EMILIA TERRAGNI

category winner

Magno Wooden Radio
INDONESIA

Designed and conceived by Singgih S Kartono;
manufactured by locals in Java
NOMINATED BY HENRIETTA THOMPSON

Witness Flat
NETHERLANDS

Designed by Studio Makkink & Bey for la Galerie de Pierre Bergé
NOMINATED BY CAROLINE ROUX

Light Wind
NETHERLANDS

Designed by Demakersvan
NOMINATED BY IAN JOHNSTON

Green Felt Protest Suit
UK

Designed by Tony Mullin
NOMINATED BY ONKAR KULAR

SENZ XL Storm Umbrella
NETHERLANDS

Designed by Gerwin Hoogendoorn, Gerard Kool, Philip Hess
and Niels Heijman of SENZ
NOMINATED BY IAN JOHNSTON

Rotational Moulded Shoe
UK

Designed and produced by Marloes Ten Bhömer;
design of the rotational moulding machine: Nick Williamson
NOMINATED BY ONKAR KULAR

Cloakroom at the Museum Boijmans van Beuningen
NETHERLANDS

Designed by Studio Wieki Somers for Museum Boijmans van Beuningen
Rotterdam; in partnership with Haunting Dogs Full of Grace
NOMINATED BY CAROLINE ROUX

Venus Natural Crystal Chair
JAPAN

Designed by Tokujin Yoshioka Design
NOMINATED BY AMBRA MEDDA AND FLEUR WATSON

Steelwood Family
ITALY

Designed by Ronan and Erwan Bouroullec for Magis
NOMINATED BY FRANCESCA PICCHI

3D Stencil
AUSTRALIA

Designed by Trent Jansen Studio
NOMINATED BY BRIAN PARKES

PlantLock
UK

Designed by Duncan Kramer and Dan Monck of the Front Yard Company
NOMINATED BY SAM HECHT

blown-fabric lanterns
JAPAN

Designed by Nendo; produced by Asahi Kasei Fibers Corporation
NOMINATED BY FRANCESCA PICCHI

Ski helmet for girls
NORWAY

Designed by Per Finne Industrial Design for Kari Traa
NOMINATED BY ANNA THORUD HAMMER

Grassworks
NETHERLANDS

Designed by Jair Straschnow
NOMINATED BY DANIEL CHARNY, PHILIPPE GARNER AND GARETH WILLIAMS

The Pallet Project furniture
UK

Designed by Nina Tolstrup of Studiomama
NOMINATED BY HENRIETTA THOMPSON

Mu Folding Plug
UK

Designed by Min-Kyu Choi
NOMINATED BY TONY CHAMBERS, DANIEL CHARNY,
MARCUS FAIRS, SAM HECHT AND SHANE WALTER

Carbon Fibre Chair
JAPAN

Designed by Shigeru Ban Architects; material by TENAX;
provided by Teijin Ltd
NOMINATED BY FRANCESCA PICCHI

Extrusions
UK

Designed by Heatherwick Studio
NOMINATED BY CAROLINE ROUX

Setu office chair
GERMANY

Designed by Studio 7.5; manufactured by Herman Miller
NOMINATED BY SAM HECHT

Repair Project
PORTUGAL

Designed and conceived by Linda Brothwell; commissioned by the
British Council for Experimenta Design, Lisbon
NOMINATED BY EMILY CAMPBELL

The Idea of a Tree
AUSTRIA

Designed by Katharina Mischer and Thomas Traxler of mischer'traxler
NOMINATED BY THOMAS GEISLER

CASE Abyss
NORWAY

Designed by Abyssus Marine Services for SeaBird Technologies
NOMINATED BY ANNA THORUD HAMMER

2010

360° Work Chair
GERMANY

Designed by Konstantin Grcic and manufactured by Magis
NOMINATED BY PAOLA ANTONELLI AND CAROLINE ROUX

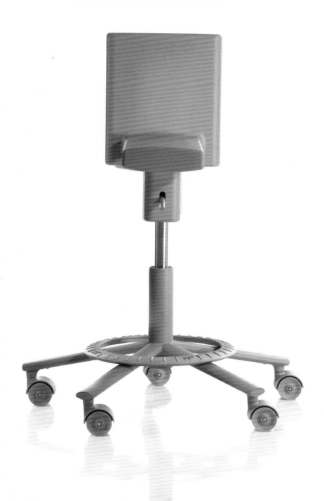

Kyoto Box
KENYA

Designed by Jon Bøhmer
NOMINATED BY TONY CHAMBERS

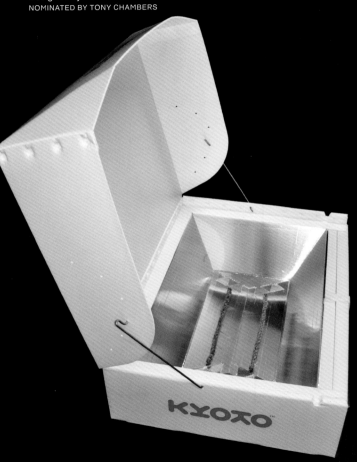

Houdini chair
GERMANY

Designed by Stefan Diez and manufactured by e15
NOMINATED BY FRANCESCA PICCHI AND EMILIA TERRAGNI

Breathe furniture

AUSTRALIA

Designed by Helen Kontouris and manufactured by SunWeave International
NOMINATED BY BRIAN PARKES

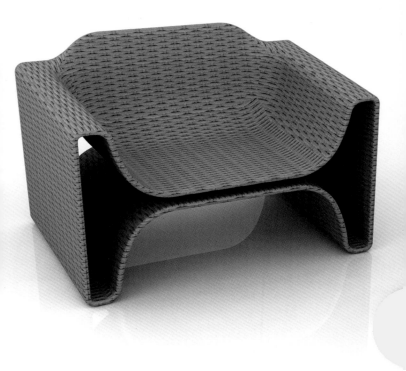

Design Bugs Out Commode
UK

Designed by PearsonLloyd; manufactured by Kirton Healthcare
NOMINATED BY DAVID KESTER

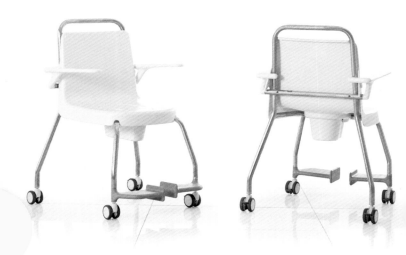

Beehaus

UK

Designed by Johannes Paul, James Tuthill, William Windham
and Simon Nicholls of Omlet
NOMINATED BY DAVID KESTER

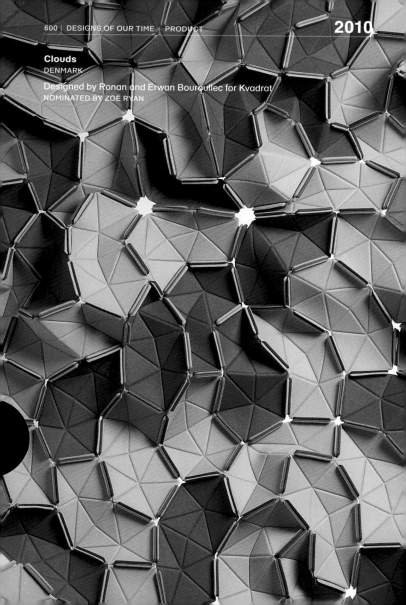

Clouds
DENMARK

Designed by Ronan and Erwan Bouroullec for Kvadrat
NOMINATED BY ZOË RYAN

PACT underwear
USA

Designed by Yves Béhar and produced by Jason Kibbey
and Jeff Denby of PACT
NOMINATED BY LYNDA RELPH-KNIGHT

Parcs furniture
UK

Designed by PearsonLloyd and manufactured by Bene
NOMINATED BY THOMAS GEISLER

Design and Democracy: Blanke Ark
NORWAY

Designed by Blueroom, Innovativoli and Kadabra
NOMINATED BY NINA BERRE

Worldmade Sport wheelchair
UK

Designed by David Constantine, Stefan Constantinescu, Ray Mines
and Jen Howitt Browning; manufactured by Motivation
NOMINATED BY DANIEL CHARNY

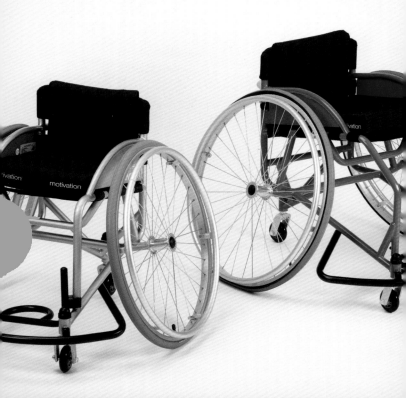

Sugru
UK

Designed by Jane Ní Dhulchaointigh; researched and developed by
James Carrigan, Dr Steve Westall, Dr Ian Moss and Tom Dowden
NOMINATED BY HENRIETTA THOMPSON

Real Time

THE NETHERLANDS

Designed by Maarten Baas

NOMINATED BY ED ANNINK, MARCUS FAIRS,
FRANCESCA PICCHI AND HENRIETTA THOMPSON

The Story of Stuff
USA

Written and narrated by Annie Leonard; produced by Free Range Studios
NOMINATED BY ED ANNINK

Soma
ISRAEL

Designed by Ayala Serfaty
NOMINATED BY CAROLINE ROUX

Hope chandelier
ITALY

Designed by Francisco Gomez Paz and Paolo Rizzatto for Luceplan
NOMINATED BY FRANCESCA PICCHI

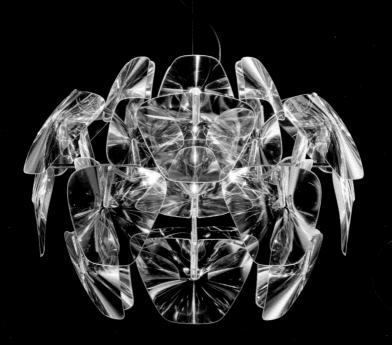

Polytopia
AUSTRALIA

Designed by Lucas Chirnside
NOMINATED BY BRIAN PARKES

Samsung N310 Mini Notebook
JAPAN

Designed by Naoto Fukasawa and manufactured by Samsung
NOMINATED BY SAM HECHT

L'Eau d'Issey Ettore Sottsass edition
FRANCE

Designed by Issey Miyake
NOMINATED BY SAM HECHT

2010

Palindrome Series
UK

Designed by Peter Marigold
NOMINATED BY ALEXANDRA CUNNINGHAM

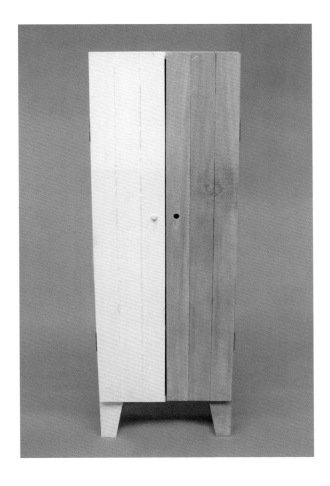

In-Betweening Clock
UK

Designed by Hye-Yeon Park
NOMINATED BY GARETH WILLIAMS

Freecom Mobile Drive CLS
GERMANY

Designed by Sylvain Willenz; manufactured by Freecom
NOMINATED BY ARIC CHEN

Contemplating Monolithic Design
JAPAN/UK

Designed by Sony Design and Barber & Osgerby;
exhibition design by Universal Design Studio
NOMINATED BY ZOË RYAN

ACT Fire Extinguisher
NORWAY

Designed by Sigrun Vik
NOMINATED BY ANNA THORUD HAMMER

Plumen 001
UK

Concept and design direction by Hulger; designed by Samuel Wilkinson
NOMINATED BY SAM HECHT AND SHANE WALTER

overall winner

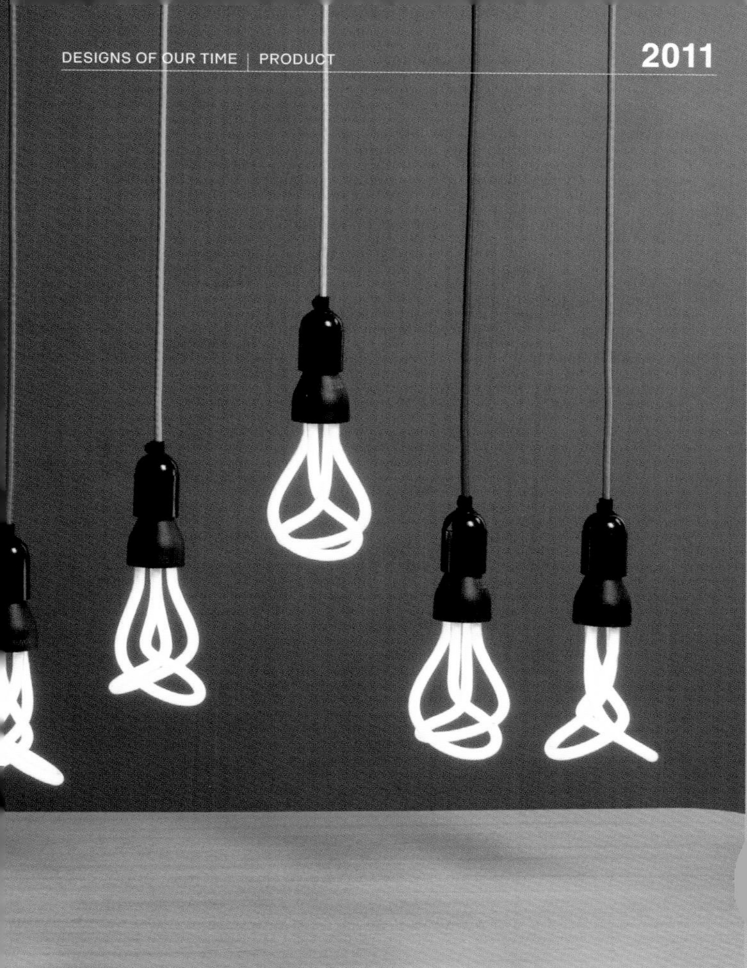

Pavegen
UK

Designed by Laurence Kemball-Cook and Philip Tucker
NOMINATED BY SEBASTIAN CONRAN

Playing with LEGO Bricks and Paper
JAPAN/DENMARK

Designed by MUJI and LEGO
NOMINATED BY SAM HECHT

Amplify chandelier
USA

Designed by Yves Béhar and fuseproject for Swarovski
NOMINATED BY MICHELLE OGUNDEHIN

PramPack
NORWAY

Designed by Kadabra Produktdesign; invented by Anne Morkemo;
manufactured by STOKKE
NOMINATED BY ANNA THORUD HAMMER

Dyson Air Multiplier
UK

Designed by James Dyson
NOMINATED BY SEBASTIAN CONRAN

Collec+ors collection
AUSTRALIA

Designed by Khai Liew, Julie Blyfield, Kirsten Coelho, Jessica Loughlin,
Bruce Nuske, Gwyn Hanssen Pigott and Prue Venables
NOMINATED BY BRIAN PARKES

Dune furniture
AUSTRIA

Designed by Rainer Mutsch; manufactured by Eternit
NOMINATED BY THOMAS GEISLER

2011

Branca Chair
ITALY

Designed by Industrial Facility, Sam Hecht, Kim Colin and Ippei Matsumoto; manufactured by Mattiazzi
NOMINATED BY DANIEL CHARNY

Flying Future
GERMANY

Designed by Ingo Maurer
NOMINATED BY FRANCESCA PICCHI

Blueware Collection
UK

Designed by Glithero; developed with Vauxhall Collective
NOMINATED BY HENRIETTA THOMPSON

See Better to Learn Better
USA/MEXICO

Designed by Yves Béhar and fuseproject, in partnership with Augen Optics
NOMINATED BY MICHELLE OGUNDEHIN

Vigna Chair
ITALY

Designed by Martino Gamper and manufactured by Magis
NOMINATED BY FRANCESCA PICCHI

Quarz Series
AUSTRIA

Designed by Max Lamb; manufactured by Lobmeyr
NOMINATED BY THOMAS GEISLER

IntimateRider
USA

Designed by Alan Tholkes
NOMINATED BY DANIEL CHARNY

Drop table
ITALY

Designed by Junya Ishigami and manufactured by Living Divani
NOMINATED BY FRANCESCA PICCHI

Diamant Series coffins
DENMARK

Designed by Jacob Jensen Design; manufactured by Tommerup Kister
NOMINATED BY HENRIETTA THOMPSON

Plytube
UK

Designed by Seongyong Lee
NOMINATED BY HENRIETTA THOMPSON, GARETH WILLIAMS AND JANE WITHERS

Endless chair
NETHERLANDS

Designed by Dirk vander Kooij
NOMINATED BY ED ANNINK

iPad
USA

Designed by Apple Inc.

NOMINATED BY PATRICK BURGOYNE, SEBASTIAN CONRAN,
JEREMY LESLIE, LYNDA RELPH-KNIGHT AND DAVID ROWAN

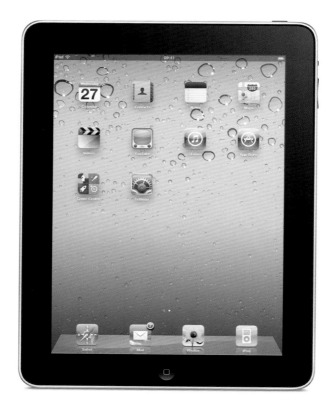

Sayl task chair
USA

Designed by Yves Béhar and fuseproject; manufactured by Herman Miller
NOMINATED BY SAM HECHT

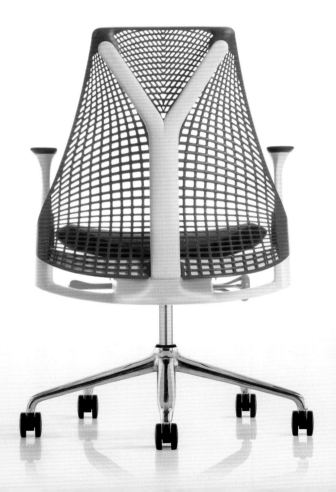

2011

Wall Piercing
ITALY

Designed by Ron Gilad and manufactured by Flos
NOMINATED BY PAOLA ANTONELLI AND ZOË RYAN

Yii
TAIWAN

Conceived by National Taiwan Craft Research Institute (NTCRI)
and Taiwan Design Centre (TDC); creative direction by Gijs Bakker
NOMINATED BY FRANCESCA PICCHI

Spun chair
UK

Designed by Heatherwick Studio and manufactured by Magis
NOMINATED BY DANIEL CHARNY AND DAVID ROWAN

Thin Black Lines series
JAPAN

Designed by Nendo; exhibited by Phillips De Pury & Company
at the Saatchi Gallery
NOMINATED BY CAROLINE ROUX AND HENRIETTA THOMPSON

2011

One Arm Drive wheelchair system
UK

Designed by Jon Owen and Mark Owen;
manufactured by Nomad Wheelchairs Ltd
NOMINATED BY DAVID ROWAN

Leveraged Freedom Chair
USA

Designed by MIT Mobility Laboratory; developed in collaboration with
Association for the Physically Disabled In Kenya, BMVSS Jaipur, Continuum,
Indian Institute of Technology, Transitions Foundation of Guatemala
and Whirlwind Wheelchair International
NOMINATED BY DANIEL CHARNY

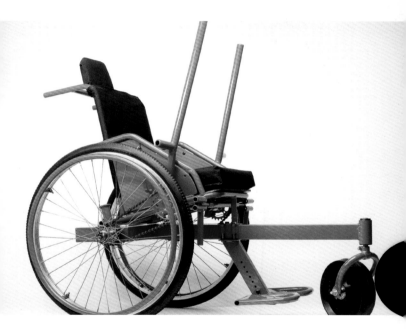

Universal Gown
UK

Designed by Ben de Lisi
NOMINATED BY DAVID KESTER

Origin Part I: Join
NETHERLANDS

Designed by BCXSY in collaboration with Mr Tanaka
NOMINATED BY HENRIETTA THOMPSON

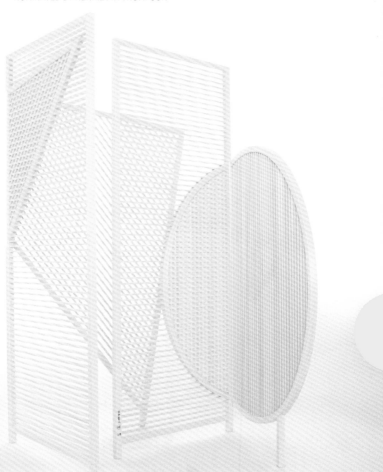

Solo Bench
BRAZIL

Designed by Domingos Tótora
NOMINATED BY ADÉLIA BORGES

Earthquake Table
ISRAEL

Designed by Arthur Brutter and Ido Bruno; product development by
Bezalel Labs Research & Development Company Ltd; manufactured
by A. D. Meraz Industries Ltd
NOMINATED BY DANIEL CHARNY

Carbon Black wheelchair
UK

Designed by Andrew Slorance; manufactured by I-imagine
NOMINATED BY DANIEL CHARNY

Nest Learning Thermostat
USA

Designed and manufactured by Nest
NOMINATED BY SAM HECHT

White Collection lights
FINLAND

Designed by Ville Kokkonen of Artek; manufactured by Artek
NOMINATED BY CAROLINE ROUX

Harbour Chair
UK

Designed by André Klauser and Ed Carpenter;
manufactured by Very Good & Proper
NOMINATED BY EMILIA TERRAGNI

The Crates series
CHINA

Designed and manufactured by Jingjing Naihan Li of Naihan Li & Co.
NOMINATED BY ARIC CHEN AND CAROLINE ROUX

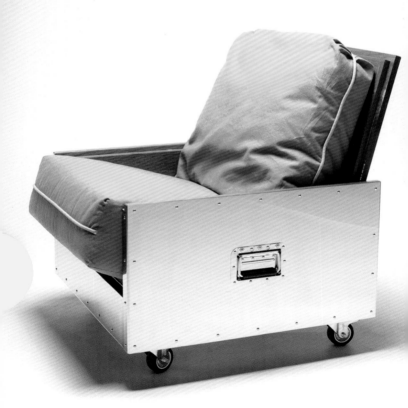

2012

1.3 Chair
UK

Designed by Kihyun Kim and manufactured by Zeitraum
NOMINATED BY GARETH WILLIAMS

Ascent
UK

Designed by Barber & Osgerby; commissioned by Haunch of Venison
NOMINATED BY LYNDA RELPH-KNIGHT

Heracleum light
NETHERLANDS

Designed by Studio Bertjan Pot and manufactured by Moooi;
Electrosandwich® technology by Marcel Wanders
NOMINATED BY ANTOINETTE KLAWER

NSEPS (Not So Expanded Polystyrene)
UK

Designed by Attua Aparicio Torinos and Oscar Wanless of Silo
NOMINATED BY LIZ FARRELLY AND GARETH WILLIAMS

2012

Oak Inside furniture

NETHERLANDS

Designed by Christien Meindertsma; commissioned by Thomas Eyck;
manufactured by Roosje Hindeloopen
NOMINATED BY THORSTEN VAN ELTEN

A-frame and Corb
UK

Designed by Ron Arad and manufactured by pq
NOMINATED BY DANIEL CHARNY

Defibtech Lifeline VIEW AED
USA

Designed and manufactured by Defibtech
NOMINATED BY DANIEL CHARNY

Olympic Torch 2012
UK

Designed by Barber & Osgerby; commissioned by
the London Organising Committee of the Olympic and
Paralympic Games (LOCOG); engineered by Tecosim UK;
manufactured by The Premier Group
NOMINATED BY SEBASTIAN CONRAN

Jambox
USA

Designed by Yves Béhar and fuseproject; senior designer: Gabe Lamb;
manufactured by Jawbone
NOMINATED BY PETE COLLARD

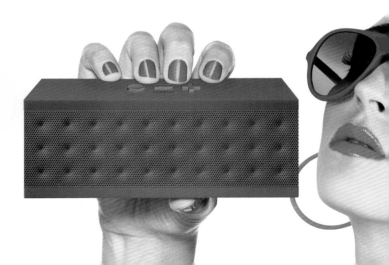

Hövding cycle helmet
SWEDEN

Designed and manufactured by Hövding
NOMINATED BY WAYNE HEMINGWAY

Hemp Chair
GERMANY

Designed by Studio Aisslinger
NOMINATED BY TIM PARSONS

Osso chair
FRANCE

Designed by Ronan and Erwan Bouroullec; manufactured by Mattiazzi
NOMINATED BY TIM PARSONS AND EMILIA TERRAGNI

Moon Rock table
UK

Designed by Bethan Laura Wood for Nilufar Gallery
NOMINATED BY CAROLINE ROUX

Botanica
NETHERLANDS

Designed by Studio Formafantasma; commissioned by Fondazione Plart
NOMINATED BY ZOË RYAN

Lightwood chair
UK

Designed by Jasper Morrison; manufactured by Maruni
NOMINATED BY PETE COLLARD AND JAMES MAIR

Chassis chair
GERMANY

Designed by Stefan Diez and manufactured by Wilkhahn
NOMINATED BY TIM PARSONS

Orb-it vacuum cleaner
USA

Designed by Black + Decker
NOMINATED BY SEBASTIAN CONRAN

The Solar Sinter
UK

Designed by Markus Kayser Studio
NOMINATED BY DANIEL CHARNY, CONNY FREYER,
ONKAR KULAR AND GARETH WILLIAMS

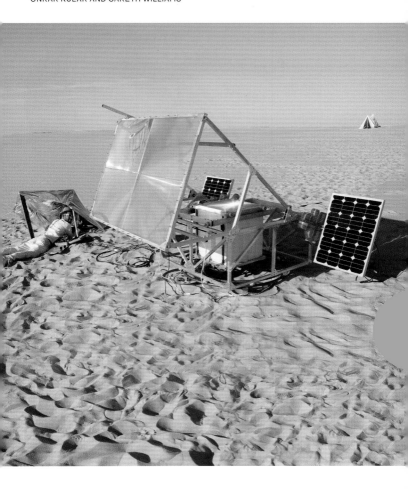

TMA-1 headphones
DENMARK

Designed by KiBiSi and manufactured by AIAIAI
NOMINATED BY SAM HECHT

Tip Ton chair

UK/SWITZERLAND

Designed by Barber & Osgerby; manufactured by Vitra
NOMINATED BY CAROLINE ROUX AND ZOË RYAN

Shade
UK

Designed by Simon Heijdens; commissioned by Art Institute of Chicago
NOMINATED BY ZOË RYAN

XXXX_Sofa
NETHERLANDS

Designed by Yuya Ushida and manufactured by Ahrend
NOMINATED BY PAOLA ANTONELLI

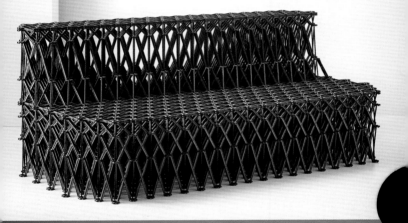

Totem lights
UK

Designed by Bethan Laura Wood in collaboration with Pietro Viero
NOMINATED BY CAROLINE ROUX

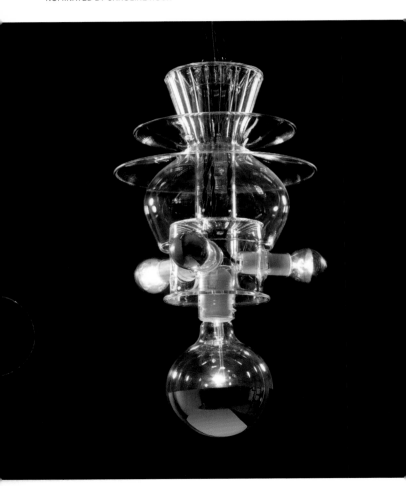

Waver armchair
GERMANY/SWITZERLAND

Designed by Konstantin Grcic and manufactured by Vitra
NOMINATED BY THOMAS GEISLER

Thixotropes
UK

Designed by Conny Freyer, Sebastien Noel and Eva Rucki of Troika;
commissioned by Selfridges
NOMINATED BY LOUISE SHANNON

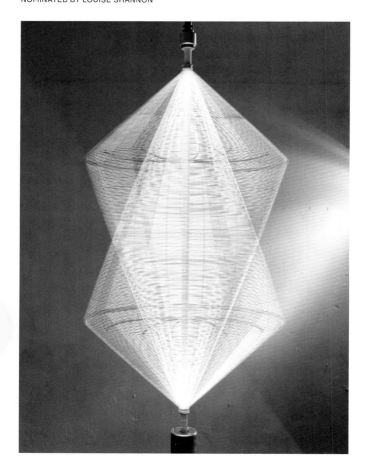

Textile Field at the Victoria and Albert Museum
FRANCE

Designed by Ronan and Erwan Bouroullec, in collaboration with Kvadrat
NOMINATED BY IAN CARTLIDGE AND LYNDA RELPH-KNIGHT

Mine Kafon
NETHERLANDS

Designed by Massoud Hassani
NOMINATED BY ED ANNINK, THORSTEN VAN ELTEN AND JANE WITHERS

Little Sun
GERMANY/DENMARK

Designed by Olafur Eliasson and Frederik Ottesen
NOMINATED BY OLIVIA SOLON

Liquid Glacial table
UK

Designed by Zaha Hadid for David Gill Galleries
NOMINATED BY RONALD T LABACO, HOLLY HOTCHNER AND CAROLINE ROUX

Future Primitives
BELGIUM

Designed by Muller Van Severen for Biennale Interieur 2012
NOMINATED BY MAX FRASER

Re-Imagined Chairs
UK

Designed by Nina Tolstrup and Jack Mama of Studiomama
NOMINATED BY MAX FRASER

w127 winkel lamp
GERMANY/SWEDEN

Designed by Dirk Winkel and manufactured by Wästberg
NOMINATED BY SAM HECHT

Beolit 12 portable speaker
DENMARK

Designed by Cecilie Manz and manufactured by Bang & Olufsen
NOMINATED BY BERNARD MCCOY

A-Collection furniture
FRANCE/DENMARK

Designed by Ronan and Erwan Bouroullec
and manufactured by HAY
NOMINATED BY SEBASTIAN CONRAN

Colour Porcelain
NETHERLANDS/JAPAN

Designed by Scholten & Baijings and manufactured by 1616 Arita
NOMINATED BY MAX FRASER AND ZOË RYAN

Child ViSion glasses
UK

Designed by Goodwin Hartshorn for the Centre for Vision in the
Developing World (CVDW) with Dow Corning Corporation
NOMINATED BY JEREMY MYERSON

Switch and socket collection
FRANCE

Designed by Inga Sempé for Legrand
NOMINATED BY TIM PARSONS

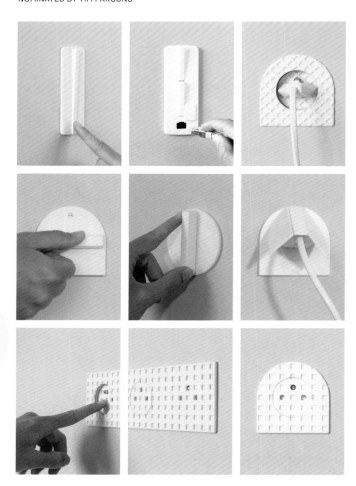

Medici chair

GERMANY

Designed by Konstantin Grcic and manufactured by Mattiazzi
NOMINATED BY JOHANNA AGERMAN ROSS

category winner

100 Chairs
ITALY

Designed by Marni
NOMINATED BY CAROLINE ROUX

Kiosk 2.0
BELGIUM

Designed by Unfold
NOMINATED BY DANIEL CHARNY

Palma kitchenware

UK/JAPAN

Designed by Jasper Morrison in collaboration with Oigen
NOMINATED BY JOHANNA AGERMAN ROSS

Faceture vases
UK

Designed by Phil Cuttance
NOMINATED BY MAX FRASER

Well Proven Chair
UK

Designed by James Shaw and Marjan van Aubel
NOMINATED BY TIM PARSONS

Plug lamp
SWEDEN

Designed by Form Us With Love with ateljé Lyktan
NOMINATED BY BERNARD MCCOY

Pierre Hardy Travel Sprays
FRANCE

Designed by Pierre Hardy for Frédéric Malle Editions de Parfums
NOMINATED BY TONY CHAMBERS

Surface Tension Lamp
SWEDEN/NETHERLANDS

Designed by Front and manufactured by Booo
NOMINATED BY MAX FRASER AND CAROLINE ROUX

Flyknit Racer running shoe
USA

Designed by Nike
NOMINATED BY RONALD T LABACO AND HOLLY HOTCHNER

Kit Yamoya anti-diarrhoea kit by ColaLife
UK

Designed by Tim Llewellyn for pi global; original concept and
field implementation by Simon Berry and Jane Berry
NOMINATED BY DANIEL CHARNY

The Sea Chair
UK/BRAZIL

Designed by Studio Swine and Kieren Jones
NOMINATED BY JEREMY TILL

Engineering Temporality furniture
NETHERLANDS

Designed by Tuomas Markunpoika
NOMINATED BY JANA SCHOLZE

Papafoxtrot toys
UK

Designed by PostlerFerguson
NOMINATED BY ONKAR KULAR

Magic Arms: 3D-printed robotic exoskeleton
USA

Designed by Tariq Rahman and Whitney Sample of
Nemours/Alfred I. duPont Hospital, with help from Stratasys Ltd
NOMINATED BY DANIEL CHARNY

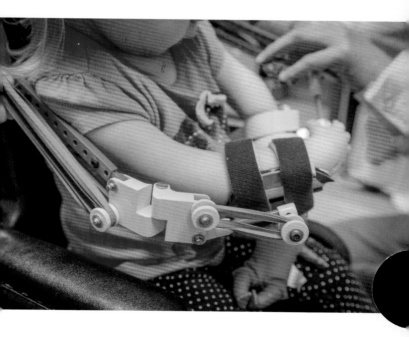

Gravity Stool
NETHERLANDS

Designed by Jólan van der Wiel
NOMINATED BY MAX FRASER AND GARETH WILLIAMS

Replicator 2
USA

Designed by MakerBot
NOMINATED BY TIM ABRAHAMS AND EMILIA TERRAGNI

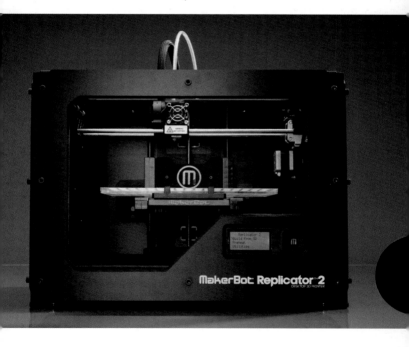

Tié paper chair
CHINA

Designed by PINWU
NOMINATED BY TIM PARSONS

London 2012 Olympic Cauldron
UK

Designed by Heatherwick Studio
NOMINATED BY DANIEL CHARNY, WAYNE HEMINGWAY AND LYNDA RELPH-KNIGHT

Esource
UK

Designed by Hal Watts
NOMINATED BY EVONNE MACKENZIE AND JANE WITHERS

Tekio lighting
UK

Designed by Anthony Dickens
NOMINATED BY MAX FRASER

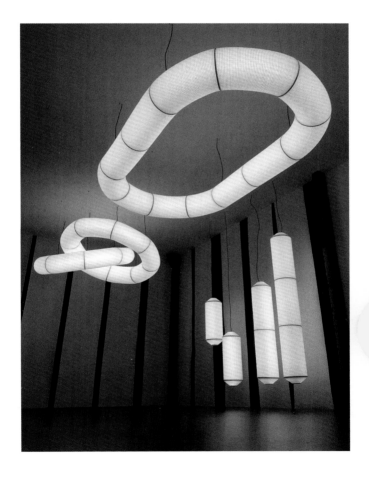

LiquiGlide ketchup bottle
USA

Designed by Dave Smith of the Varanasi Research Group at MIT
NOMINATED BY ALEX BEC

Little Printer
UK

Designed by BERG
NOMINATED BY JEREMY LESLIE, OLIVIA SOLON AND SHANE WALTER

Corniches
FRANCE/SWITZERLAND

Designed by Ronan and Erwan Bouroullec and manufactured by Vitra
NOMINATED BY SAM HECHT

Simple Collection
UK

Designed by Philippe Malouin; exhibited at ProjectB Gallery
and curated by Maria Christina Didero
NOMINATED BY ARIC CHEN

String Lights
UK

Designed by Michael Anastassiades for Flos
NOMINATED BY MAX FRASER, SAM HECHT, EMILIA TERRAGNI AND GARETH WILLIAMS

PET Lamp
SPAIN

Designed by Álvaro Catalán de Ocón
NOMINATED BY TIM PARSONS

2014

Bodleian Libraries Chair
UK

Designed by Barber & Osgerby and manufactured by Isokon Plus
NOMINATED BY LYNDA RELPH-KNIGHT

Udukuri furniture/Iro Collection
JAPAN

Designed by Jo Nagasaka for Established & Sons
NOMINATED BY MAX FRASER

Nest Protect smoke and carbon monoxide alarm
USA

Designed by Nest
NOMINATED BY ANDY LAW

Clever Caps

BRAZIL

Designed by Claudio Patrick Vollers and Henry Suzuki;
manufactured by Clever Pack

NOMINATED BY ADÉLIA BORGES

GoPro Hero3 Black video camera
USA

Designed by GoPro
NOMINATED BY ANDY LAW

Form 1 3D printer
USA

Designed by Formlabs
NOMINATED BY DANIEL CHARNY

Alba vase collection
ITALY

Designed by Massimiliano Adami and manufactured by Serralunga
NOMINATED BY CHIARA ALESSI

Lunaire lamp
FRANCE

Designed by Ferréol Babin for FontanaArte
NOMINATED BY CHIARA ALESSI

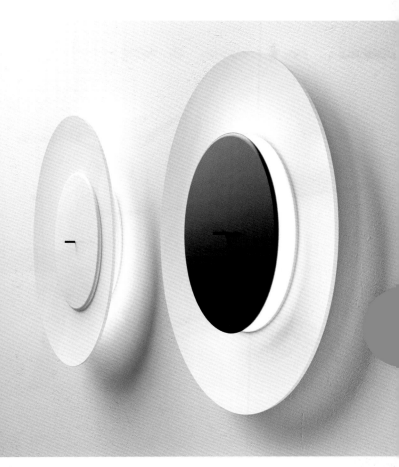

Plume cycle mudguard
UK/USA

Designed by Patrick Laing and Dan McMahon
NOMINATED BY VICKY RICHARDSON

Luffa Lab
UK

Designed by Mauricio Affonso
NOMINATED BY JOCELYN BAILEY

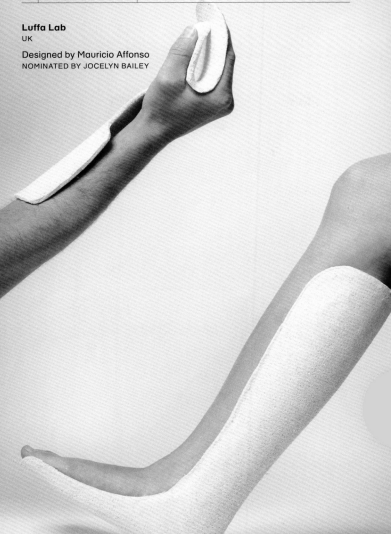

2014

Ripple table
UK

Designed by Benjamin Hubert in collaboration with Corelam
NOMINATED BY MAX FRASER

A Behaviour Changing (ABC) Syringe

UK

Designed by Dr David Swann
NOMINATED BY JEREMY MYERSON

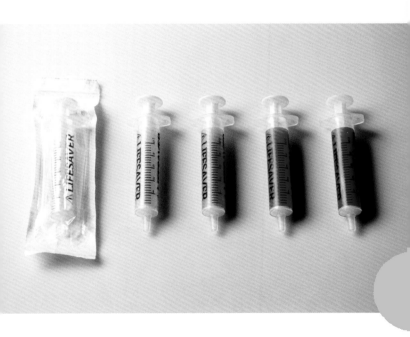

Chair4Life (C4L) modular wheelchair
UK

Designed by Renfrew Group for the NHS National Innovation Centre (NIC)
NOMINATED BY DANIEL CHARNY

The Seaboard GRAND
UK

Designed by Roland Lamb and Hong-Yue Edom for ROLI Ltd
NOMINATED BY DANIEL CHARNY AND LIZ FARRELLY

The Alchemist's Dressing Table
UK

Designed by Lucie Gledhill
NOMINATED BY JOCELYN BAILEY

2014

Pro chair family
GERMANY

Designed by Konstantin Grcic and manufactured by Flötotto
NOMINATED BY SAM HECHT

The Bradley Timepiece
USA

Designed by Eone
NOMINATED BY ANDY LAW

Phonebloks
NETHERLANDS

Designed by Dave Hakkens
NOMINATED BY DANIEL CHARNY AND THOMAS GEISLER

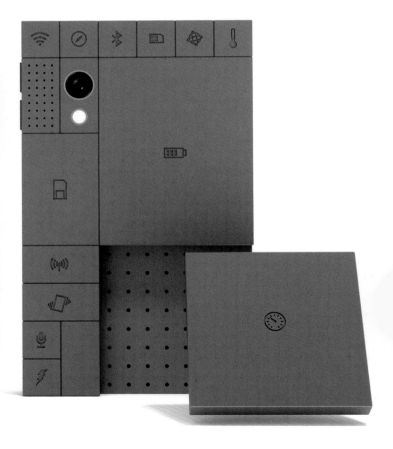

Silk Pavilion
USA

Designed by Mediated Matter Group and MIT Media Lab
NOMINATED BY ANTHONY DUNNE

UN North Delegates' Lounge Interior
NETHERLANDS

Designed by Hella Jongerius with Rem Koolhaas, Irma Boom,
Gabriel Lester and Louise Schouwenberg; manufactured by
Royal Tichelaar Makkum, Vitra and Knoll
NOMINATED BY PAOLA ANTONELLI AND ZOË RYAN

Risk Centre

UK

Designed by Onkar Kular and Inigo Minns; curated by
Magnus Ericson and exhibited at Arkitekturmuseet

NOMINATED BY CATHERINE INCE

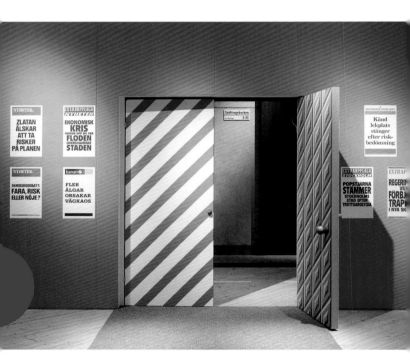

Fairphone
NETHERLANDS

Designed by Bas van Abel
NOMINATED BY LIZ FARRELLY AND MAX FRASER

Man Machine
GERMANY

Designed by Konstantin Grcic for Galerie kreo
NOMINATED BY CHIARA ALESSI

Endgrain
UK

Designed by Yael Mer and Shay Alkalay of Raw-Edges
NOMINATED BY CATHARINE ROSSI

Dragonfly
ITALY

Designed by Odo Fioravanti and manufactured by Segis
NOMINATED BY CHIARA ALESSI

Field Experiments: Indonesia
USA/AUSTRALIA/CANADA

Designed by Benjamin Harrison Bryant, Paul Marcus Fuog
and Karim Charlebois-Zariffa
NOMINATED BY EMILIA TERRAGNI

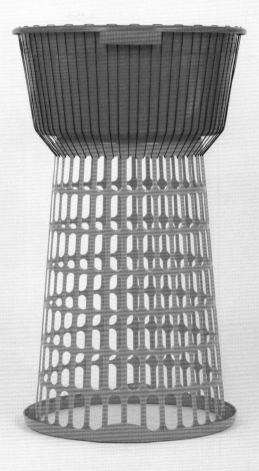

The Extrapolation Factory
USA

Founded by Elliott P Montgomery and Chris Woebken
NOMINATED BY ANTHONY DUNNE

Miito
DENMARK

Designed by Nils Chudy and Jasmina Grase
NOMINATED BY MAT HUNTER AND ALEX MILTON

Moocall SMS Calving Alert Sensor
IRELAND

Designed by Lyndsey Bryce and Christopher Murphy with Niall Austin
NOMINATED BY ALEX MILTON

Project Daniel
USA

Designed by Not Impossible
NOMINATED BY DANIEL CHARNY

10 100 1000
MEXICO

Project by La Metropolitana, Francisco Torres and Luis David Arredondo
NOMINATED BY RENATA BECERRIL

Current Table
NETHERLANDS/SWITZERLAND

Designed by Marjan van Aubel with Solaronix
NOMINATED BY SUVI SALONIEMI

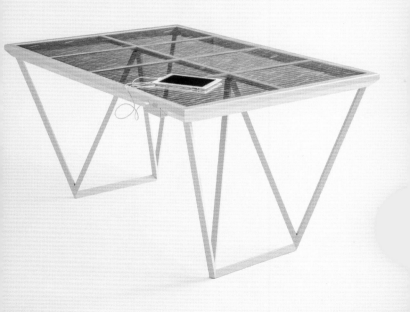

Blue Diversion toilet
AUSTRIA/SWITZERLAND

Designed by EOOS with Eawag (Swiss Federal Institute of Aquatic Science and Technology)
NOMINATED BY THOMAS GEISLER

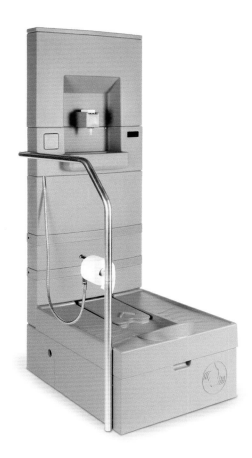

Air-purifying billboard – Como 1200 Árboles
PERÚ

Designed by University of Engineering and Technology of Peru (UTEC)
and FCB MAYO Perú (Humberto Polar)
NOMINATED BY MAX FRASER

Grow-It-Yourself Mushroom Materials
USA

Designed by Ecovative
NOMINATED BY ANDY LAW AND PAOLA ANTONELLI

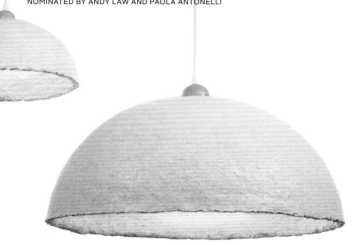

Sabi Space
UK

Designed by MAP Project Office for Sabi
NOMINATED BY MAT HUNTER

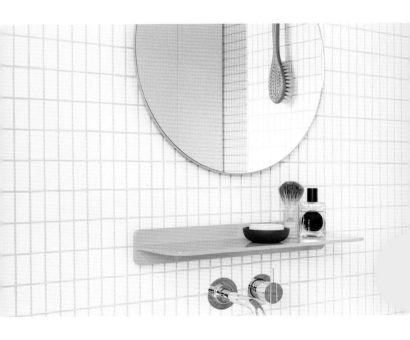

BrydgeAir
SINGAPORE

Designed by Brydge Keyboards
NOMINATED BY JEREMY WHITE

BRCK
KENYA

Designed by Erik Hersman, Reg Orton and Philip Walton
NOMINATED BY PAOLA ANTONELLI

DIY Gamer Kit
UK

Designed by Technology Will Save Us
NOMINATED BY FREDERICO DUARTE

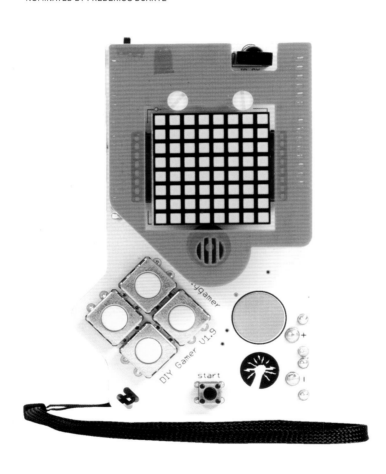

Kano computer kit
UK

Designed by Kano and MAP Project Office
NOMINATED BY BEN TERRETT

Strap Chair
NETHERLANDS/FRANCE

Designed by Scholten & Baijings; manufactured by Moustache
NOMINATED BY EMILIA TERRAGNI

Turn On
GERMANY/UK

Designed by Joel Hoff; manufactured by HAY
NOMINATED BY SAM HECHT

Human Organs-on-Chips

USA

Designed by Donald Ingber and Dan Dongeun Huh
NOMINATED BY PAOLA ANTONELLI

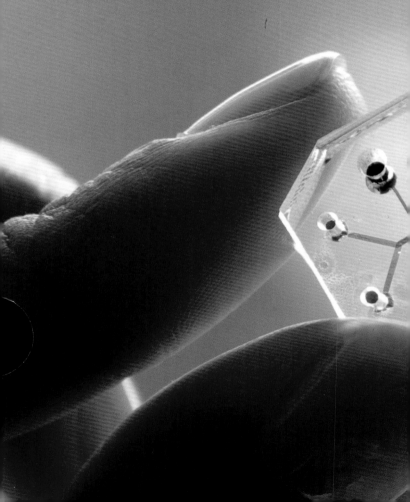

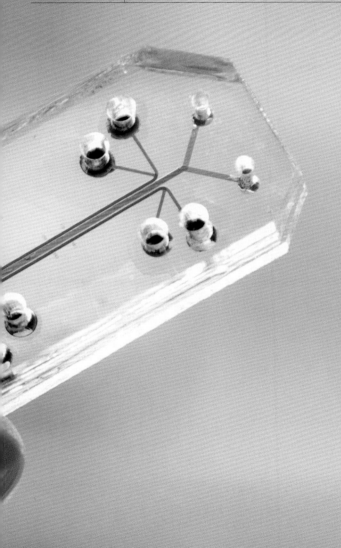

QardioArm
USA/UK

Designed by Qardio and Clara Gaggero Westaway,
Adrian Westaway and Duncan Fitzsimons
NOMINATED BY RAMA GHEERAWO

Double O bicycle light
UK

Designed by Paul Cocksedge Studio
NOMINATED BY WAYNE HEMINGWAY

MUJI kitchen appliances
JAPAN

Designed by Naoto Fukasawa for MUJI and Ryohin Keikaku Co. Ltd
NOMINATED BY SEBASTIAN CONRAN AND MAX FRASER

O&G Studio Design and Manufacturing
USA

Designed by Jonathan Glatt and Sara Ossana
NOMINATED BY ANDY LAW

adidas x Parley running shoe
UK/USA

Designed by adidas sustainability; design teams: Alexander Taylor,
Parley for the Oceans and Sea Shepherd
NOMINATED BY MAX FRASER

île/w153 lamp
FRANCE

Designed by Inga Sempé for Wästberg
NOMINATED BY TIM PARSONS

Post/Biotics
UK

Designed by Vidhi Mehta with Josiah Zayner and scientist Theresa Schacher
NOMINATED BY RAMA GHEERAWO

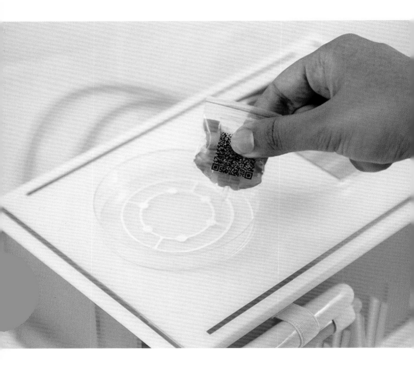

category winner

Space Cup
USA

Designed by Mark Weislogel and Andrew Wollman with John Graf and Donald Pettit, NASA Johnson Space Center, for Ryan Jenson of IRPI LLC
NOMINATED BY PAOLA ANTONELLI

Mono-Lights
NETHERLANDS

Designed by OS Δ OOS
NOMINATED BY BERNARD MCCOY

Joto
UK

Designed by Jim Rhodes, Jamie Wieck, Barney Mason, Carmen Domingo and Guy Moorhouse at Those
NOMINATED BY MAT HUNTER

Tokyo Tribal
SINGAPORE

Designed by nendo for industry+
NOMINATED BY ADÉLIA BORGES

Adaptive Manufacturing
NETHERLANDS

Designed by Olivier van Herpt and Sander Wassink
NOMINATED BY LIDEWIJ EDELKOORT

Design Museum Dharavi

INDIA

Co-founded by Amanda Pinatih and Jorge Mañes Rubio, with Kruti Suraiya, Shyam Kanle and Puneet Bareja
NOMINATED BY AANCHAL SODHANI TULI AND GARETH WILLIAMS

The Smog Free Project
NETHERLANDS

Designed by Studio Roosegaarde with European Nano Solutions and
Bob Ursem for City of Rotterdam, Stichting Doen and Port of Rotterdam
NOMINATED BY SHANE WALTER

Echo
USA

Designed by Amazon
NOMINATED BY MATT WEBB

LEGO City Fun in the Park – City People Pack
DENMARK

Designed by Andrew Butler Coghill; senior designer: the LEGO Group
NOMINATED BY DANIEL CHARNY

2016/
JAPAN

Creative direction by Scholten & Baijings and Teruhiro Yanagihara
for 1616 Arita
NOMINATED BY ZOË RYAN

Drinkable Book
USA

Designed by Brian Gartside with graphic designer Aaron Stephenson and chemist Dr Theresa Dankovich, PhD, for Folia Water
NOMINATED BY MAX FRASER

Species II chair
UK

Designed by Patrik Fredrikson and Ian Stallard for David Gill Gallery
NOMINATED BY PETE COLLARD

WITT – Harvesting Motion into Energy
UK

Designed by Martin and Mairi Wickett, with Schaefer,
Gibbs Gears and Innovate UK
NOMINATED BY TESSA DARLEY

Kodak Super 8 Camera
USA

Designed by Yves Béhar, Ilgu Cha and Sarah Neurnberger of fuseproject
for Steven Overman and Danielle Atkins at Kodak
NOMINATED BY PETE COLLARD AND CATHERINE INCE

The BBC micro:bit
UK

Designed by Technology Will Save Us with element14,
Lancaster University and ScienceScope for the BBC's Make It Digital
initiative; supported by ARM, Barclays, Freescale, Microsoft,
Nordic Semiconductor, Samsung and Wellcome Trust
NOMINATED BY SEBASTIAN CONRAN

Alphabet of Light
DENMARK

Designed by BIG (Bjarke Ingels Group) for Artemide
NOMINATED BY BERNARD MCCOY

Solid Textile Board Benches
UK

Designed by Max Lamb in collaboration with Kvadrat for Really
NOMINATED BY EMILIA TERRAGNI

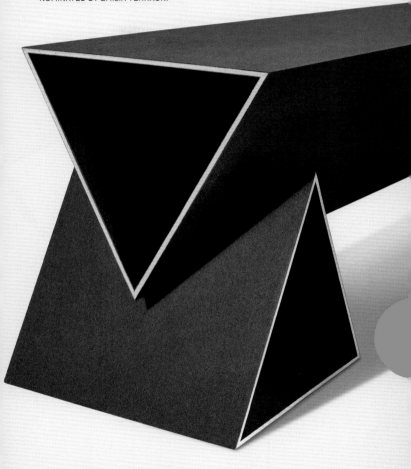

Avy Search and Rescue Drone
NETHERLANDS

Designed by Paul Vastert, David Wielemaker, Christian McCabe
and Patrique Zaman
NOMINATED BY INGEBORG DE ROODE

The Pilot Translating Earpiece
USA

Designed by Waverly Labs
NOMINATED BY PHILIP MICHAEL WOLFSON

Sufferhead Original Stout
NIGERIA

Designed by Emeka Ogboh
NOMINATED BY UGOCHUKWU-SMOOTH C NZEWI

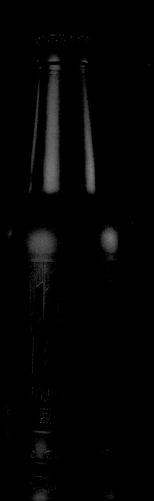

Wedge Dowel
SWEDEN

Designed by IKEA
NOMINATED BY BEN TERRETT

Nimuno Loops
UK

Designed by Anine Kirsten, Max Basler and Jaco Kruger
NOMINATED BY MICHA WEIDMANN

BuffaloGrid
INDIA

Designed by Daniel Becerra
NOMINATED BY MATT WEBB

Dansbana! Vårby gård
SWEDEN

Designed by Anna Fridolin, Anna Pang and Teres Selberg of Dansbana!
for Huddinge kommuni
NOMINATED BY KIERAN LONG

Flax Chair
NETHERLANDS

Designed by Christien Meindertsma for LABEL/BREED
NOMINATED BY MATEO KRIES

AIR-INK
INDIA

Designed by Graviky Labs
NOMINATED BY NICOLAS ROOPE

Remolten
CHILE

Designed by gt2P (Great Things To People) with Friedman Benda
NOMINATED BY FREDERICO DUARTE

SNOO Smart Sleeper
USA

Designed by Yves Béhar and fuseproject for Dr Harvey Karp's Happiest Baby
NOMINATED BY WAYNE HEMINGWAY

product

transport

Fiat 500
ITALY

Designed by Roberto Giolito of Fiat
NOMINATED BY ANDREW NAHUM

SkySails
GERMANY

Designed by SkySails
NOMINATED BY PHILIPP RODE

Airbus A380
FRANCE/UK/CHINA

Designed by Airbus and PriestmanGoode
NOMINATED BY HELEN EVENDEN AND PHILIPP RODE

TomTom Portable GPS car navigation system
NETHERLANDS

Manufactured by TomTom NV
NOMINATED BY PHILIPP RODE

London Serpentine SolarShuttle
UK

Designed by Christoph Behling of SolarLab Research & Design
NOMINATED BY HELEN EVENDEN

Mex-x wheelchair
GERMANY

Designed by Meyra
NOMINATED BY DANIEL CHARNY

category winner

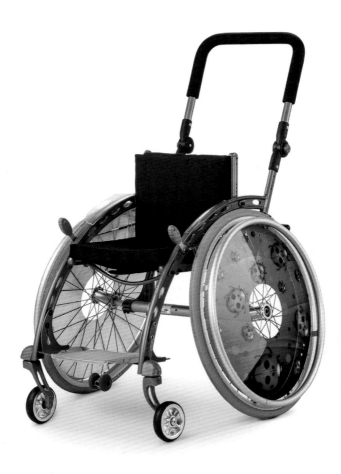

Vélib' Communal bicycle service
FRANCE

Concept by JCDecaux; designed by Patrick Jouin
NOMINATED BY TONY CHAMBERS AND PHILIPP RODE

London Congestion Charging Extension
UK

Designed by Transport for London
NOMINATED BY PHILIPP RODE

Streetcar
UK

Designed by Streetcar
NOMINATED BY PHILIPP RODE

High Speed 1 and St Pancras International terminal
UK

Designed by High Speed 1 by London and Continental Railway
NOMINATED BY PHILIPP RODE

Flyak kayak
PORTUGAL

Designed by Nelo and Mar-Kayaks in partnership with Foil Kayak
NOMINATED BY SEBASTIAN CONRAN

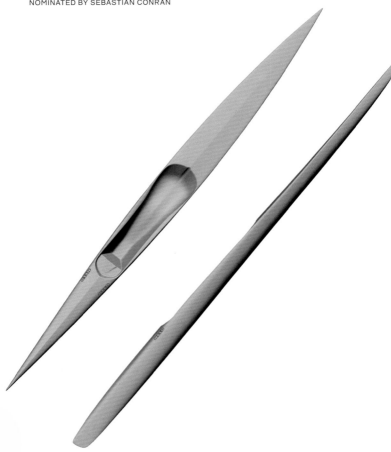

Aquaduct tricycle
USA

Designed by IDEO, Global Design and Consultancy Agency
NOMINATED BY ZOË RYAN

Balance Sport Wheelchair
USA

Designed by Eric Larson, Ricky Biddle, Ben Shao and Austin Cliffe
NOMINATED BY DANIEL CHARNY

Line-J Medellín Metro Cable
FRANCE/COLOMBIA

Designed by Poma for Metro de Medellín
NOMINATED BY PHILIPP RODE

Lötschberg Base Tunnel
SWITZERLAND

Designed by Frutigland and Westschweiz; architects: Uli Huber,
Rolf Mühlethaler and Claudine Lorenz; engineering by Team 3K
and Nunatak Architects; commissioned by BLS AlpTransit AG
NOMINATED BY PHILIPP RODE

Trek District bicycle
USA

Designed by Trek
NOMINATED BY SAM HECHT

Charge Spot
USA

Designed by NewDealDesign for Better Place
NOMINATED BY DANIEL CHARNY

car2go
GERMANY

Designed by Daimler AG
NOMINATED BY PHILIPP RODE

KTM 690 Stunt motorcycle
AUSTRIA

Designed by Kiska
NOMINATED BY SEBASTIAN CONRAN

The Greenbird: wind-powered vehicles
UK

Designed and engineered by Richard Jenkins and Dale Vince;
supported by Ecotricity
NOMINATED BY MORITZ WALDEMEYER

Th!nk City electric car
NORWAY

Designed by Th!nk
NOMINATED BY SEBASTIAN CONRAN

Urbikes – Fourth Generation Urban Bicycle
SPAIN

Designed by Eduard Sentís and manufactured by Modular BPS
NOMINATED BY DANIEL CHARNY

GINA Light Visionary Model car
GERMANY

Designed by BMW
NOMINATED BY ED ANNINK

E430 electric aircraft
CHINA

Designed and manufactured by Yuneec International
NOMINATED BY SEBASTIAN CONRAN

Honda EV-N Concept car
JAPAN

Designed by Kanna Sumiyoshi for Honda
NOMINATED BY YORGO TLOUPAS

Gocycle electric bicycle
UK

Designed and manufactured by Karbon Kinetics Ltd
NOMINATED BY SEBASTIAN CONRAN

Mission One Superbike
USA

Designed by Yves Béhar and fuseproject for Mission Motors
NOMINATED BY YORGO TLOUPAS

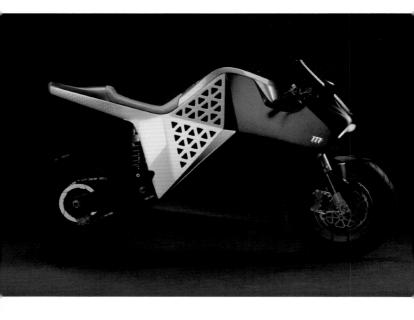

Nissan Land Glider
JAPAN

Designed by Nissan Motor Co. Ltd
NOMINATED BY SEBASTIAN CONRAN

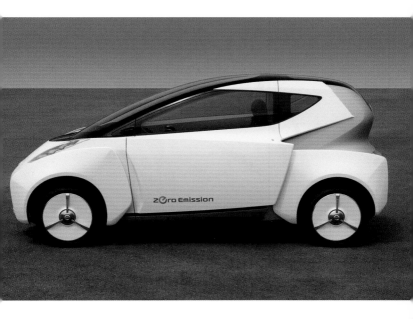

Riversimple car
UK

Designed by Riversimple
NOMINATED BY MARK ADAMS

Fiat 500 TwinAir
ITALY

Designed by Fiat
NOMINATED BY DALE HARROW

EN-V concept car
USA

Designed by General Motors
NOMINATED BY DALE HARROW

DeZir concept car
FRANCE

Designed by Laurens van den Acker for Renault
NOMINATED BY DALE HARROW

VanMoof No.5 bicycle
NETHERLANDS

Designed by VanMoof
NOMINATED BY ANTOINETTE KLAWER

2011

Barclays Cycle Hire
UK

Designed by Transport for London and Serco Group
NOMINATED BY SEBASTIAN CONRAN, WAYNE HEMINGWAY AND WILL HUDSON

YikeBike
NEW ZEALAND

Designed by Grant Ryan
NOMINATED BY DALE HARROW AND ANDREW NAHUM

Taurus Electro G4 aircraft
SLOVENIA

Designed by Pipistrel Ajdovščina; development engineer and G4 project team
leader: Tine Tomažič; head of research: Professor Dr Gregor Veble
NOMINATED BY PAUL MARCHANT

Bike Hanger
USA

Designed by Manifesto Architecture
NOMINATED BY BERNARD MCCOY

Emergency ambulance – redesign
UK

Designed by Helen Hamlyn Centre for Design and Vehicle Design Department at the Royal College of Art
NOMINATED BY DANIEL CHARNY

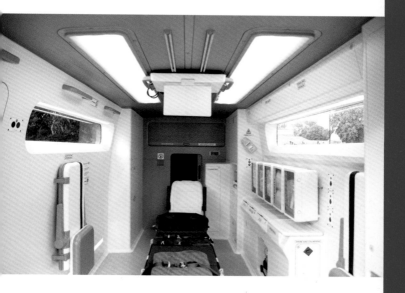

mia electric car
FRANCE

Designed by Murat Günak and David Wilkie; manufactured by mia electric
NOMINATED BY SAM HECHT

787 Dreamliner aircraft
USA

Designed and manufactured by Boeing
NOMINATED BY PAUL MARCHANT

T27 electric car
UK

Designed by Gordon Murray Design
NOMINATED BY SEBASTIAN CONRAN

Autolib'
FRANCE

Concept by Bertrand Delanoë, Mayor of Paris; designed by Société Autolib'
Métropole; operated by Société Autolib' Métropole, part of Bolloré Group
NOMINATED BY WAYNE HEMINGWAY

BMW i3
GERMANY

Designed by BMW
NOMINATED BY MATTEO CONTI

Morph Wheel
UK/USA

Designed by Vitamins and manufactured by Maddak
NOMINATED BY JOCELYN BAILEY AND DANIEL CHARNY

London 2012 Olympics wayfaring

UK

Designed by Transport for London, LOCOG and Jedco

NOMINATED BY PATRICK BURGOYNE

Touch & Travel
GERMANY

Designed by DB Mobility Logistics AG
NOMINATED BY PHILIPP RODE

Donky Bike
UK

Designed by Ben Wilson
NOMINATED BY SAM HECHT AND JEREMY MYERSON

Exhibition Road Project
UK

Designed by Dixon Jones for Borough of Kensington and Chelsea
NOMINATED BY HANNAH REDLER

N-One Car
JAPAN

Designed by Honda
NOMINATED BY SAM HECHT

Air Access
UK

Designed by PriestmanGoode
NOMINATED BY PAUL MARCHANT

Mando Footloose chainless bicycle
UK/SOUTH KOREA

Designed by Mark Saunders and manufactured by Mando
NOMINATED BY PAUL MARCHANT

XL1 concept car
GERMANY

Designed by Peter Wouda of Volkswagen
NOMINATED BY PAUL MARCHANT AND ANDREW NAHUM

category winner

ME.WE concept car
FRANCE

Designed by Jean-Marie Massaud and Toyota ED2
NOMINATED BY BERNARD MCCOY

Hybrid/24 electric bicycle
UK

Designed by A2B
NOMINATED BY SAM HECHT

IFMOVE bicycle
TAIWAN

Designed by Michael Lin, Stijn Deferm, Kain Gailiver and Rex Liu
of Pacific Cycles Inc.
NOMINATED BY RUNGTAI LIN

e-Go single-seater aircraft
UK

Designed by Giotto Castelli, Tony Bishop, Rob Martin and Malcolm Bird
NOMINATED BY PAUL MARCHANT

BMW i8 car
GERMANY

Designed by Adrian van Hooydonk, Senior Vice President, BMW Group Design
NOMINATED BY DALE HARROW AND ANDREW NAHUM

Tesla Model S electric car
USA

Designed by Elon Musk, Product Architect, with the Tesla design team led by Franz von Holzhausen
NOMINATED BY KIM COLIN

Loopwheels
UK

Designed by Sam Pearce and Jelly Products
NOMINATED BY SEBASTIAN CONRAN

Google Self-Driving Car
USA

Designed by YooJung Ahn, Jared Gross and Philipp Haban
NOMINATED BY SEBASTIAN CONRAN

D-Air Bag Street safety equipment
ITALY

Designed by Vittorio Cafaggi for Dainese
NOMINATED BY SEBASTIAN CONRAN

MOTIV.e City Car
UK

Designed by Gordon Murray Design for Yamaha Motor Company
NOMINATED BY DALE HARROW

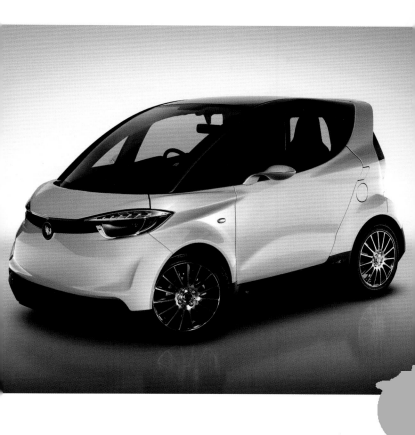

OKO e-bike
DENMARK

Designed by KiBiSi for Biomega
NOMINATED BY BERNARD MCCOY AND PAUL MARCHANT

Lumos Helmet
USA/HONG KONG

Designed by Eu-wen Ding and Jeff Haoran Chen
NOMINATED BY PAUL MARCHANT

Tesla Model 3
USA

Designed by Elon Musk with the Tesla design team,
led by Franz von Holzhausen
NOMINATED BY TESSA DARLEY

TX: The Electric Taxi
UK

Designed by Geely for London Taxi Company
NOMINATED BY PAUL MARCHANT

Gogoro Smartscooter and GoStation
TAIWAN

Designed by Horace Luke
NOMINATED BY RUNG-TAI LIN

BeeLine – smart navigation for bikes
USA

Designed by Mark Jenner and Tom Putnam with Map Project Office
NOMINATED BY SEBASTIAN CONRAN

Autonomous-Rail Rapid Transit (ART)
CHINA

Designed by CRRC
NOMINATED BY ARIC CHEN

Olli
USA

Designed by Local Motors
NOMINATED BY PHILIPP RODE

GITA
USA

Designed by Piaggio Fast Forward, led by Greg Lynn
NOMINATED BY NICOLAS ROOPE

Mahjouba Initiative
MOROCCO

Designed by Eric van Hove
NOMINATED BY UGOCHUKWU-SMOOTH C NZEWI

Seabubbles
FRANCE

Designed by Alain Thébault and Anders Bringdal
NOMINATED BY MURIEL BRUNET

Honda Moto Riding Assist
JAPAN

Designed by Honda
NOMINATED BY MAX FRASER

Light Traffic
USA

Designed by Carlo Ratti at Senseable City Lab at
Massachussetts Institute of Technology (MIT)
NOMINATED BY MAX FRASER

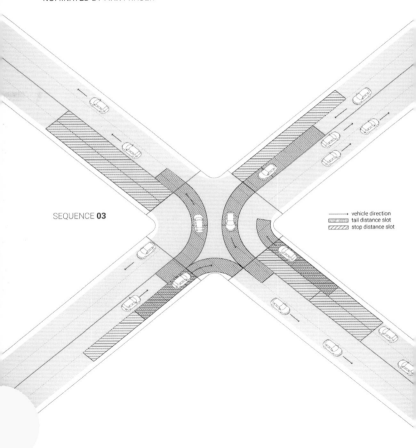

SEQUENCE **03**

vehicle direction
tail distance slot
stop distance slot

Scewo
SWITZERLAND

Designed by Thomas Gemperle, Adrien Weber, Naomi Stieger,
Stella Mühlhaus, Bernhard Winter and Pascal Buholzer at the
Swiss Federal Institute of Technology
NOMINATED BY WAYNE HEMINGWAY

12. NEMBRO LIBRARY
Architecture, 2008
Nembro's public library is part new-build, part conversion of the town's former primary school. Designed by Florence-based firm Archea Associati, the new structure is a transparent glass box surrounded by a second facade of red glazed earthenware tiles. The small tiles pivot on a steel framework, allowing them to rotate, acting as a sunshade for the interior.

13. NORDPARK RAILWAY STATIONS
Architecture, 2008
Designed by Zaha Hadid, these four stations along the Nordpark cable railway leading up to Innsbruck's northern chain of mountains demonstrate how architecture can be used to give a public transport system a cohesive identity. Hadid's lush geometry, echoing the Bergisel Ski Jump she completed for the city in 2002, can be understood as a restatement of what Otto Wagner did for Vienna's urban railway and Hector Guimard's work for the Paris Métro.

14. CHOCOLATE MUSEUM
Architecture, 2008
Designed for the Nestlé factory, this simple pavilion was developed by Rojkind Arquitectos as a visitor centre to promote the food and drink company's chocolate products. It was designed and built in just ten weeks. The playfully folded surfaces were designed to invite a range of associations, ranging from an origami bird, brightly coloured folk-art sculpture, or perhaps even a spaceship.

15. THE MAIN STADIUM FOR
THE 2008 OLYMPIC GAMES
Architecture, 2008
The 2008 Beijing Olympics were used by China to signal its emergence as a political and economic superpower. With 100,000 seats, the new National Stadium represents the most innovative stadium design since the free-form tent structure used for the 1972 Munich Olympic stadium. The apparently random steel structure, dubbed the 'Bird's Nest Stadium', is an instantly recognisable landmark and a setting in which spectators are made to feel part of the event.

16. FAHLE HOUSE
Architecture, 2008
The Fahle House occupies a prominent site in the city of Tallinn. The former cellulose and paper factory was designed by architect Erich Jacoby in 1926, but had been derelict for years. Dominated by the tall and voluminous boiler house at its heart, it was adapted to become a residential and cultural centre by KOKO Architects. Historic interior details and surfaces were preserved wherever possible, with the location of long-destroyed boilers marked using circles on the ceiling and floors.

17. NEW MUSEUM
Architecture, 2008
When the New Museum of Contemporary Art planned their new home on the Bowery, it limited their search to younger architects who had not built anything in New York. The chosen architects, Kazuyo Sejima and Ryue Nishizawa of SANAA, designed the museum as a series of galleries stacked on top of each other. Shafts provide natural light in the column-free galleries and public terraces look out over the city. The anodised aluminium expanded mesh on the facade pays homage to the Bowery's industrial history.

18. BMW WELT
Architecture, 2008
Wolf Prix was one of the most provocative voices in the Viennese architectural community of the 1970s. His solar-powered delivery centre for BMW, located at the company's Munich headquarters, was part of the brand's strategy of celebrating the act of buying a car. Visitors can watch as car owners collected their purchases from underneath the mirrored glass and steel roof, driving away via a spherical ramp that connects directly to the autobahn.

19. EAST BEACH CAFE
Architecture, 2008
The East Beach Cafe in Littlehampton was Thomas Heatherwick's first architectural commission. Replacing a derelict beach kiosk, the café is fabricated from structural steel that has been treated to form a protective coating of rust, sliced diagonally into ribbons that wrap up and over the building as if blown into place by the coastal winds. The facade is filled with glass doors and windows, forming a layered shell that is open to the seafront.

20. HONGLUO CLUBHOUSE
Architecture, 2008
Located an hour's drive from Beijing, the Hongluo Clubhouse is on the shore of Hongluo Lake with an impressive view of the mountains. Approached by means of a bridge, the clubhouse forms an island in the middle of the lake, on which it appears to float. The sunken entrance to the clubhouse drops below the lake's surface, leaving the visitor feeling as if they are walking through water to access the building.

21. CASA LEVENE SINGLE FAMILY HOUSE
Architecture, 2008
Built on a steeply sloping, wooded site to the north-west of Madrid, the Levene house was designed for Richard Levene, director of the *El Croquis* magazine. Rather than clearing the site, mature trees have been retained and carefully used to create patterns of light and shade that give the house its special quality. The main entrance and public rooms are at the top of the slope; as the house steps down the slope, it descends through three floors of bedrooms.

22. STEPHEN LAWRENCE CENTRE
Architecture, 2008

Built in memory of the murdered architecture student Stephen Lawrence, this community centre is dedicated to improving opportunities for young black people in south London. David Adjaye's design is based on a ground-floor plan by artist Chris Ofili, and is intended to encourage young people to enter the site and make use of the building. The moiré pattern on the glass facade is also based on a drawing by Ofili.

23. CASTLEFORD BRIDGE
Architecture, 2009

In the former mining town of Castleford, McDowell+Benedetti's bridge was designed as part of a wider regeneration of the waterfront. Created in collaboration with the Alan Baxter practice and Arup, the 130-metre-long structure curves around an old mill on the Aire river, giving visitors a view of white water flowing over a weir. Cumaru timber decking and benches run the full length of the bridge, providing a welcome place to sit and chat as well as a new route across town.

24. CAIXAFORUM
Architecture, 2009

A major cultural centre, CaixaForum blends old and new in the centre of Madrid. A multi-storey extension extends from the preserved facade of a disused power station, its sculpted roofline reflecting the surrounding topography. At ground-floor level, the base of the building has been excised so that it appears to be suspended in mid-air. Clad in angular steel panels, the soffit of the apparently gravity-defying building forms the entrance to the galleries and concert halls inside.

25. ACCORDIA HOUSING
Architecture, 2009

A major residential development comprising 212 houses and 166 apartments, Accordia illustrates that it is possible to build housing at scale without compromising on quality. The masterplan architects, Feilden Clegg Bradley Studios, worked in close collaboration with MaccreanorLavington and Alison Brooks Architects to create a range of housing in terraced and mews arrangements that incorporate a mix of internal courtyards, rooftop verandas and shared communal avenues to create a district where people want to live.

26. 10X10 LOW COST HOUSING PROJECT
Architecture, 2009

Initiated by Design Indaba, the 10x10 Low Cost Housing Project was established with the aim of stimulating debate around the delivery of low-income housing in Cape Town. Ten teams of South African architects were paired with international designers to come up with affordable, sustainable and innovative responses. The first qualifying solution came from Luyanda Mpahlwa of MMA Architects,

who borrowed from traditional mud-and-wattle building techniques to develop a sand-bag construction system.

27. WESTMINSTER ACADEMY
Architecture, 2009

Located in west London, Westminster Academy challenges preconceptions about what a British school should look like. Through consultation with children, staff and the local community, architects AHMM were able to ensure the building worked for everyone concerned. Their multidisciplinary approach involved graphic designers Studio Myerscough to ensure that graphical elements were carefully integrated with the building rather than added as an afterthought.

28. SPADINA WAVEDECK
Architecture, 2009

The Spadina WaveDeck is the first of a series of timber structures planned for the Toronto lakefront, aimed at revitalising the area's economic fortunes. A cross between a bridge and a boardwalk, the WaveDeck breaks with the waterfront's uniform nature to create an undulating and curving space. Wooden surfaces and stainless-steel rails lend a sense of craft and of the standards appropriate for a public amenity.

29. BUBBLETECTURE H
Architecture, 2009

An environmentally themed visitor centre near Osaka, Bubbletecture H reflects Japanese architect Shuhei Endo's exploration of the geometry of bubbles. Endo deliberately used building material that requires very little maintenance, such as the Cor-Ten steel cladding which covers the centre's auditorium, library and workshop. The cedar that lines the interior walls came from the adjacent forest, while the building is covered with moss and turf, allowing it to subtly change over time in line with the surrounding landscape.

30. LINKED HYBRID
Architecture, 2009

A 220,000 square metre pedestrian-oriented complex sited adjacent to the old city walls of Beijing, Linked Hybrid consists of a ring of structures linked together with sky bridges. Described as an 'open city within a city', the site features a number of public roof gardens in addition to shops and restaurants. Geothermal wells provide the complex with cooling in summer and heating in winter, making it one of the largest green residential projects in the world.

31. KAIT WORKSHOP
Architecture, 2009

This single-storey pavilion was designed as a multi-purpose workshop for the Kanagawa Institute of Technology campus in the suburbs of Tokyo. The brief called for a building where students could work on self-initiated projects while still allowing for collaboration with the local community. junya. ishigami+associates's solution consists of a free-form structure that appears to completely blur the edges between the inside and outside world. The effect is created by a total of 305 pillars, each different in size and shape.

32. EIGHT INSCRIBED HOUSES
AND THREE COURTYARDS
Architecture, 2009

Designed by Las Palmas-based studio Romera y Ruiz Arquitectos, this social housing development is a clever response to the tight constraints of the plot. The eight houses on the site fit together ingeniously while three hidden internal courtyards, each painted a strikingly different colour, provide natural ventilation and link internal circulation routes. A pleated facade, formed by a series of shutters, shades the windows from sunlight and provides shelter from prevailing winds.

33. NORWEGIAN NATIONAL
OPERA AND BALLET
Architecture, 2009

The international competition to design the Oslo opera house was won by architects Snøhetta in 2000. Their proposal is notable for the way it combines world-class cultural facilities with a commitment to public space. Clad in white Carrara marble, the angular and sloping forms allow visitors to wander to the top of the building and take in views across the water. The opera house's memorable silhouette cements its landmark quality.

34. SERGIO CARDELL PLAZA TRAM STOP
Architecture, 2009

Commissioned by the Valencian public railway company, this tram stop is at the centre of a new tram line linking the centre of Alicante with the residential areas of San Juan. Formerly a traffic roundabout, the new tram stop was transformed by Subarquitectura to become a new and accessible public space. A number of fractal pathways, designed to avoid existing trees on the site, give passengers thirty-two possible ways to approach the tram stop.

35. MUSEUM OF CONTEMPORARY
ART DENVER
Architecture, 2009

David Adjaye's first public building in the United States, the Museum of Contemporary Art Denver is designed to be as flexible as possible. The art galleries are three separate stacks, with the space between the stacks and the outside walls used for circulation. Two of the stacks support the members' room and the educational space, while the third supports a roof garden by landscape architect Karla Dakin that hosts the museum's dedicated outdoor art programme.

36. HUTONG BUBBLE 32
Architecture, 2010

Beijing's rapid development has altered the city's landscape on a massive scale, continually eroding the delicate urban tissue of the old city. Hutong Bubble 32 is the first of a proposed series of bubble-shaped additions to Beijing's traditional hutong neighbourhoods, allowing for urgent infrastructural upgrading without necessitating demolition. The result is a bold, small-scale intervention that introduces a contemporary solution into the most traditional of settings.

37. NEUES MUSEUM
Architecture, 2010

Completed in 1849, the Neues Museum sustained heavy bomb damage during the Second World War. In 1997, the British architect David Chipperfield won the competition to return the shell to its former glory. Working with conservation specialist Julian Harrap, Chipperfield chose to repair and maintain the existing fabric where possible, painstakingly restoring murals, frescoes, mosaics and long-lost colour schemes. Where there was nothing left to restore Chipperfield designed bold new spaces, notably the museum's magnificent central stairwell.

38. THE HIGH LINE
Architecture, 2010

A model of urban redevelopment, the High Line project is an elevated public park on Manhattan's West Side. Built in the 1930s to carry freight trains, the railway spans twenty-two city blocks, weaving over streets and between buildings within sight of the Hudson River. Disused since 1980, this grassy industrial corridor was in danger of being demolished until a scheme to convert it into a park began in 2005. Inspired by its post-industrial beauty, the architects developed an 'agritecture' strategy that echoes the theme of nature reclaiming a piece of urban infrastructure.

39. TEA TENERIFE ESPACIO DE LAS ARTES
Architecture, 2010

TEA is a multi-functional exhibition centre in the heart of Santa Cruz de Tenerife. Swiss architects Herzog & de Meuron developed an architectural concept with interflowing spaces to allow for different activities. A public path cuts diagonally through the complex, connecting these spaces to the outside world and inviting in passing pedestrians. The path transforms into a triangular, semi-covered area at the heart of the building, creating a public plaza that is open and accessible to all.

40. RAVEN ROW
Architecture, 2010

Raven Row is a contemporary art centre in Spitalfields that combines two eighteenth-century silk mercers' houses with an early 1970s concrete-framed office building. Built around 1690, the Grade I-listed buildings have been added to, converted, neglected and repaired over the years. The multi-layered history of the site was sensitively reworked by 6a Architects, whose narrative treatment hinted at the buildings' eventful lives: charred timber was used to evoke the fire that ravaged the houses in the 1970s.

41. PORCHDOG HOUSE PROTOTYPE
Architecture, 2010

Conceived in the aftermath of 2005's Hurricane Katrina, this prototypical house was developed by Architecture for Humanity to help families whose homes were destroyed. The challenge was to create a house that was both affordable and flood resistant while still responding to the historic character of the area. The prototype merges traditional and modern by taking a typical Biloxi house and cutting it in half to form an elevated, two-storey dwelling that is stronger and safer than a timber structure.

42. BRITISH EMBASSY, WARSAW
Architecture, 2010

Following the events of 11 September 2001, many new governmental buildings tended towards grim fortress-like characteristics. In contrast, Tony Fretton's design for the British Embassy in Warsaw has a serene character that belies its secure qualities. The architect exploited the set-back from the road required to counter the threat of bombing to provide an idyllic landscape setting. Equally crucially, the building's external walls are designed to withstand the impact of explosive devices while maintaining an accessible and light appearance.

43. MAXXI: NATIONAL MUSEUM OF THE XXI CENTURY ARTS
Architecture, 2010

The MAXXI museum houses two institutions, MAXXI Arte and MAXXI Architecture. Zaha Hadid's concept for the complex draws its cue from the building's purpose as a centre for the display of visual arts, with overlapping flows and pathways to create a dynamic space. Black steel staircases and bridges fly across a void where walls become floors and even threaten to become ceilings. The layout encourages the visitor to explore MAXXI as a series of continuous spaces.

44. BRANDHORST MUSEUM
Architecture, 2010

Architects tend to shy away from introducing strong colours to the outside of their buildings. Not so the British-German architecture practice of Sauerbruch Hutton, who brought some of their trademark boldness to the Brandhorst Museum in Munich. Their elegant scheme consists of a simple elongated building of three interconnecting stacks, each distinguished by differently coloured cladding. The unique polychromatic facade consists of 36,000 ceramic rods glazed in twenty-three different colours.

45. MONTERREY HOUSING
Architecture, 2010

An international 'do-tank' based in Chile, ELEMENTAL focuses on finding socially driven solutions to the challenge of housing the world's ever-increasing population. Commissioned by the Mexican government to build a new housing complex in Monterrey, ELEMENTAL refined their unique 'half a home' strategy first developed in Iquique, Chile: building half-finished prefabricated structures, designed to facilitate onwards self-build expansion. The resulting social housing takes on a self-defined character as residents built the other half according to their own needs.

46. YOULHWADANG BOOK HALL
Architecture, 2010

The YoulHwaDang Book Hall is the latest in a cluster of buildings designed for the Paju Book City development outside Seoul. Housing a bookshop, café and apartments, its principal contribution to Paju takes the form of a public square. The facade presents is a highly sophisticated yet free composition.

47. MELBOURNE RECITAL CENTRE AND MTC SOUTHBANK THEATRE
Architecture, 2010

When ARM Architecture was given the challenging brief of creating a new home for the Melbourne Recital Centre and the Melbourne Theatre Company (MTC), they created two distinct yet connected buildings. The theatre's facade features white steel tubing in geometric patterns that appear to be two- or three-dimensional depending on the viewer's position. Since most people visit the theatre in the evening, ARM gave the buildings a shape and dynamism made for the night.

48. NINGBO HISTORY MUSEUM
Architecture, 2010

Designed by Chinese architect Wang Shu, the Ningbo History Museum combines local construction methods with a contemporary architectural language inspired by the surrounding landscape. The building is conceived as an archaeological mountain located on ruins, and covered with miscellaneous recycled bricks and roof tiles from the settlements that once occupied the area. The masons involved in its construction were taught the ancient technique of *wa pan*, a process of recycling used building materials that is all but forgotten in China.

49. BALANCING BARN
Architecture, 2011

Balancing Barn was the first building to be completed for Living Architecture, a not-for-profit initiative that offers the public the chance to rent architect-designed holiday houses. Made from reflective metal sheeting in a nod to the local building vernacular, MVRDV's Balancing Barn apparently defies gravity by extending spectacularly over a grassy slope. In a whimsical touch that belies the sophisticated engineering required, a swing hangs beneath the cantilevered structure.

50. STONEBRIDGE HILLSIDE HUB
Architecture, 2011
Stonebridge Hillside Hub is a mixed-use landmark building forming the final phase of a fourtneen-year regeneration of the Stonebridge Estate in north-west London. The Hub brings together the disparate elements of the estate, including a community centre, with a public piazza at the front and a private landscaped garden behind. Two wings contain mixed-tenure residential apartments, a primary care centre, café and convenience store.

51. 1111 LINCOLN ROAD
Architecture, 2011
A mixed-use development, 1111 Lincoln Road is a radical rethinking of the concrete car park. With a retail unit and private residence on the upper levels, the structure can also be used for parties, shoots, fashion shows, concerts and other activities, with amazing views as a backdrop. Ceilings vary between standard parking height and double, or even triple, height, and walking on the unenclosed, sculptural staircase in the centre is a panoramic, ceremonial experience.

52. TAPE INSTALLATIONS
Architecture, 2011
Between 2009 and 2010 the Croatian-Austrian collective Numen/For Use used nothing but rolls of sticky tape to create site-specific installations. Multiple layers of transparent tape act like tendons stretched between rigid points and columns, resulting in complex, amorphous shapes reminiscent of organic lifeforms. The concept originated from a set design for a dance performance, in which dancers stretched the tape as they moved, resulting in a (tape) recording of their choreography.

53. NOTTINGHAM CONTEMPORARY
Architecture, 2011
Housing a range of public amenities including cinemas, theatres and galleries alongside commercial and educational zones, Nottingham Contemporary occupies one of the oldest sites in the city. Designed by Caruso St John, the building is clad in patterned verdigris-scalloped panels inspired by the facades of the nearby Lace Market. The pattern is taken from a specific example of Nottingham lace, which was scanned, modified and converted into a three-dimensional mould.

54. LADAKH COMMONWEALTH PEACE PAVILION AND CLASSROOM INITIATIVE
Architecture, 2011
Located 4,000m above sea level, the Commonwealth Peace Pavilion is an outdoor classroom space for the Druk White Lotus School in Ladakh. Constructed from disused military parachutes, these structures are based on traditional Ladakhi yak tents, which resist harsh winds and intense sun and incorporate local weaving and dyeing. It was developed by the BaSiC Initiative, who collaborated with local pupils and Buddhist nuns to create the structure.

55. OPEN AIR LIBRARY
Architecture, 2011
The Open Air Library is a stunning example of community activism. The project began when local residents of Salbke launched an urban planning experiment in collaboration with Leipzig-based KARO Architeckten to bring back their library. A life-size prototype was constructed from beer crates, and filled with 20,000 donated books. This temporary construction gave residents an opportunity to see how the library could reinvigorate their town centre and bring about a new sense of community. Inspired by the project, local residents successfully campaigned to raise the money for a permanent library.

56. UNIVERSITY OF OXFORD: DEPARTMENT OF EARTH SCIENCES
Architecture, 2011
WilkinsonEyre's building for the University of Oxford's Department of Earth Sciences features a distinctive narrative exterior wall, made from carefully selected horizontal bands of limestone. In this way, the building tells the story of its occupants in the same way a fossil communicates about a particular geological era. This gives the building a strong geological 'identity' that also acts as an organisational device, dividing the stone-clad laboratory wing from the glazed office wing.

57. A FOREST FOR A MOON DAZZLER
Architecture, 2011
When architect Benjamin Garcia Saxe's mother first left the city, she built a space where she could look at the moon from her bed. Garcia Saxe reinterpreted her self-made dwelling, creating a bamboo ceiling that opens to the night sky. Although aimed at satisfying an emotional wish, Garcia Saxe's design is nonetheless practical at its core. The building is created from two inexpensive yet identical modules that can be combined in a number of adaptable configurations.

58. VOID HOUSE
Architecture, 2011
A family home, the Void House takes its name from the large ground-level void which provides access to the garden beyond. By removing the

ground floor entirely, this void is directly accessible from the street and becomes a semi-public space. Internally, open rooms are arranged around a central staircase, as if the entire house were viewable from any point within.

59. BURJ KHALIFA
   Architecture, 2011
At 828m tall, Burj Khalifa redefined the possibilities of skyscrapers. Designed by the architects and engineers from the Chicago office of Skidmore, Owings & Merrill, the tower combines local influences with cutting-edge technology to achieve high performance in a desert climate. Modelled in a wind tunnel to minimise wind forces, the skyscraper is composed of sculpted volumes arranged in a spiralling pattern around a central buttressed core. The Y-shaped floor plan maximises views of the Arabian Gulf.

60. UK PAVILION SHANGHAI EXPO 2010
   Architecture, 2011
In 2007 Heatherwick Studio won the competition to design the UK Pavilion for the Shanghai 2010 Expo. The centrepiece was the Seed Cathedral, which highlighted the work of the Royal Botanic Gardens in Kew. The 20-metre-high building was constructed from 60,000 long transparent optical rods, each containing a seed from Kew Gardens. The rods gently quivered in the breeze, like a dandelion or sea urchin, drawing light into the pavilion during the day and directing it outwards at night.

61. CONCRETE CANVAS SHELTERS
   Architecture, 2011
Developed by Peter Brewin and William Crawford while still at university, Concrete Canvas Shelters are an innovative solution to the problem of housing displaced communities. It consists of an inflatable inner liner with a unique outer fabric impregnated with dry concrete powder. Once inflated, the outside layer simply needs water to cause it to harden. A shelter can be erected by two untrained people in under an hour and is ready for use in twenty-four hours.

62. VITRAHAUS
   Architecture, 2011
VitraHaus is a dozen stacked and extruded architectural renditions of a basic house form. Designed by Swiss architects Herzog & de Meuron for furniture manufacturer Vitra, it is used to display objects designed primarily for the home. Inside, there are surprising transitions between rooms, and glazed gable ends on each level offer views of the exterior landscape: the idyllic Tüllinger Hills, the railway tracks and the urbanised plain of the Rhine.

63. MEDIA-TIC BUILDING
   Architecture, 2011
Media-TIC is an innovative mixed-use office building in Barcelona's science and technology district. The building's skin consists of layers of ethylene tetrafluoroethylene (ETFE), which are filled with nitrogen-based fog. The cushioned facades inflate or deflate according to the strength of the sun, making it very energy-efficient. Structurally, the building is based around a huge load-bearing exoskeleton, or superstructure, from which all the floors are suspended.

64. THE HEPWORTH WAKEFIELD
   Architecture, 2012
Set on an island amid abandoned mills, the sculptural form of the Hepworth Wakefield appears to rise directly from the River Calder. On entering the building, the building's nature reveals itself, as visitors rise through a staircase and foyer into a series of top-lit galleries. David Chipperfield's crystalline conjunctions of rhomboid forms evoke the work of its namesake, Wakefield-born sculptor Barbara Hepworth.

65. NATIONAL PARK OF MALI BUILDINGS
   Architecture, 2012
To mark the fiftieth anniversary of Mali's independence, the National Park in Bamako was improved with new amenities. The complex, consisting of low-rise pavilions set around an oval playground, is surrounded by huge baobab trees amid spectacular savanna outcrops. The walls are topped by a delicate steel-truss roof, which overhangs to provide shade for the facades and creates natural thermal ventilation for the spaces below.

66. MOSES BRIDGE, FORT DE ROOVERE
   Architecture, 2012
Fort de Roovere is part of a historic system of Dutch moat defences first constructed in 1698. When architects RO&AD were asked to design a new bridge over the restored fort, they faced a problem: how to minimise its visual impact against the historic landscape. Their solution was to sink the bridge into both the embankment and the water, rendering it virtually invisible. The effect is that of walking through, rather than over, the water.

67. THE IRON MARKET
   Architecture, 2012
The Iron Market has been a symbol of Haitian community aspiration for over 120 years, but suffered extensive fire damage in 2008 and was devastated in the 2010 earthquake. The London-based firm of John McAslan + Partners led a team, including local artisans, to resurrect the entire Iron Market within a year of the earthquake. The scheme preserved and repaired all key details, using original materials wherever possible.

68. MAGGIE'S CENTRE GARTNAVEL
Architecture, 2012
The aim of a Maggie's Centre is to create an environment of practical and emotional support for people with cancer. Set in woods in the grounds of Gartnavel hospital, this single-storey building's flowing sequence creates relaxed spaces and minimises corridors and hallways. Since the first Maggie's opened in 1996, a series of innovative buildings by world-class architects have been commissioned with the belief that exceptional architecture can help people feel better.

69. CARE HOME
Architecture, 2012
Formed of three adjoining volumes, this care home provides eighty-eight rooms and studio bedrooms with views over the landscape. Each floor has staff and support areas, as well as a communal living room looking into the courtyards. Homely furnishings, accessible fittings and clear signage complement large amounts of controlled daylight and fresh air. Externally, a concrete plinth and pre-cast concrete rails at each floor level give a strong horizontal emphasis to the building.

70. FOLLY FOR A FLYOVER
Architecture, 2012
Located between two concrete road bridges in east London, Folly for a Flyover transformed a previously neglected site into a space for local residents, attracting over 20,000 visitors for the nine weeks it was open in summer 2011. The warmth of the wooden facade was designed to deliberately contrast with the bleak infrastructure that surrounded it; the aim was 'to suggest the story of a stubborn landlord who had refused to move as the motorway was built'.

71. GUANGZHOU OPERA HOUSE
Architecture, 2012
At the centre of a new cultural and commercial quarter in Guangzhou, Zaha Hadid's opera house is as dramatic as the performances inside. Taking the form of two softly angular pebbles approached by inclined walkways, the gravity-defying granite- and glass-clad steel structure is made possible by innovatively engineered traditionally sand-cast steel joints. Complex internal foyer spaces and balconies twist around the central concrete auditorium, offering views of the spectacular skyline.

72. SPACEPORT AMERICA
Architecture, 2012
A terminal building and aircraft hangar for the world's first commercial space airport, Spaceport America has an undulating desert-coloured roof that blends into the arid landscape. It is partially dug into the ground to increase thermal insulation and protect the building from the eroding desert winds, while skylights and solar panels take advantage of the strong sun.

73. LONDON 2012 VELODROME
Architecture, 2012
Designed for the 2012 Olympic Games, the form of the state-of-the-art London 2012 Velodrome directly echoes the geometry of the track it contains. The track is constructed from 56km of pale Siberian pine and designed to create record-breaking conditions, installed to millimetre precision by specialist carpenters. The temperature and other environmental conditions are also carefully controlled to facilitate top cycling speeds.

74. BUTARO HOSPITAL
Architecture, 2012
Developed by MASS Design Group in partnership with healthcare charity Partners In Health, Butaro District Hospital is an innovative 150-bed hospital that serves over 400,000 people. The design uses natural ventilation to reduce the transmission of airborne diseases, with the hilltop site specifically chosen to maximise airflow. Traditional ward layout was rethought, with beds moved away from perimeter walls to centrally placed half-height walls, making room for larger windows.

75. YOUTH FACTORY
Architecture, 2012
Youth Factory is a new type of urban social space, taking the form of an undulating landscape with brilliantly coloured translucent structures. The ground dips and crests to encourage skateboarders and adventurous cyclists, while more formal learning and performance spaces are sheltered by a large cloud-like canopy. Mérida is famous for its Roman ruins: the Youth Factory sits on a raised foundation to protect the delicate remains beneath.

76. BOOK MOUNTAIN
Architecture, 2013
A tower of books encased in a glass pyramid, the Book Mountain is a new take on the public library. It contains a spiralling trail of staircases, pathways and terraces that create a 480-metre-long route through five floors of bookshelves towards a café beneath the pyramid's apex. In an age where virtual reading is rapidly replacing the desire for physical books, MVRDV have created an unashamed celebration of browsing bookshelves.

77. THE LIBRARY BUILDING
Architecture, 2013
The Library Building is a powerful example of what can be achieved when public and private development interests are combined. The striking white building, stacked to resemble the books it contains, doubles as both library and performance space. An open spiral staircase gives visitors a good view of the books, but also provides seating with great views of the stage.

78. THE SHARD
Architecture, 2013

As the tallest addition to the London skyline, the Shard divides public opinion. Standing above London Bridge railway station, Renzo Piano's 72-storey tower is topped by a 15-storey public viewing gallery, demarcated by glass facets that incline inwards but do not meet. For detractors, it is a modern incursion into an ancient city. For supporters, it evokes Canaletto's paintings of London spires. Regardless, the Shard is a triumph of engineering, managing to thread its piles through ancient foundations.

79. TOUR BOIS LE PRÊTRE TOWER
Architecture, 2013

The renovation of Bois le Prêtre Tower is a persuasive argument against the demolition of much-maligned tower blocks. Architects Lacaton & Vassal saved this tower by retro-fitting an outer layer of balconies and walls of glass directly to the structure. The project was completed for nearly half the equivalent cost of demolition and rebuilding, and residents did not need to be rehoused during the renovation. The project stands as evidence that social housing can have a more sustainable future.

80. IKEA DISOBEDIENTS
Architecture, 2013

With plans to publish 208 million copies in 2013, the IKEA catalogue may soon exceed even the number of Gideon Bibles. The ubiquity of this mundane, homogenous ideal-home fiction provides stark evidence of the immense impact of IKEA's domestic ideology. Andrés Jaque demands that we rebel. In this short project, Jaque identifies households where domestic reality does not match the domestic ideal. Architecture does not need bricks and mortar to comment on fractured and difficult realities.

81. HOME-FOR-ALL
Architecture, 2013

Following the devastating 2011 earthquake and tsunami in north-eastern Japan, the concept of home gained a very different meaning. Noting how homelessness is hard to emulate in emergency shelters, architect Toyo Ito initiated a recovery project entitled Home-for-All, which sets out to create home-like spaces shared by the community. Resembling a watchtower and built from salt-damaged cedar, the Rikuzentakata Home-for-All represents a last outpost before a vast flat land that used to be home for thousands of people.

82. DAIKANYAMA T-SITE
Architecture, 2013

Resurrecting the allure of the bookshop as a social place in an age of online media, Daikanyama T-Site's campus is a self-assured neighbourhood retail centre in Tokyo. Refreshing in its considered mix of the formal and informal elements of architecture, interior design and product displays, and low cost and fast track in development, the three-building complex represents a new retail paradigm in Japan.

83. FRANKLIN D. ROOSEVELT
FOUR FREEDOMS PARK
Architecture, 2013

Opening almost seventy years after the famous speech from which it got its name, the Four Freedoms Park occupies a prime position on Roosevelt Island in New York City's East River. Designed by American architect Louis Kahn in 1973, construction only began in 2010 thanks to the efforts of former US ambassador, William vanden Heuvel. Strikingly geometrical in form yet sensitive to context, the open-air plaza looks over the water towards Manhattan.

84. METROPOLITAN ARTS CENTRE (MAC)
Architecture, 2013

The first major work by Belfast architects Hackett Hall McKnight, the Metropolitan Arts Centre (MAC) is literally and figuratively a beacon in the revitalisation of downtown Belfast. A multipurpose facility serving the visual and performing arts, it heralds its presence by a slim basalt tower topped with a luminous lantern. In a city where civic space has been contested, militarised and segregated, the MAC provides a new kind of meeting place.

85. KUKJE GALLERY
Architecture, 2013

The form of SO-IL's building for the Kukje Gallery in Seoul reads as clearly as the stairways and cylindrical elevator shaft that have been pulled outside it. However, the innovation comes from the bespoke metal chainmail that 'shrink-wraps' it all, consisting of 510,000 handmade stainless-steel links. Precisely tailoring the mesh to fit elastically over the building was an accomplishment in itself.

86. SUPERKILEN
Architecture, 2013

Stretching through the Nørrebro neighbourhood of Copenhagen, Superkilen is a new breed of urban park that raises questions about what constitutes civic space in the twenty-first century. Architect Bjarke Ingels has scattered miscellaneous street furniture – benches, fountains, lamps and ping-pong tables – from sixty different nations across a brightly coloured carpet of pink glass and rubber. Sourced from a range of different cultures and contexts, the park is a commentary on Copenhagen's diversity.

87. ASTLEY CASTLE
Architecture, 2013

Invited by architectural charity the Landmark Trust to create a holiday house from the ruined structure of the medieval Astley Castle, London-based Witherford Watson Mann skilfully placed a two-storey contemporary house within the original sandstone walls. Clay brickwork fills gaps in the structure, creating a visible contrast between new and old. The modern structure takes up only a part of the footprint of the original castle; the rest is left open to create outdoor rooms.

88. GALAXY SOHO
Architecture, 2013
Galaxy SOHO is a 330,000-square-metre office, retail and entertainment complex in the heart of Beijing. A composition of five flowing, curvilinear volumes linked by stretched bridges transforms this historic part of the city into a futuristic landscape. Commissioning architects like Zaha Hadid is no longer rare in China, but for a commercial private sector project consisting primarily of offices it represents a creative achievement.

89. MUSEUM OF CONTEMPORARY
ART (MOCA) CLEVELAND
Architecture, 2013
MOCA Cleveland is a lean, tactical model for arts organisations in straitened economic times. A deliberately enigmatic construction in this inner-city suburb of hospital and university buildings, MOCA's tent-like carapace is covered with a skin of diagonal panels that reflect neighbourhood activity. The public share all four floors with more private zones (including offices, storage and delivery), giving visitors a sense of MOCA's day-to-day functions.

90. MUSEUM OF INNOCENCE
Architecture, 2013
The Museum of Innocence is one of Nobel Prize laureate Orhan Pamuk's most famous books, featuring a character that collects all the things that his lover has touched. As was Pamuk's original intention, the story became a real-life museum in Istanbul's Beyoğlu neighbourhood. Stepping through the doors, visitors enter a space filled with cabinets of curiosities, each representing a different chapter in the book. Lighting and spatial design is used to communicate the melancholy that runs through the novel, creating an experience that falls between reality and fiction.

91. A ROOM FOR LONDON
Architecture, 2013
A wonderfully surreal sight on the London skyline, A Room for London is one of a number of projects by Living Architecture, a not-for-profit initiative promoting world-class modern architecture. Taking the form of a boat grounded on the roof of the Southbank Centre's Queen Elizabeth Hall, the idea for the temporary structure came from colonial narratives of travel and displacement, in particular Joseph Conrad's novella *Heart of Darkness* - a story that begins beside the Thames.

92. THALIA THEATRE
Architecture, 2013
Built in the 1840s for the Count of Farrobo to host theatrical events as well as spectacular parties, the Thalia Theatre had been in a state of ruin since it burnt down in 1862. The renovation, led by Gonçalo Byrne Arquitectos and Barbas Lopes Arquitectos, preserves the monumental nature of the ruin by covering the exterior with smooth concrete, while retaining the interior in its original condition.

93. MUSEO JUMEX
Architecture, 2014
Clad in local travertine and ending in a sawtooth rooftop, David Chipperfield's understated yet monolithic Museo Jumex achieves a remarkable presence and scale. The vertical organisation of the spaces, from basement, entrance lobby, cafeteria, open-air terrace and galleries provide careful reflections on the relationship between light, space and the exhibited art.

94. MARSAN MEDIATHEQUE
Architecture, 2014
Designed by French architects archi5, the Mediatheque is an interactive media library. Taking the form of a covered square at the centre of an austere quadrangle in a former barracks, it tackles the challenge of covering such a large span by making its facades transparent. One corner of the clean envelope of geometric lines opens on to Mont-de-Marsan's urban context, while the classical internal layout is offset by non-orthogonal lines more commonly seen in nature.

95. CHILD CHEMO HOUSE
Architecture, 2014
This children's chemotherapy unit is a rare example of inventive architects tackling a healthcare brief that is both technically challenging and highly emotive. Designed by Tezuka Architects, Child Chemo House is akin to a small village with numerous shared spaces. Home to entire families for several months at a time, the structure enables maximum connectivity and (when separated by necessity) maximum visibility between children undergoing chemotherapy and their families, reducing trauma for children, siblings and parents alike.

96. FRAC NORD-PAS DE CALAIS
Architecture, 2014
FRAC Nord-Pas de Calais is the result of a competition to transform a derelict workshop dating from 1949 into a new home for the archives and exhibition spaces of the Nord-Pas de Calais region. Architects Lacaton & Vassal chose to leave the original structure empty, housing the archives in an adjoining prefabricated 'twin' using ETFE cushions and corrugated polycarbonate panels.

The result meets all the requirements in the brief but with an extra 9,000 square metres of exhibition space.

97. MAKOKO FLOATING SCHOOL
Architecture, 2014

Half-building, half-boat, the Makoko Floating School is a prototype for building in watery regions that lack permanent infrastructure. Designed by Nigerian-born architect Kunlé Adeyemi as a school for inhabitants of Makoko, a former fishing village in Lagos where over 100,000 people live in houses on stilts. Consisting of a basic A-frame structure supported by plastic barrels, the Floating School's canted flanks are louvred for shelter, while solar panels provide power.

98. HEYDAR ALIYEV CENTRE
Architecture, 2014

An instant landmark, Zaha Hadid's Heydar Aliyev Centre is a rare convergence of architectural vision, computational intelligence and extreme engineering. Its swooping roof, containing an auditorium, library and museum, morphs into walls that spread into the surrounding landscape, while planes of water cascade through zigzag paths and flowered parterres. The upper surface of the state-of-the-art shell is supported by thousands of unique struts, whose continuous curves fold like an extended Möbius strip.

100. ST MORITZ CHURCH INTERIOR RENOVATION
Architecture, 2014

John Pawson's work has long been identified with the ecclesiastical, white-washed style of the seventeenth-century church architecture in the Netherlands. Although this has always been an influence on Pawson's work, he has rarely had a chance to practise his technique on a real church. The St Moritz Church is a small masterpiece. Every ingredient works with every other to produce a symphony of calm: the mind is set free, and the architecture contributes to a moment of spiritual philosophy.

101. THE NEW CREMATORIUM AT THE WOODLAND CEMETERY
Architecture, 2014

In the undulating terrain of the UNESCO World Heritage-listed Woodland Cemetery, Johan Celsing's New Crematorium offers a discreet presence. Unlike most buildings of this kind, its human scale gives it a welcoming and respectful appearance. At the entrance, mourners gather under a generous brick canopy, in close proximity to the woodland. In a small ceremony room with a vaulted ceiling, the light washes over a wall of white-glazed perforated bricks.

102. PRAÇA DAS ARTES PERFORMING ARTS CENTRE
Architecture, 2014

The Praça das Artes Performing Arts Centre is a collage of interlocking concrete blocks in downtown São Paulo. Its lead architect, Brasil Arquitetura's founding partner Marcelo Ferraz, worked with Lina Bo Bardi on the SESC Pompéia in 1977. Like SESC, the success of the Praça das Artes lies in the creation of a new civic space. In a gesture that gives back to the city, a generous courtyard flows under the building, connecting surrounding streets and opening up the building to the public realm.

103. LA TALLERA
Architecture, 2014

La Tallera is a new cultural centre just south of Mexico City. Formerly the studio of the Mexican muralist David Alfaro Siqueiros, the conversion was given life by Escobedo's architectural sleight of hand. Two of Siqueiros' vast murals were rotated from their original position, and a perimeter wall removed. Previously, the murals could only be glimpsed from the street, but now, the once private patio has been made public.

104. PAUL SMITH SHOP FACADE
Architecture, 2014

Invited to design a shopfront for fashion designer Paul Smith, 6a Architects presented something very different from traditional shopfronts. The facade is of a cast-iron raised pattern of large interlocking circles in a deep burnt sienna. Close up, the patterns seem like the weave of a fabric. Four round glass window vitrines protrude into the street, while the entrance is set back with curved cast-iron panels, creating a simple but striking overall composition.

105. NEWHALL BE HOUSING SCHEME
Architecture, 2014

At first glance, this residential development looks like an elegant, modern terraced-housing block. The clever and playful geometry of oblique lines and folding surfaces gives rhythm to volumes made from simple materials and inspired by local rural buildings. The back-to-back arrangement of homes creates terraced courtyards, maximising internal living space and flexibility. Loft spaces are either finished, or can be retrofitted by homebuyers to create additional bedrooms.

106. LES TURBULENCES, FRAC CENTRE
Architecture, 2014

Les Turbulences is a radical reworking of former military premises in Orléans. Architects Jakob + MacFarlane used the slightly skewed, U-shaped plan of the old buildings to cast a non-standard grid across the open courtyard. This lattice erupts into a single irregular volume with nodes protruding upwards and sideways to ocular skylights. Outside, polygonal concrete units rise to a carapace of opaque and perforated aluminium panels, the latter illuminated from within at night.

107. LA ÚLTIMA ESPERANZA – THE LAST HOPE
Architecture, 2015

La Última Esperanza is the final iteration of a long-term collaboration between the Ecuadorean studio Al Borde and the Cabuyal community in the Manabí district of Ecuador. Previous collaborations had already produced a school and a community centre. For the final iteration, Al Borde created an architecture school, empowering the community to create new buildings for themselves, independent of any formal architectural training. By transferring skills back to the local community, this exceptional project challenges notions about the role of the architect in society.

108. HOUSE FOR TREES
Architecture, 2015

House for Trees occupies an introverted lot in Ho Chi Minh City, consisting of five concrete towers topped by greenery. The towers are, in effect, tree pots. Set at slightly different heights, each upper zone conceals a deep layer of soil to assist proper drainage, a critical issue in this tropical and rapidly developing urban environment. They stake out a communal courtyard, with ground-level shared rooms and access to the more private upstairs spaces provided by external bridges.

109. DESERT COURTYARD HOUSE
Architecture, 2015

While Wendell Burnette Architects' design for this residential property in Arizona's Sonoran Desert employs the qualities of light, mass, privacy and transparency to great effect, it is the use of rammed-earth walls that elevates the building above the norm. This ancient technique uses natural raw materials, including soil from the site, to create a sustainable material with high thermal mass and a direct relationship to the surrounding landscape.

110. FONDATION LOUIS VUITTON
Architecture, 2015

Designed by Frank Gehry, the Fondation Louis Vuitton in Paris is an art museum and cultural centre sponsored by the LVMH group and its subsidiaries. Housing temporary exhibitions and concerts in a 'glass cloud' of twelve curved sails, the building appears to emerge as a cascade from the Bois de Boulogne. A contemporary evocation of the grand greenhouses of the mid nineteenth century, the building's multiple terraces break down the distinction between inside and outside.

111. MARKTHAL ROTTERDAM
Architecture, 2015

MVRDV's design for a new market hall in Rotterdam comprises a forty-metre arched roof that contains 228 apartments, a range of leisure facilities and, below the arch, a food market. A colourful one-hectare mural, Cornucopia, by artists Arno Coenen and Iris Roskam covers the inside of the arch. Digitally printed on 4,000 perforated aluminium panels, it depicts oversized images of market produce, as well as flowers and insects that refer to seventeenth century Dutch still-life paintings.

112. ONE CENTRAL PARK
Architecture, 2015

Sydney's latest urban renewal redevelopment is a game-changing example of tower architecture. Designed by Jean Nouvel in collaboration with French botanist and artist Patrick Blanc, over 250 native Australian species are spread over fifty per cent of the building's facade; the vertical gardens and surrounding parkland add up to 30,000 square metres of greenery. Nouvel's architectural mastery is demonstrated by the addition of an oversize cantilevering terrace and heliostat.

113. FORFATTERHUSET KINDERGARTEN
Architecture, 2015

Fun yet thoughtful, this kindergarten comprises five small buildings and a series of playgrounds wrapped by a continuous, undulating curtain of vertical brick strips. Placed slightly apart from each other, the bricks offer privacy and protection from the sun, while still affording views into the inner courtyards or the street. Three terraces run at different heights around the buildings, providing a sense of enclosure and seclusion by the extension of the brick veil.

114. ARENA DO MORRO
Architecture, 2015

Located in the Mãe Luiza favela, the Arena do Morro is a subtle adjustment of an existing sports facility to create new multipurpose rooms for community use. After in-depth planning studies of the neighbourhood, Herzog & de Meuron installed a generous white roof across the site. This canopy is emblematic of the new project. It is made of standard aluminium panels, tapered at either end to enhance views into the interior.

115. PHILHARMONIC HALL
Architecture, 2015

When the Barcelona-based practice Barozzi/Veiga won the commission to design the Philharmonic Hall back in 2007, the idea was to put Szczecin back on the map with a distinctive building. Their design is reminiscent of the crystalline fantasies of expressionist architect Bruno Taut. The silhouette nods to architectural tradition, but the overall effect is unmistakably contemporary. It is often compared to an iceberg – white and bulky, but at the same time somewhat unreal, thanks to its subtly layered facade.

116. SAW SWEE HOCK STUDENT CENTRE
Architecture, 2015
This multi-faceted red-brick building demonstrates a sensitive approach born of a deep understanding of the site and its inhabitants. Located at the London School of Economics' historic Aldwych campus, the Saw Swee Hock Student Centre brings all of the university's student facilities under one roof. The angular geometry of the building is informed by the challenging nature of the triangular site. Sensuous materials combine with free-flowing spaces and a generous stairway to create meeting places at every level.

117. GARDEN SCHOOL
Architecture, 2015
OPEN Architecture's design for the Fangshan campus of Bejiing No.4 High School is a thoughtful response to China's notoriously rigid and hierarchical education system. The Garden School's variety of circulation spaces stand in stark contrast to the strict orthogonal layout of most Chinese schools. The design accommodates varying modes of social interaction and, through its diversity of forms, nourishes the imagination and encourages a more holistic approach to personal development.

118. WATERBANK CAMPUS
Architecture, 2015
The Waterbank Campus at Endana Secondary School in Kenya is notable for the way in which it aims to be a catalyst for social and environmental transformation. Built using local materials and expertise, Waterbank doubles the amount of accommodation and range of amenities compared to conventional classroom typologies. The campus is designed to harvest rainwater, which feeds into a central reservoir that supplies classrooms, canteens, staff housing and night-time latrines.

119. UC INNOVATION CENTER
Architecture, 2015
The UC Innovation Center is an 8,176-square-metre building on the campus of the Universidad Católica de Chile in Santiago. The client requested a building with a contemporary look, but the designers, ELEMENTAL, wanted to avoid the environmental and design pitfalls of the hackneyed glass-fronted edifice. The resulting building consists of several volumes of stacked concrete with impressively deep recessed openings to provide natural air flow. In addition to creating a conducive research environment, this design reduced energy costs by two-thirds.

120. SANCAKLAR MOSQUE
Architecture, 2015
A plain, rectangular stone tower is the only visible trace of a mosque submerged in the slope of a hill. This unprecedented structure is a site-sensitive place of worship, respecting the topography of the surrounding valley. This architecture does not make demands but rather mediates between the individual and god. Solemnity is attained through simplicity, modesty and abstraction: a few round steps constitute the minbar, and a bare niche forms the mihrab.

121. LONG MUSEUM WEST BUND
Architecture, 2015
Located on the site of a coal-loading point from the 1950s, the Long Museum is a distinctly modern gallery that echoes its industrial past. The building provides a series of spatial delights that vary from monumental triple-height volumes to intimate rooms. A series of large, interlocking vaults have real structural power, creating galleries that are more architecturally distinct than the prevalent 'white box'.

122. GRANBY WORKSHOP
Architecture, 2016
Granby Workshop is a social enterprise that experiments with manufacturing processes to create hand-made objects for the home. It is led by art, design and architecture collective Assemble with the Granby Four Streets CLT, which has brought a neglected community in Toxteth back to life over the past two decades. Profits are returned to the workshop or used to support other local projects, offering an alternative to top-down, developer-led regeneration.

123. FONDAZIONE PRADA
Architecture, 2016
The Fondazione Prada is a reinterpretation of the past that unites old and new. The vast complex, formerly a gin distillery, combines brewing cisterns and industrial warehouses (one clad in gold leaf) with new structures to house temporary exhibitions, collections, archive, a cinema and restaurant. In recent decades art has been placed in either a neutral 'white box' or the now clichéd refurbished industrial building, but the Fondazione is a place of many stories and conditions.

124. SUSTAINABLE HOUSING
Architecture, 2016
It is estimated that Mexico needs nine million new homes. To address this, Tatiana Bilbao developed a prototype for low-income housing across Mexico. Budgeted at $8,000 per unit, each house grows from a cinder-block core, with basic services and minimal rooms, plus a double-height living/dining room. The structurally stable core can be extended with lighter materials, such as wooden pallets, to accommodate growing families and small business endeavours.

125. NIDA HOUSE

Architecture, 2016

The Nida House makes the most of its beautiful surroundings with minimum resources. Made of concrete, glass and wood, this detached house uses concentric square platforms, arranged like an inverted pyramid, with the smaller private rooms at the bottom and social spaces on the top levels, leaving the perimeter free. A central spiral staircase leads to a top platform open to the sky, like an elevated piazza overlooking the Pacific.

126. THE GREEN

Architecture, 2016

A community centre in south-east London, The Green offers a timely example of how architects can work proactively with a community to create a highly successful outcome. Intelligent use of insulation makes the building more energy-efficient, which helps to keep running costs to a minimum. Such cost considerations were central to a detailed consultation process between the architects and the community, including workshops to consider various day-to-day scenarios that could illustrate the centre's future revenue potential.

127. DREAMLAND MARGATE

Architecture, 2016

With its scenic railway, roller disco and restored dodgem cars, the Dreamland Margate amusement park has been recreated through a lovingly recreated exercise in recycling, upcycling and nostalgia. The roller disco has its original ceiling, while the booths alongside it are decked in original Formica samples unearthed in a warehouse in Blackpool. Picnic benches are made from reclaimed timbers, while many of the vintage rides were sourced across Europe.

128. BETTER SHELTER

Architecture, 2016

Great design responds to needs, and the refugee crisis is one of the biggest of our era. Better Shelter is a ground-breaking example of putting values ahead of value and benefit above profit. This social enterprise draws on IKEA's expertise in flat-pack technology to create more robust shelters for refugees, with a commitment to continuous improvement. Harnessing their vast experience, IKEA has shown that design is not only about improving conditions, but also about taking responsibility and, as such, contributing towards a better world.

130. SL11024

Architecture, 2016

Set on a challenging wedge-shaped hillside site on the dense border of the UCLA campus in Westwood, the SL11024 university campus houses an active community whose living patterns defy boundaries of home and work. The combination of residential accommodation and communal spaces gives a lively civic openness to this thirty-one-unit student and faculty housing complex.

131. ARENA FOR LEARNING

Architecture, 2016

Led by Yvonne Farrell and Shelley McNamara, Grafton Architects have long made education a key part of their practice. In the desert climate and seismic zone of Lima, Peru, their Arena for Learning campus for UTEC blurs the boundaries between teaching and research through an open circulation strategy. Laboratories are displayed as exhibition spaces, placing the educational ethos of the institution at its heart.

132. HARBIN OPERA HOUSE

Architecture, 2016

Emulating the mountains that surround this northern Chinese city, the Harbin Opera House's silhouettes are wrapped judiciously around 1,600-seat and 400-seat theatres. Sinuous ash-clad interiors seem to melt beneath a crystalline glass atrium. The project shows MAD principal Ma Yansong at the peak of his powers: the building produces an artificial landscape that, like a traditional Chinese painting, reconciles the natural and manmade.

133. VIA 57 WEST

Architecture, 2016

With VIA 57 West, Bjarke Ingels has invented a bravura hybrid typology for Manhattan, cross-breeding the historic row-house streetscape with the glamour and sculptural singularity of the skyscraper. BIG's first building in the Americas slopes diagonally from the lowest corner of the block, by the Hudson River, up to its full height at its Midtown corner. The diagonally-sloping structure offers residents views of the city and of the river as well as a generous communal courtyard.

134. TATE MODERN BLAVATNIK BUILDING

Architecture, 2016

The expanded Tate Modern should not be seen just as an extension, but rather as the continuation and fulfilment of Herzog & de Meuron's original design. Here the sharing of space is not seen just as a matter of coexistence or of passive browsing, but as an experience at once physical, spatial, visual and spiritual. These qualities were already present in the first phase of Tate Modern, but the extension gives them new dimensions.

135. DESIGN THAT SAVES LIVES

Architecture, 2016

In April 2013, the Rana Plaza building near Dhaka in Bangladesh collapsed, killing 1,132 mostly female workers. To ensure there was no repeat of this tragedy, a consortium of clothing brands approached Arup to help assess the structural safety of thousands of Bangladeshi garment factories, which employ more than four million people and are critical to the country's economy. The resulting project has led to safer workplaces, demonstrating what design can do when it focuses on genuine issues.

136. LYCÉE SCHORGE SECONDARY SCHOOL
Architecture, 2017
The Lycée Schorge Secondary School reconsiders
what we think of as modernity by reimagining
tradition. The design consists of nine modules
which accommodate a series of classrooms and
administration rooms in a radial layout which wrap
around a public courtyard. The school not only
sets a new standard for educational excellence
in the region, but it also provides a source of
inspiration by making innovative use of locally-
sourced building materials and traditional
construction methods.

137. HEGNHUSET, MEMORIAL
AND LEARNING CENTRE
Architecture, 2017
At the heart of this youth camp sits a remarkable
building that answers the apparently impossible
question: how do you inhabit a place where something so bad has happened, while still bearing
testimony to the victims? The Hegnhuset at Utøya,
where Anders Breivik murdered sixty-nine young
Labour activists, is a very architectural response.
A double colonnade surrounds the brutally severed
form of the café where many activists were killed,
while still incorporating a new library and canteen.

138. FONDACO DEI TEDESCHI
Architecture, 2017
The sixteenth-century Fondaco dei Tedeschi
served as Venice's post office before being bought
by the Benetton Group in 2008. Over eight years
the building has been carefully restored and
altered to create a department store like no other.
OMA's renovation allows tourists and locals alike
to engage with the layers of Venice's history: from
the medieval courtyard wall, eighteenth-century
brickwork and the 1930s concrete supports
to twenty-first-century additions.

139. WARKA WATER
Architecture, 2017
Moisture exists in the air everywhere, no matter
how arid the climate. Warka Water cleverly combines a rain butt, fog catcher and dew collector
in the form of a twelve-metre-tall bamboo tower
that supports a sleeve of water-gathering mesh
able to amass 100 litres of clean drinking water
every day. Italian designer Arturo Vittori developed
the project in a remote village in north-eastern
Ethiopia, mimicking nature's water-collecting
techniques, as seen in beetle's shells, lotus
flowers and spider's webs.

140. WELTSTADT – REFUGEES' MEMORIES
AND FUTURES AS MODELS
Architecture, 2017
This year-long project saw 150 young refugees
working with eight Berlin workshops to create
models of buildings at a 1:10 scale. The models
show what these people left behind and remem-
ber: homes, schools, factories, restaurants.

By using recycled materials, they are made to
appear realistic. This process of memory-making
is not just one of reconstruction: next to ruins
unmistakably demolished by war are houses,
some partly furnished, that serve as reminders
of good times and dreams of the future.

141. SALA BECKETT THEATRE AND
INTERNATIONAL DRAMA CENTRE
Architecture, 2017
This project transformed Barcelona's old Peace
and Justice Cooperative Building into a new
home for the Sala Beckett Theatre. A series of
interventions preserved the spatial characteristics
of the original 1920s building, while adding new
floors to serve the needs of a modern theatre
company. The theatre is given a street presence
with a large corner opening and a large foyer
connects the building's three levels of classrooms,
exhibition halls, offices, rehearsal rooms and
performance spaces.

142. CROFT LODGE STUDIO
Architecture, 2017
A dilapidated 300-year-old cottage in Leominster,
Herefordshire, has been rebuilt as a studio space
with guest accommodation to surprising effect.
This imaginative project encapsulates the remains
of the eighteenth-century building, leaving many
of its original features – including dead ivy, rotten
timbers and old birds' nests – intact. The ruin has
been wrapped in a new outer envelope of black
corrugated metal. Completed for just £160,000,
this modest project displays an intriguing and
skilful approach to conservation.

143. THE ENVIRONMENTAL ENHANCEMENT
OF THE FIVE DRAGONS TEMPLE
Architecture, 2017
Given China's spotty record with historic
preservation, architect Wang Hui's Five Dragons
project for a rural temple complex in Shanxi
province dating to the Tang dynasty offers a
ray of hope. For years, the long-derelict temple
and grounds were walled off and inaccessible, a
form of 'protection' that alienated local villagers.
By designing a series of understated squares,
courtyards and walkways, Wang has restored
the temple compound to its place at the centre
of village life.

144. PORT HOUSE
Architecture, 2017
The early twentieth-century Antwerp Docks fire
station was originally to have been crowned with
a tall tower. Now it is adorned with a striking,
self-supporting, ship-like superstructure, faced
with 2,000 diamond-shaped windows – some
clear, some opaque, and many faceted. Designed
by Zaha Hadid, it provides energy-efficient office
accommodation for port staff who, previously,
had been scattered around this historic diamond-
trading city, which today handles a quarter of
Europe's container shipping.

145. SMITHSONIAN NATIONAL MUSEUM
OF AFRICAN AMERICAN HISTORY
AND CULTURE
Architecture, 2017

Occupying the location of a former slave market on the National Mall, this museum opened after efforts to commemorate African American history that date back to a campaign led by black Civil War veterans. The multi-tiered corona form of the building evokes traditional Yoruban caryatid columns, while the ornamental exterior panels draw from historical lattice ironwork found in the American South, often created by enslaved Africans. Carefully positioned apertures create framed views of both the Lincoln Memorial and the Washington Monument, reminding visitors that the origin story of America is inseparable from the African American experience.

146. WIND AND RAIN BRIDGE
Architecture, 2017

Wind and Rain Bridge is a combination of indigenous construction techniques and thoughtful design that resulted in a powerful piece of rural place-making. Donn Holohan, together with students from the University of Hong Kong, worked with a village community in an isolated region of southern China, who became dislocated after a major flood in 2014. Completed in 2016, the scheme brought together contemporary engineering technologies with the skills of local people.

147. MRS FAN'S PLUG-IN HOUSE
Architecture, 2017

Mrs Fan's Plug-In House is a proposal for regenerating Beijing's historic hutong districts through the use of prefabricated elements. Built in 2016, the Plug-In House originated as a pilot renovation project which aimed to demonstrate that historic buildings could be upgraded in a way that did not necessitate blanket demolition. The Plug-In House can be fully customised and assembled on site; it is made of prefabricated panels that can be locked onto another using a hex socket.

148. THE CALAIS BUILDS PROJECT
Architecture, 2017

The Calais Builds Project captured the needs, culture and hopes of the residents of the Jungle refugee camp. Along with local migrants and students from the University of Limerick, architect Gráinne Hassett designed and built a major community infrastructure, including a Women and Children's Centre and the Baloo's Youth Centre. The buildings were functional and provided safety and dignity when it was most needed, but were demolished by the French Government and their inhabitants once again displaced.

152. VOLUME
Digital, 2008

An audio-visual installation located at the Victoria and Albert Museum, Volume was a unique sculpture of light and sound. Consisting of an array of LED columns, speakers and motion sensors, the installation was designed to respond to human movement. Visitors could step inside the array and to see their actions rendered in light and sound. The piece was a collaboration between design collective United Visual Artists (UVA) and Massive Attack's 3D and Neil Davidge.

153. THE REPLENISHING BODY KIOSK
Digital, 2008

The Replenishing Body Kiosk was an interactive video installation inspired by the fact that the human body is sixty per cent water. It was created by Ross Phillips and Nick Knight of SHOWstudio as a gallery installation in partnership with Evian. Using a twenty-five section touchscreen grid, visitors were invited to make a one-second video of part of their body in close-up. Each one-second clip was added on top of previous footage, creating a composite video portrait that continually replenished itself.

154. FIXMYSTREET
Digital, 2008

Created by online community mySociety, FixMyStreet is used to report, view or discuss local problems like graffiti, fly tipping, broken paving or street lighting. Users enter a location on the website, click on the map and describe the problem: an email is automatically sent to the relevant council. As the information is public, people can see what others have reported or can even go and fix it themselves. In this way, the internet is efficiently used to improve lives through civil actions at a local level.

155. SHARKRUNNERS
Digital, 2008

An online game, Sharkrunners encouraged players to act as virtual shark researchers along the Californian coast. It was created by Area/Code, who connect imaginary game spaces with real-world events, sensors and data. The ships were virtual, but the sharks were actual great white sharks with GPS units attached to their dorsal fins. Telemetry provided their position and movement, so every shark that players encountered in the game corresponded to a real shark in the real world.

156. LE SACRE DU PRINTEMPS
Digital, 2008

Created by media artist Klaus Obermaier, Le Sacre du Printemps is an interactive interpretation of Stravinsky's *The Rite of Spring*. Using interactive stereoscopic camera systems, the stage performance of dancer Julia Mach was digitally manipulated and projected on a screen.

These projections responded to movement, imagery and speed, triggered and influenced by the orchestra. The audience watched the projections through stereoscopic lenses, enabling them to feel closer to the performance.

157. TRULIA HINDSIGHT
Digital, 2008

A property website, Trulia Hindsight is a technologically sophisticated mapping and data visualisation of urban growth. Using the year properties were built as its starting point, the website shows the growth of streets, neighbourhoods and cities over time. A slider control allows users to see when the majority of development occurred, or to focus on only homes built before or after specific years.

158. PRIVATE VIEW EXHIBITION
FOR TRUSSARDI,
PALAZZO TRUSSARDI ALLA SCALA
Digital, 2008

In 2007, the leather luxury goods company Trussardi commissioned Paul Cocksedge Studio to create an exhibition for their space at the Salone del Mobile in Milan. Cocksedge placed the brand's icons behind walls covered with a filter that blocks the visible light spectrum but allowed infrared light to pass through. Although the walls of the exhibition appeared black to the human eye, visitors could discover the hidden objects using digital cameras and camera phones.

159. BURBLE LONDON
Digital, 2008

Launched during London Fashion Week 2007, the Burble was a seventy-metre-tall structure consisting of 1,000 extra-large helium balloons, supported by 140 carbon-fibre hexagonal units. Each balloon contains a micro-controller and multi-coloured LEDs. The structure could be composed and assembled by members of the public themselves. The Burble was originally designed to sway by itself in the evening breeze, but its coloured patterns and shape could also be controlled by an articulated handlebar.

160. TED WEBSITE
Digital, 2008

Relaunched in 2007, TED.com shares inspiring talks with the world for free. TED's mission – 'ideas worth spreading' – is realised through the website, offering thousands of presentations from cultural giants, including Bill Clinton, Richard Branson, Jane Goodall, Philippe Starck, Frank Gehry and Bono – with more added each week. As of January 2008, the talks had been viewed nearly thirty million times by more than twelve million people worldwide.

161. UNLIMITED
Digital, 2008

Created by London-based digital agency Poke, Orange Unlimited was, at the time, the world's longest website. Merging the boundaries between maths, programming, art and design, the seemingly infinite website was developed by a multidisciplinary team that included film composer and sound designer Nick Ryan, illustrator Rex Crowle and generative math artist Marius Watz. As visitors scrolled down, they followed a never-ending rainbow featuring a vast spectrum of interactive characters in an effective promotion of the brand's offer of unlimited minutes.

162. 'TERMINAL 5 IS WORKING'
Digital, 2009

The opening of Heathrow's Terminal 5 in March 2008 got off to a shaky start. Asked to repair T5's image, BBH created a campaign that featured untouched, realistic photographs of travel through the terminal that had been taken only the day before. These formed a backdrop to text that featured on digital display boards, bearing positive messages such as 'Yesterday at T5, 89% of flights arrived on time'.

163. APPEEL
Digital, 2009

Described as a 'virus spreading through interacting individuals', Appeel demonstrated the basic principles of interactivity. A wall was covered by a large number of coloured stickers, positioned on a grid. People were invited to remove the stickers, leaving white spots in the layout, thereby individually and collectively changing the wall's appearance. These stickers then took a life of their own as they were positioned randomly, or carefully, to compose new images or write messages.

164. 'HOUSE OF CARDS' MUSIC VIDEO
Digital, 2009

The music video for the Radiohead song 'House of Cards' is ground-breaking in that it was made without cameras or lights. Instead, moving three-dimensional images (such as singer Thom Yorke) were captured as data using innovative scanner technology. Although the production itself is noteworthy, the code used to make it was released to the public so that they could make their own version.

165. KINETIC SCULPTURE –
THE SHAPES OF THINGS TO COME
Digital, 2009

Kinetic Sculpture is an installation at the BMW Museum in Munich consisting of 714 individually controlled metal balls suspended from thin steel wires. Within a grid covering six square metres, they appear to float, rising and falling in an elegant seven-minute sequence. Initially abstract and chaotic, the pattern evolves into more recognisable forms until finally, they create the outline of a vehicle. The result is a poetic translation of the design process.

166. 'INTEGRAL' INTERACTIVE MUSIC VIDEO
Digital, 2009

The music video for the Pet Shop Boys song 'Integral' is notable for the way it featured QR codes. Developed by design agency Rumpus Room, these QR codes could be read by camera phones, allowing the user to download URLs. As well as allowing fans to engage with the band's performance on a deeper level, the released content also informed them about issues surrounding civil liberties – specifically ID cards within the UK.

167. FID.GEN BARCODES
Digital, 2009

Fid.Gen Barcodes is a generative design tool for creating and tailoring fiducial markers, used in computer vision based interactive projects applying the open source package reacTIVision. A design product for creators rather than consumers, Fid. Gen transforms the way in which physical things are linked to the digital world by the application of barcodes. Even though they are designed as machine-readable objects, the markers are reminiscent of quirky abstract characters.

168. LITTLEBIGPLANET
Digital, 2009

LittleBigPlanet is a unique game combining an amazing adventure with a huge social community. The game revolves around the player's control of small avatars, known as Sackboys or Sackgirls, in a variety of platforming scenarios. Though the game has pre-built levels for players to explore, its customisable nature is of equal importance, from altering the player's character to building entirely new objects and levels, and then sharing them online as part of the LittleBigPlanet community.

169. THIS HAPPENED EVENTS SERIES
Digital, 2009

This Happened was a series of events providing a forum for surveying and debating interaction design. The audience and speakers consisted of a mix of established practitioners, students, commercial clients and cultural institutions. The main objective was to analyse and discuss ideas within current working practices, with the aim of encouraging people to open up their minds to new and creative working methods.

170. DINNER TABLE GAME
Digital, 2009

Commissioned for the exhibition Science of Survival at the Science Museum, Dinner Table used a top projection onto a three-dimensional surface to create the illusion of a real dinner table. The aim was to gather a healthy plate of food for yourself, while at the same time learning how our choices are shaped by global food supply and affect other people around the world – or, in this case, at the table.

171. MAKE: MAGAZINE
Digital, 2009

The first magazine devoted entirely to DIY technology, Make: unites, inspires and informs a growing community of resourceful people who undertake amazing projects in their backyards, basements and garages. It is a platform and meeting point for DIY designers and engineers covering all levels of design, with a daily update on new projects around the world alongside high-quality articles and instructions.

172. CLOUD
Digital, 2009

Resembling an art installation, the digital sculpture Cloud at Heathrow's Terminal 5 reinterpreted the flip-dots used in the 1970s and 80s train station and airport signs. Covered with 4,638 flip-dots that could be individually triggered by a computer, Cloud could be programmed to play a mesmerising sequence of animated patterns across the entire skin of the sculpture. The dots, silver on one side and black on the other, generated a sound reminiscent of travel.

173. DIGITAL BY DESIGN
Digital, 2009

Troika's book Digital by Design is a survey of the most exciting 'smart' objects and the designers who pushed the boundaries of interactive technology and 'intelligent' design. The book is structured in a way that provides the reader with a brief yet comprehensive view of the projects and the people behind the work. It brought together a broad group of works that explore the latest in digital technologies where the ultimate output was placed in the hands of the user.

174. ABSOLUT QUARTET
Digital, 2009

A unique web-based musical experience, Absolut Quartet was a large-scale music-making machine created by roboticists Jeff Lieberman and Dan Paluska. Visitors to a website could enter a 4-8 second theme, from which the machine would generate, in real time, a unique musical piece based on the input melody to complete the quartet. The main instrument was a ballistic marimba which launched rubber balls two metres into the air, precisely aimed to bounce off forty-two chromatic wooden keys.

175. L-E-D-LED-L-ED
Digital, 2010

L-E-D-LED-L-ED consisted of hundreds of bead-shaped light emitting diodes (LEDs) that could slide back and forth along a series of parallel horizontal wires. Viewers were encouraged to touch and feel the installation, using their imagination to create a pattern or picture. To create the installation, designers Dilight developed a new and innovative process that reconverted the electric current passing through the horizontal wires, generating light by means of coiled wire inside each bead.

176. GRAFFITI TAXONOMY: PARIS
Digital, 2010

For Graffiti Taxonomy: Paris, Evan Roth spent four days photographing over 2,400 graffiti tags from each of Paris' twenty districts. To investigate the stylistic diversity of the graffiti, the ten most commonly used letters (A, E, I, N, O, R, S, T and U) were identified for further study. From each letter grouping, eighteen tags were isolated to represent the range of approaches to that specific character.

177. THE EYEWRITER
Digital, 2010

The EyeWriter project is an open-source, collaborative research effort to empower people suffering from amyotrophic lateral sclerosis (ALS). It combines a pair of low-cost, eye-tracking glasses with custom software that allows artists and graffiti writers to draw using only their eyes. The EyeWriter was developed with LA graffiti writer, publisher and activist, Tony Quan, who was diagnosed with ALS in 2003, leaving him almost completely physically paralysed – except for the movement of his eyes.

178. BLOOM
Digital, 2010

Part instrument, part composition and part artwork, Bloom explored uncharted territory in the realm of applications for the iPhone and iPad. The innovative controls allowed anyone to create elaborate patterns and unique melodies by simply tapping the screen. A generative music player takes over when Bloom is left idle, creating an infinite selection of compositions and accompanying visualisations. As one of the designers, Brian Eno, said, 'You can play [Bloom], and you can watch it play itself.'

179. OPENFRAMEWORKS
Digital, 2010

This open-source, cross-platform program library was designed to assist the creative process by providing a simple and intuitive framework for experimentation. It allows beginners and experts alike to develop real-time software interfaces that move far beyond traditional screen-based interaction into physical space. From the energy and responses of the openFrameworks community, the library has spawned a new generation of artists making expressive, organic, provocative and unique interactive artworks.

180. BBC iPLAYER
Digital, 2010

Launched on Christmas Day 2007, BBC's on-demand service iPlayer allows UK audiences to catch up with their favourite BBC television and radio programmes from the past seven days, at a time that suits them. Audiences have a choice of streaming or downloading their chosen programme; with series catch-up, selected programmes are also made available for the entire season.

181. PACHUBE
Digital, 2010

The Pachube service enabled people to monitor, store, discover and share environmental data from sensors connected to the internet. Just like a physical 'patch bay' (or telephone switchboard), Pachube made it simple to build applications, products and services bridging physical and virtual worlds. For example, buildings, interactive environments, networked energy meters, virtual worlds and mobile sensor devices could all talk and respond to one another.

182. AMAZON KINDLE DX
Digital, 2010

Amazon's Kindle DX was not the first e-book reader, but it was the first time that service, form and content came together at a point of mainstream marketability. The integration of the service and the device is almost magical, giving remote access to books, journals, magazines and other publications without having to resort to your computer or mobile phone. Finally a book had been invented that you can read with one hand.

183. YCN LIBRARY
Digital, 2010

Created by the Young Creative Network (YCN), the YCN Library was designed to spark interaction with the local community. Members first had to sign up at the YCN's physical headquarters at Rivington Street. Afterwards, they were free to borrow any title, which was delivered online. Details of publications on loan to other members could be viewed. Regular guest reading lists were presented in person in the space and also online, keeping the collection fresh – and the members inspired.

184. PANDA EYES
Digital, 2010

Designed for a WWF campaign that asked leading artists and designers to create new work based on the famous panda collection boxes, Panda Eyes was first displayed in Selfridges' shop window. It consisted of 100 rotating panda collection boxes that detected and tracked a viewer's presence using a thermal camera mounted overhead. Turning towards the viewer no matter how quickly they moved, the pandas' constant stare was slightly confrontational and unnerving, urging visitors to consider their impact on the environment.

185. THE INCIDENTAL
Digital, 2010

The Incidental is a user-generated website and news pamphlet created by and for the design community. Launched for the Milan Furniture Fair in 2009, it reached an estimated 20,000 people, offering opinion, news and recommendations by tapping into people's reactions to the fair. A new version for the 2009 London Design Festival included an open-house publishing base, encouraging people to drop by, comment, tweet, email or text. This user-generated content was redesigned, self-printed, folded and packaged in four daily editions.

186. ONEDOTZERO_ADVENTURES
IN MOTION FESTIVAL IDENTITY
Digital, 2010

The identity for the onedotzero_adventures in motion festival harnessed online conversations stimulated by onedotzero's global community. Specially produced generative software created a 'living' identity from which all visual communication is born: paused to create print assets or recorded to create film assets. The open-source software was available free to download and adapt. As a result, the identity continued to evolve through the festival's international tour.

187. PAINT
Digital, 2011

Substituting paint for pixels in this installation, Paint was created using an LED wall, motion sensors and an acute understanding of how people interact with objects. Developed to mark the launch of Nokia's N8 phone, participants pick up an empty paint bucket and place it in a virtual filling station. A camera at the top takes a snap of the user, which is used to 'fill up' the bucket. Players then 'throw' their painted face all over the nearby wall.

188. THE JOHNNY CASH PROJECT
Digital, 2011

The Johnny Cash Project is a living communal portrait of the musician known as the 'man in black'. Working with a simple image template and using an embedded custom drawing tool, participants create a unique and personal portrait of Johnny Cash. Their work is then combined with art from around the world, and integrated into a collective whole: a crowd-sourced music video for 'Ain't No Grave' rising from a sea of one-of-a-kind portraits.

189. THE ELEMENTS IPAD APP
Digital, 2011

The Elements was the first complete e-book developed from the ground up for iPad. The interactive app started as a living periodic table where every element was represented by a smoothly rotating sample: to read about tin, for example, the user tapped on the tin

soldier; to read about gold, on the gold nugget. Immediately, users saw a rotating sample of the element filling the screen, photographed with razor sharpness.

190. ROCK BAND 3
Digital, 2011

In earlier incarnations of this game, players used instrument-shaped controllers to mime to classic and modern rock soundtracks in their homes. Rock Band 3 made some important advances. The addition of a pro mode and realistic instruments, including full drum kits, keyboards and guitars styled like Fender Stratocasters, delivered a level of gameplay so realistic that the experience moved from pure entertainment to an educational interaction.

191. REACTABLE MOBILE
Digital, 2011

Reactable first attracted worldwide attention in 2007 when Björk toured with this strange, hypnotic new instrument. Developed by the Music Technology Group at Pompeu Fabra University in Barcelona, Reactable is a circular, table-top instrument, using translucent acrylic pucks to control a modular synthesiser. Reactable Mobile is a more accessible version, available as a downloadable app. The software combines sampling and multi-touch technologies to give access to this intuitive means of creating music to anyone with a touchscreen.

192. WALLPAPER* CUSTOM COVERS
Digital, 2011

For their August 2010 edition, Wallpaper* magazine gave subscribers the opportunity to create their own cover. The user-facing online design application used pre-designed elements, icons and graphics, which were then converted into high-resolution files. Using state-of-the-art digital printing and military-precision planning, 21,000 unique covers were printed on seven different paper stocks. Even subscribers who didn't design their own received a unique cover, developed by a program that randomised these elements.

193. FLIPBOARD
Digital, 2011

Conceived as the world's first social magazine, Flipboard aimed to fundamentally improve how people discover, view and share content across social networks. Readers could create their own sections based on content from Facebook, Twitter, Flickr and Google Reader, and quickly flip through the latest updates from friends and trusted sources. Launched as a free iPad app in July 2010, the single magazine-style format meant readers no longer had to click on link after link.

194. ANGRY BIRDS
Digital, 2011

A multi-platform mobile game, Angry Birds is remarkably simple: launch flightless birds at egg-stealing pigs to earn points by hitting critical weak points that bring their houses down. Angry Birds' success lies in its intuitive simulation of real-world physics and the ease with which players understood the flight trajectory of the birds and the structural properties of the buildings under attack. By the end of 2010, Angry Birds had been downloaded over fifty million times.

195. WIRED MAGAZINE IPAD APP
Digital, 2011

Wired has pushed the possibilities of iPad-optimised content further than most magazines. Specialist content includes individually designed pages to suit portrait or landscape orientations and material developed with a touchscreen device in mind, such as animated 360-degree images. Developed in collaboration with Adobe, the original US version offered a first glimpse of the possibilities of online publishing in May 2010, with *Wired UK* following in December.

196. E. CHROMI:
LIVING COLOUR FROM BACTERIA
Digital, 2011

When seven Cambridge undergraduates designed E. coli bacteria that could secrete colours visible to the naked eye, they named this new variety E. chromi. Designers Alexandra Daisy Ginsberg and James King worked alongside the team to explore its potential. Together they designed a timeline for how this foundational technology might affect our lives over the next century, from printing inks to disease monitoring and pollution mapping.

197. CELLSCOPE
Digital, 2011

CellScope uses mobile-phone-enabled telemicroscopy to link patients with doctors, no matter where they are in the world. The CellScope team developed an automated, compact and portable system capable of image capture, image processing and communication with medical experts. Patients thus become active participants in their own care and doctors can customise drugs and dosing based on real-time feedback.

198. MIMOSA
Digital, 2011

Commissioned for the 2010 Salone del Mobile, Mimosa was an interactive installation consisting of slim organic-LED (OLED) panels arranged to form flowers. A motion sensor mounted above reacted to movement from nearby people, opening and closing the delicate petals and changing the light conditions. The piece was inspired by mimosa plants, which open and close in response to environmental conditions.

199. GUARDIAN EYEWITNESS IPAD APP
Digital, 2011

Selected by Apple as one of the apps to showcase the iPad to the world, Eyewitness provided free access to the Guardian's award-winning photography. It showcased the best photos in superb detail, allowing users to fully appreciate the work each photographer had put in. Features included technical insights from photographers, and the ability to save photos as favourites and share them on social media.

200. SPEED OF LIGHT
Digital, 2011

Commissioned to mark the tenth anniversary of broadband in the UK, Speed of Light was a series of installations exploring communication and modernity at a former industrial warehouse on the South Bank. United Visual Artists stripped fibre optics back to their minimum: thin strands of glass and flickering beams of light. Dramatising the experience of fibre-optic communication, the installation transformed an input from the audience into a pathway of light through the exhibition.

201. HIGH ARCTIC:
AN EXPEDITION EXPERIENCE
Digital, 2012

A gallery installation within the National Maritime Museum, High Arctic aimed to convey the scale, beauty and fragility of the unique Arctic environment. An 820-square-metre immersive, responsive environment, Ultraviolet transported visitors to a space that sat somewhere between the physical and digital realms. The show used ultraviolet torches and computer-vision techniques to create simple, yet powerful messages about the rapidly-vanishing frozen landscape.

202. GUARDIAN IPAD EDITION
Digital, 2012

Shortly after the iPad was launched, the Guardian reimagined its weekly newspaper app to fit the new format. The front page was a grid featuring colour-coded section heads. This allowed generous space for selected stories, creating a hierarchy of news that reinforced the Guardian's reputation as a thoughtfully edited newspaper. The app was downloaded 100,000 times in the first four days after it was launched.

203. THE STANLEY PARABLE
Digital, 2012

An overnight viral internet sensation on its launch, the Stanley Parable video game was created by Davey Wreden in his bedroom. The player's interaction with the game results in multiple structures and endings, creating feelings of both control and doubt, since the player chooses but can do nothing that has not been programmed. Labelled an 'art game', the Stanley Parable poses questions about the nature of game systems and the relationship between gamer and designer.

204. MUSICITY
Digital, 2012

Musicity was a purpose-built mobile app that allowed visitors to different London locations to hear original tracks composed by musicians including Paul White, Stac and Subeena. The recording artists were commissioned to create music based on an aspect of the city that inspired them. This could only be listened to and downloaded when visiting those places. Musicity created a unique union of music, architecture and experience that offered a new way to explore the urban environment.

205. MICROSOFT KINECT FOR
XBOX 360 AND KINECT SDK
Digital, 2012

Kinect allows users to control an Xbox by spoken command or motion alone. It includes a sensor that tracks full body movement, a camera, a depth sensor made up of an infrared projector and a monochrome sensor that allows Kinect to see the room in 3D. The Kinect Software Development Kit (SDK) recognises the wider possibilities of this technology – for example, to help surgeons access patient records hands-free during surgery.

206. SUWAPPU
Digital, 2012

Suwappu – from the Japanese for 'swap' – is a series of eight character toys, whose upper and lower halves can be swapped to create hybrids. Their features are decipherable by image-recognition software in the accompanying Suwappu smartphone application: face markings control how the characters interact and perform, while leg markings generate the characters' environments.

207. HOMEPLUS VIRTUAL STORE
Digital, 2012

In August 2011, Homeplus, a South Korean supermarket, opened their first virtual store in an underground station in the capital Seoul. From large illuminated billboard displays that mimic supermarket shelves, customers selected their purchases by scanning barcodes with their smartphones and using a mobile app. Once the customer's shopping was complete, their 'digital trolley' would be sent and the products delivered to their home that same day.

208. BBC HOMEPAGE VERSION 4
Digital, 2012

By 2011, the BBC website homepage was attracting nine million unique visitors each week. However, audience research showed eighty per cent of visitors were funnelled to the news and sport pages, while other sections were hard to find. The new homepage welcomes visitors with a horizontally scrolling navigation bar with links to breaking news and sport stories, popular programmes and other content. It also detects the user's location to automatically display the local time and weather.

209. BECK'S THE GREEN BOX PROJECT
Digital, 2012

The Green Box Project commissioned new digital works by thirty artists and designers. The art could only be viewed through Beck's Key, an augmented reality app, when holding your smartphone or iPad against specially designed green boxes in public locations. Beck's championed young artists for over twenty-five years (among them Damien Hirst and Tracey Emin) by commissioning limited-edition bottle labels, so the Green Box Project was a new way to promote the brand.

210. LETTER TO JANE
Digital, 2012

A quarterly independent arts magazine for the iPad, Letter to Jane gave artists an open platform on which to share their personal creative work and ideas. The application's clean, pared-down style featured intuitive navigation that allowed the reader to focus on the content, and the app made good use of images, text, audio and video to allow that content to take centre stage.

211. FACE SUBSTITUTION
Digital, 2012

Face Substitution explores digital face replacement. It tracks the face of a subject in real time, while simultaneously drawing another face on top of the subject's. Intelligent blending helps match the subject's lighting and skin tone while preserving the target's facial features. Initially developed as a technical demonstration, the technology has now been popularised by several social media applications.

212. CITYTRACKING PART 2
Digital, 2013

CityTracking is an online map-making platform that allows users to create artistic interpretations of geographic data. CityTracking Part 2 combines open-source geographical data with a range of visual filters. It introduces three new artistic templates: Watercolour, Toner and Terrain. Toner reduces the map to minimalist black and white, Terrain emphasises the topography of a region and Watercolour offers a purely artistic handmade aesthetic.

213. ENGLISH HEDGEROW AUGMENTED
REALITY PLATE
Digital, 2013

English Hedgerow is a fine bone china plate whose surface design appears to come to life when viewed through a dedicated iPhone app that uses augmented reality technology. The app brings traditional surface design into the digital age for one of the oldest surviving manufacturers of chintz-style ceramics in the UK.

214. FREE UNIVERSAL CONSTRUCTION KIT
Digital, 2013
The Free Universal Construction Kit is a set of digital files that can be used to 3D-print adapter bricks for various construction toys, allowing children to combine otherwise incompatible commercial products. The designers hoped to encourage a debate about the limitations of mass-produced commercial products. As 3D printing penetrates the mainstream, everyone has opportunities to create their own custom adaptations of high-street products.

215. A SUPERSTITIOUS FUND
Digital, 2013
A Superstitious Fund is an investment algorithm that traded autonomously on the stock market making decisions based on superstitions, numerology and lunar phases. The project was inspired by the loss of up to $2.4 billion from the US economy every year due to fears over the date, Friday the 13th. Working with financial advisers, fortune-tellers and lawyers, Chung created a program that feared the number 13 and a full moon, among other uniquely human foibles.

216. RAIN ROOM
Digital, 2013
Rain Room was an interactive field of falling water installed at the Barbican's Curve Gallery in London. It reacted to the movements of visitors, stopping the flow of water as they passed beneath. The installation was controlled by 3D-tracking cameras which tracked people walking underneath, closing and opening valves in response.

217. CANDLES IN THE WIND
LIGHTING INSTALLATION
Digital, 2013
Candles in the Wind is an installation that recreated the effect of candlelight using 256 programmable LEDs and circuit-board display units, each of which are carefully programmed to match the flicker of a naked flame. The light created is difficult to distinguish from the real thing, demonstrating the potential of the LED technology to recreate natural effects.

218. WIND MAP
Digital, 2013
The Wind Map is an online digital visualisation of the wind, showing real-time information about current weather patterns across North America as an ever-changing graphic illustration. Streaming live data from the America's National Digital Forecast Database, the program animates surface wind patterns for the next hour and shows the highest and average wind speeds.

219. CHIRP APP
Digital, 2013
Chirp is a smartphone app that shares information using sound. The system encodes data within short audio bursts that can be heard and trans-lated by other devices nearby. Each audio 'chirp' lasts about two seconds and includes dozens of notes played rapidly in a certain order, like digital birdsong. The receiver's device decodes the sequence into letters, which create a link to a website.

220. ZOMBIES, RUN! APP
Digital, 2013
Zombies, Run! is a smartphone app that creates an interactive game experience for runners. In a post-apocalyptic world, the living dead roam the streets ready to catch anyone who doesn't run fast enough. The project was inspired by the programmers' own experiences as failed runners. Drawing on 1950s B-movie culture, they designed an app that encourages people to exercise more by making it fun.

221. DIGITAL POSTCARDS
AND POSTCARD PLAYER
Digital, 2013
Put a Digital Postcard into the Postcard Player, press a 'button' printed on the card and music begins to play. The postcards use conductive ink which enables them to act like switches, sending instructions to the player about what tracks to play. The experience is more like holding a record sleeve than swiping a touchscreen, with flicking through a set of postcards analogous to browsing a record collection.

222. RASPBERRY PI
Digital, 2013
The Raspberry Pi is a $25 computer designed to make programming more accessible to children. Since its launch, over five million units have been sold worldwide. The credit-card sized computer was adopted quickly by schools, as well as DIY designers and hackers, to build projects involving robot electronics, remote-controlled devices and household gadgets.

223. WINDOWS PHONE 8
OPERATING SYSTEM
Digital, 2013
In 2012, Windows Phone 8 was the newest version of Microsoft's smartphone operating system. The graphical user interface includes a system called Live Tiles, which enables users to personalise the screen layout using a coloured grid. Users could allocate these blocks of colour to their favourite applications, streaming real-time information and updates to their home screen. The system offers a choice of twenty different colours, and the option to resize each tile.

224. GOV.UK WEBSITE
Digital, 2013
GOV.UK is the streamlined website for all UK government online services. The design focuses on the differing needs of users rather than the demands of the provider. Although centrally operated, government departments were previously

spread across thirty-three websites. The new service brings all departments under a single domain with a clear, uniform design language, improving legibility and navigation. The site uses Margaret Calvert's New Transport typeface, a contemporary version of the font used for UK road signage from the 1960s.

226. DASHILAR APP
Digital, 2013

Dashilar is a three-dimensional map created to guide visitors around the densely populated district of that name during Beijing Design Week 2013. The map's fine red outlines have a delicate illustrative quality, evoking the history of the area, and the app is exquisitely executed. Its real value, however, lies in the way it demonstrates the uniqueness of a disappearing way of Beijing life.

227. LIGHT FIELD CAMERA
Digital, 2013

Blurring the line between image capture and photo processing, the Light Field Camera enables photographers to change the focus of a picture after it has been taken. By using a micro-lens array, the camera records the entire three-dimensional light field. It can then calculate where the rays will reach if they travel beyond the lens. Once uploaded to a computer, the focus of an image can be manipulated from close foreground through to background.

228. OCULUS RIFT VIRTUAL REALITY DEVELOPMENT KIT
Digital, 2014

Virtual reality has long been the holy grail of gaming and entertainment. In 2014, Oculus Rift – a Kickstarter start-up – was considered the most successful attempt to date. With sharp picture quality, sensors and a camera to track the position of your head and body, the wearer can lean in to look at something from a particular angle or even peer around corners in sync with the virtual environment, providing a fully immersive experience.

229. TOUCH BOARD
Digital, 2014

The Touch Board is an easy-to-use piece of electronics kit that can turn almost any material or surface into a sensor. By connecting anything conductive to one of its twelve electrodes, it can play a sound via its onboard MP3 player or a note via its musical instrument digital interface (MIDI). It can also respond to a simple finger touch via its capacitive sensing technology.

230. SIDEKICK CREATIVES CROWDFUNDING SERVICE
Digital, 2014

The success of crowdfunding websites has created a need for designers to produce presentations that will help secure funding. Sidekick is a collective of seven artists, designers and filmmakers who help designers promote and sell their idea or project. Sidekick's expertise in art direction, video production and social media promotion has, by 2017, helped raise £1,231,965 from 12,734 backers over 18 campaigns.

231. PUBLIC LAB FOLDABLE MINI-SPECTROMETER
Digital, 2014

The Public Lab Foldable Mini-Spectrometer is an inexpensive tool that enables concerned citizens to collect environmental data and connect their findings with experts. Folding up in minutes, it transforms the user's smartphone into a visible, near-infrared spectrometer. Developed after the 2010 Deepwater Horizon oil spill in the Gulf of Mexico, the tool was part of an effort by Public Lab community to make the analysis of pollutants like crude oil cheaper and more accessible.

232. AEROSEE CROWDSOURCED SEARCH-AND-RESCUE DRONE
Digital, 2014

This crowdsourced search-and-rescue project for Patterdale Mountain Rescue Team harnessed the force of 350 online volunteers, who used their computers, tablets or mobiles to look for lost or stranded people by studying images of the mountainside sent by a drone. The drone could be sent out in advance of a manned helicopter, helping locate the person in danger and facilitate a quicker rescue.

233. PEEK (PORTABLE EYE EXAMINATION KIT)
Digital, 2014

PEEK is an easy-to-use, affordable and portable system for testing eyes. By 2014, there were thirty-nine million blind people in the world, eighty per cent of whom had been curable. PEEK's clip-on hardware supplies detailed images of the patient's eye, using a smartphone camera's flashlight to illuminate the back of the eye. Patient's data can be stored on the phone and emailed to a doctor for diagnosis.

234. LEGO CALENDAR
Digital, 2014

This wall-mounted planner made of Lego can be synchronised with a digital diary by taking a photograph of it with a smartphone. Vitamins Design wanted a tactile wall calendar that was on a sufficiently large scale to show the months ahead easily, but would work both online and offline. The analogue, Lego brick-formed planner became a centrally shared calendar where all the studio's commitments were logged, yet can also be shared digitally.

235. DUMB WAYS TO DIE
  Digital, 2014
Dumb Ways to Die is a public-safety film campaign commissioned to put a stop to the rising number of accidents and deaths among young people on Melbourne's train system. Launched on iTunes and YouTube, the song was an instant viral success, with over seventy-five million hits by late 2014.

236. CITYMAPPER APP
  Digital, 2014
Citymapper is an easy-to-use wayfinding app that draws on open-source transport data to update users on the quickest route across town. Users input their location and destination and the app offers multiple routes by bus, tube, taxi or by cycling and walking. It also tells users how long the journey will take, how much it will cost, and even how many calories will be burned.

237. HELLO LAMP POST
  Digital, 2014
Hello Lamp Post is a project launched in Bristol, south-west England, during the summer of 2013 to engage people with the city and its urban landscape. It was the first commission of Watershed's Playable City Award. By text message, people were encouraged to start conversations with parking meters, bridges, boats, bollards, phone boxes and postboxes, identified using the codes that are applied to pieces of street furniture to identify them for repairs.

238. GÉNÉRATIONS GAME
  Digital, 2014
Unlike a conventional video game, it is impossible to finish a game of Générations in a single lifetime. Players, at the end of their life, decide who the game will be passed on to when they die, and even if they want that person to be able to finish the game. The game was intended by its developers, French experimental game collective One Life Remains, to inspire thinking about digital heritage.

239. THE WALLS HAVE EYES
  Digital, 2015
A project originally shown at the Ethical Dilemma Café at Mozilla Festival (Mozfest) 2014, The Walls Have Eyes used three small picture frames with hidden components including Raspberry Pi computers and cameras to collect photographs of people nearby along with personal information from their phones. The images and data were displayed on a projector and printed using a dot matrix printer, giving the information that constantly leaks from our devices an obvious – and provocative – physical form.

240. THE REFUGEE PROJECT
  Digital, 2015
The Refugee Project is an interactive map that uses data collected by the United Nations to show the world movement of people between 1975 to 2012. The maps provide a visualisation of the numbers of people involved, their country of origin and their place of asylum for each year.

241. THE OCEAN CLEANUP
  Digital, 2015
This ambitious project aims to find an environmentally safe process for removing plastic waste pollution from our oceans. The initial concept is for a network of boating barriers attached to the seabed, which uses sea currents to push plastic towards a 40km-long V-shaped structure. Within it would be a platform to gather and compress the plastic, ready to be transported for recycling.

242. MONUMENT VALLEY
  Digital, 2015
Monument Valley is a beautifully crafted architectural fantasy puzzle. It follows the journey of Princess Ida through ten levels of 'sacred geometry': mazes, passages, bridges and floating structures, all seen in isometric view. The gameplay was inspired by MC Escher's paradoxical art, while the rich use of colour and illustration style were inspired by Japanese prints.

243. MEGAFACES
  Digital, 2015
Created by Asif Khan for the 2014 Winter Olympics in Sochi, MegaFaces consists of monumental three-dimensional digital portraits, each more than eight metres high. The kinetic facade consisted of 11,000 LED-tipped telescopic motors, which could extend up to 2.5 metres to create the contours of each person's face. Each portrait was created in 3D-scanning booths that toured Russia before the Games.

244. DISCLOSED
  Digital, 2015
A concept design for a mobile app, Disclosed presents information held by food retailers and producers to help the discerning shopper make decisions about what to buy. Each user can tailor the app to their own preferences, reflecting their views on health, society and the environment. From foods that are low in fat to Fairtrade goods or organic produce – or all three – the app identifies products that meet a selected criteria, making shopping more effective and speedy.

245. OF INSTRUMENTS AND ARCHETYPES
  Digital, 2015
Of Instruments and Archetypes is an exquisite set of wireless digital measuring tools that transfer instantly the dimensions of things to an on-screen digital 3D model. Made of wood and brass, the tools reduce the possibility of human error. However, the process of using the eye and hand to manipulate the tools allows the user to retain a sense of 'making' in the digital process.

246. RESPONSIVE STREET FURNITURE
Digital, 2015
Responsive Street Furniture uses smart technology to make the streets easier and safer to navigate for people with visual impairments or other disabilities. Requests for brighter street lighting, longer crossing times or audio information are made on a website, where users can register their smartphone or low-cost key fob. When they next approach a piece of Responsive Street Furniture, it will automatically respond to that request.

247. NO MAN'S SKY
Digital, 2015
Inspired by classic science-fiction, No Man's Sky is a video game about exploration and survival in an endless galaxy. The complex content was produced by a process of 'infinite procedural generation', which creates a never-ending playground for discovery. It was estimated that the game's galaxy would have over eighteen trillion planets, each with its own unique seas, landscapes, flora and fauna.

248. SHADOWING
Digital, 2015
Shadowing is an interactive activity embedded within a streetlight. Infrared video records the 'shadows' below, with projected playback triggered by the next person to walk below, creating a connection between different people and times within the same city. If nobody passes for a while, the streetlight cycles back through previous shadows.

249. REFUGEE REPUBLIC
Digital, 2016
Refugee Republic is an interactive web-based documentary about everyday life in Domiz, a Syrian refugee camp in northern Iraq. Using an illustrated map, viewers are able to look at different aspects of camp life. Layers of information in different media – audio recordings, films, photographs, drawings – help to tell the stories of some of the 58,000 people living there, helping to dispel stereotypes of life in a camp.

250. MTV MARTIN LUTHER KING DAY
Digital, 2016
To mark Martin Luther King Day on 19 January 2015, all MTV's programmes were broadcast in black and white for twelve hours. Richard Turley, Deputy Editorial Director and first Senior Vice President of Visual Storytelling, was responsible. His simple but striking change to MTV's programming was aimed at generating debate about racial prejudice in the US.

251. PHONVERT
Digital, 2016
Phonvert is a not-for-profit movement using open-source software to extend the life of 'retired' smartphones. In 2015, more than 280 million working smartphones were replaced without being recycled. Many have usable functions like cameras, accelerometers, touchscreens and Wi-Fi, but are still ending up in landfill. Installing the Phonvert app on an old smartphone allows it to be converted into useful Internet of Things products – alerting you when the post arrives, for instance.

252. SH:24
Digital, 2016
SH:24 is an online sexual health service providing free information, advice and remote testing for sexually transmitted infections. The project's objective was to filter out patients with limited symptoms, thereby freeing up thousands of appointments at GP surgeries and sexual health clinics for more complex cases. The service includes easy-to-use home sampling kits for chlamydia, syphilis, gonorrhoea and HIV, as well as text-based communication and live webchats with a nurse.

253. OPENSURGERY
Digital, 2016
OpenSurgery is an open-sourced kit for domestic keyhole surgery, combining 3D printing and laser-cutting with adapted surgical tools bought online for a fraction of the cost of commercial surgical instruments. The project was inspired by YouTube videos in which users perform operations on themselves rather than meeting the expense of professional healthcare. OpenSurgery was not intended for actual use, but rather to start a debate about access to healthcare.

254. IN THE EYES OF THE ANIMAL
Digital, 2016
In the Eyes of the Animal is a 360-degree immersion into the life of a forest. The virtual reality narrative was commissioned to help visitors experience the landscape afresh, showing how the forest might be seen from the perspective of three of its inhabitants: an owl, a dragonfly and a frog. The films were made using drones, CT scanning and bespoke 360-degree cameras, and set to a stereo soundtrack using real-world recordings.

255. THIS WAR OF MINE
Digital, 2016
Responding to the 1992–96 Siege of Sarajevo, this war-themed game focuses on civilians. The player controls a group of non-combatant survivors in a makeshift shelter in the besieged fictional city of Pogoren, Graznavia. The goal is to survive the war with whatever tools and materials the players can gather. During the day, snipers stop the characters from leaving their refuge; at night, players can scavenge for items that will help them stay alive.

256. UNMADE
Digital, 2016

Unmade is a startup knitwear company that designs and produces one-off garments in central London. Their industrial-sized knitting machines have had their software recoded to control the output process, resulting in a more sustainable, resource-aware approach to manufacture. Customers can choose the type of garment, fabric and colour from a website. The garment is manufactured only when it has been ordered, which eliminates waste.

257. PRECIOUS PLASTIC
Digital, 2016

Over 311 million tonnes of plastic is produced annually, but less than ten per cent of this is recycled. In response, Dave Hakkens has developed a series of machines, easily made with basic tools and materials, to transform plastic waste into useful products and raw materials. The blueprints for his machines are open source, meaning that anyone can recreate them within their own homes or communities.

258. CASA JASMINA TURIN
Digital, 2016

A two-year research project about the future of the connected home, Casa Jasmina aims to bring digital manufacturing, networked collaboration, the Internet of Things and open-source design into a domestic setting. Drawing new skills in Italian open-source electronics together with the country's traditional skills in furniture and interior design, Casa Jasmina features a curated space whichallows the public to explore the opportunities and realities of the digital revolution for daily life.

259. MOTH GENERATOR
Digital, 2016

In 2015, Twitter disclosed that 8.5 per cent of its users – about twenty-three million of its monthly users – were bots: software programmes that send out automated posts. The Moth Generator is a Twitter bot, but instead of sending out tweets periodically or in response to specific phrases, it responds to tweets by drawing endlessly unique 'fantastical' moths. The moths provide unexpected moments of visual delight in a sea of words, but they also pose questions about human versus computer creativity.

260. POKÉMON GO
Digital, 2017

Bursting on the scene during the 1990s with its fantastical universe of 'pocket monsters', Pokémon has become the highest-grossing media franchise of all time. Pokémon GO was developed for mobile devices as a location-based augmented-reality game, utilising GPS capabilities to allow players to capture, train and battle virtual creatures which appear on screen as if in the same real-world location as the player. The game became a global phenomenon during the summer of 2016.

261. PROFESSIONAL WOMEN EMOJI
Digital, 2017

It is impossible to ignore the role emoji have in modern day-to-day communication. Previously male emoji included a detective, a police officer and a doctor, while the options for female emoji included a princess, a bride and a girl getting a haircut – the need for a suitable representation of genders, races and interests was urgent. It was wonderful to see Google step up in 2017 and make that difference.

262. PREMIER LEAGUE ON-AIR BRANDING
Digital, 2017

The Premier League is a brand that reaches over a billion fans worldwide. In early 2016, they developed a fresh visual identity with a vivid palette of clashing colours and patterns, and a simplified version of the iconic lion logo. DixonBaxi created a 'de-corporatised' look and feel that challenged the conventions of sports graphics.

263. GOOGLE NOTO
Digital, 2017

Google Noto is a family of open-source typefaces encompassing 800 languages and over 100 different writing systems. Type designers, linguists and language communities all over the world have collaborated to create a body of typefaces that retain a cohesive feel while capturing the vitality and history of individual scripts. By allowing multilingual content to be integrated harmoniously on screen, Noto invites communication across barriers of language and culture.

264. MEET GRAHAM: THE ONLY PERSON
DESIGNED TO SURVIVE ON OUR ROADS
Digital, 2017

Meet Graham is an Australian road-safety campaign that shows how human bodies would have to evolve to survive the impact of a traffic accident. The artist Patricia Piccinini was commissioned, along with a leading trauma surgeon and a road-crash investigation expert, to create a surreal, life-like sculpture called Graham, to be displayed around the country and online. The result is an unforgettable reminder of just how fragile we are.

265. REFUGEE TEXT
Digital, 2017

Refugee Text is a chatbot that takes verified and trustworthy information and makes it available on demand to any refugee with a phone. Surprisingly, access to just such information is one of the largest unaddressed needs among refugees and humanitarian organisations alike. Refugee Text addresses this with a simple turn-key chatbot that is personalised to each person's own particular situation.

266. SAYDNAYA: INSIDE A SYRIAN
TORTURE PRISON
Digital, 2017
Borrowing methodologies from architecture,
design, film, activism and theory, Forensic
Architecture produces spatial analysis that has
provided evidence for international prosecution
teams, political organisations, NGOs and the
United Nations. For Saydnaya, researchers
worked with survivors to reconstruct the physical
structure of a prison near Damascus, and their
experiences within it. The prison model and
related audiovisual material offer an intimate
and chilling confrontation with the reality of
Syrian detention facilities.

267. RAPID LIQUID PRINTING
Digital, 2017
Even before it has had the chance to fulfil its
potential, 3D printing has been surpassed.
Its production scale (small), speed (slow) and
materials (built layer by layer) have all been
bested by Rapid Liquid Printing. The process
involves a robotic apparatus depositing extruded
lines, suspended in a tank of gel. The material
holds its own form and chemically cures as
it is injected – the object is literally drawn
into existence.

268. OTHR
Digital, 2017
The New York-based firm OTHR is not only
transforming our notion of 3D printing by producing
premium made-to-order domestic objects in porcelain, bronze and steel, but is also rethinking the
entire design and production process. Recognising
that today's studio is not necessarily a physical
space, OTHR works with leading international
designers using Dropbox and Skype to replace
in-person design meetings.

269. PIERRE CHAREAU:
MODERN ARCHITECTURE AND DESIGN
Digital, 2017
This exhibition is not only a thoughtful reflection
on Chareau's design legacy, but also a stunning
example of how technology can be used in a
subtle and beautiful way to bring work of historic
importance to life. Pieces of furniture from one
of Chareau's most famous works, the Maison
de Verre in Paris, were arranged in clusters and,
using VR goggles, visitors to the exhibition were
transported into the different spaces of the house.

274. ILLUMINATI II/NOIR COLLECTION 2007
Fashion, 2008
In 2006, Peter Ingerswen set up Illuminati II to
enable him to produce sustainable garments
made from organic, fair-trade cotton fabrics.
With his Noir collection, he used these fabrics to
turn ethical fashion into something desirable and
highly wearable. The collection featured sculpted
leather and sharp cotton suits, liquid-soft blouses
and dresses in ultra-drapy cotton, silk and leather.

275. DANIELLE SCUTT
SPRING/SUMMER 2007
Fashion, 2008
Described as 'fifties-meets-seventies power
vixens', Danielle Scutt's Spring/Summer 2007
collection combined cinched waists, signature
fitted jackets in fine wool gabardine with puff
sleeves and colossal bows that engulf the shoulder
line. The collection also featured glamorous pencil
skirts and high-waisted narrow trousers, spray-on
catsuits and second-skin jersey leotards, often in
predatory prints.

276. JIL SANDER SPRING/SUMMER 2008
Fashion, 2008
Staying true to Jil Sander's refined and
pure style, Raf Simons' Spring/Summer 2008
collection imbued beautiful clothes with a
modern sensibility. Free from superfluous detail,
the collection contrasted sleek, clean tailoring
with origami-style sleeves, coquettish sheer
fabrics and chic, loose silhouettes. Experimenting
with layers of transparent fabrics that shroud
the slender lines like clouds, the effect created
a distortion of proportions and space.

277. ISSEY MIYAKE SPRING/SUMMER 2008
Fashion, 2008
For his second season at the helm of Issey Miyake,
Dai Fujiwara made a statement of hope about
global warming, calling for ethical and forward
-looking fashion. His Spring/Summer 2008
collection featured dismantled components of the
Dyson DC20 and DC18 vacuum cleaners. Some of
the heavier clothes resembled thunderous clouds,
while others revealed an unexpected modernity
and an optimistic vision of elegance.

278. DIOR HAUTE COUTURE
SPRING/SUMMER 2007
Fashion, 2008
Inspired by Madame Butterfly's Cho-Cho-San,
John Galliano's Spring/Summer 2007 collection
featured 'geishas' with red lips and full kabuki-style
makeup, their intricate origami folds and pleats
of richly embroidered satins and silks peeking
from behind a fringe of cherry blossom or fans.
Every dress had its own intense colour – hot pink,
eau-de-nil with coral, shades of burgundy and
imperial purple.

279. GILES DEACON SPRING/SUMMER 2008
Fashion, 2008
Described as 'slightly subversive ... but always
obtainable', Giles Deacon's Spring/Summer 2008
line featured traditional tea-length dresses given
a modern twist with extraordinary floral appliqué,
feathers, crystals, layers of tulle and silk-screened
prints. The collection, which featured highly
feminine soft pinks, greys and violets, retained
sophistication with the witty use of high craft.

280. RONALDO FRAGA
AUTUMN/WINTER 2007/2008
Fashion, 2008

Ronaldo Fraga's presentation of his Autumn/
Winter 2007/2008 collection during São Paulo
Fashion Week was an evocative and provocative
fusion of catwalk, theatre and political statement.
Addressing the subject of China and its rapidly
growing global influence, Fraga captured an emotionally charged environment where contradictions
coexist: traditional and revolutionary, ancient
culture and waste pollution, timeless rituals and
unlicensed mass production.

281. YVES SAINT LAURENT
DOWNTOWN TOTE
Fashion, 2008

The bag that launched a million copies, the
Yves Saint Laurent Downtown Tote's understated
and yet identifiable design made it a favourite
with celebrities. Featuring generous hexagonal
shapes, a loose structure and multiple interior
pockets, the bag has a casual, practical element,
making it ideal for everyday use. However, the
gold hardware and exposed double zip closures
provide a subtle elegance.

282. OSMAN YOUSEFZADA
AUTUMN/WINTER 2007/2008
Fashion, 2008

By combining innovative cutting with masterful
drapery, Osman Yousefzada crafts timeless
garments in the most luxurious fabrics. The simple,
yet highly directional Autumn/Winter 2007/2008
collection showcased innovative design solutions
inspired by his interest in ethnicity and costume.

283. MA KE WUYONG (USELESS)
COLLECTION 2007
Fashion, 2008

The voluminous, sculptural garments that
make up Ma Ke's Wuyong collection celebrates
form over function and beauty before practicality
(the title 'Wuyong' translates to 'Useless').
Wuyong serves as a critique of consumerism.
Ma Ke rejects fast-fashion trends and only works
with artisans using hand looms. Her aim is to
foster a desire for objects with innate value, until
choosing the well-made and the beautiful becomes
a natural choice.

284. ARENA HOMME + COVER SHOOT
SUMMER/AUTUMN 2007, ISSUE NO.27
Fashion, 2008

As part of their long-standing creative
collaboration, in 2007 Nick Knight and Simon
Foxton were invited by *Arena Homme* + magazine
to photograph the highlights of John Galliano's
Autumn/Winter 2007/2008 menswear collection.
The outlandish collection was inspired by warriors
and mythical characters, from samurai to mino-
taurs. The cover image, for the Summer/Autumn
issue, was 'the beast of six arms', an arresting
image of brawny male physiques in action.

285. HUSSEIN CHALAYAN AIRBORNE,
AUTUMN/WINTER 2007/2008
Fashion, 2008

Hussein Chalayan's 'Airborne' womenswear
collection brought the latest in LED technology
to fashion design. Taking the idea of 'changing
seasons' as his inspiration, the collection featured
high-tech protective wear described by Chalayan
as the 'winter relief component'. These included a
dome-like hat that emitted a warm red light, as well
as motorised hoods for protection from chill winds.
The coming of spring, by contrast, consisted of
a beautiful white dress made from crystals
and 15,600 flickering LEDs.

286. PIERRE HARDY FASHION ACCESSORIES
SPRING/SUMMER 2008
Fashion, 2008

Based in Paris, Pierre Hardy regularly finds
inspiration in art and architecture. His Spring/
Summer 2008 collection draws its influences
from a wide range of sources, from the Memphis
group design to conceptual artists and even
Renaissance painter Sandro Botticelli.
The result are beautifully made accessories,
which show graphic balance as well as daring
colour schemes.

287. UNIQLO CASHMERE PROJECT
WITH PANTONE
Fashion, 2008

In 2007 Uniqlo teamed up with Pantone, the
world-renowned authority on colour, to create
collections of Pantone-inspired T-shirts and then
cashmere. The latter featured 100% cashmere
sweaters, offering two styles for men (crew neck
or cardigan) and two for women (V-neck or crew
neck), all of which were available in a palette of
twenty of special Pantone Colours.

288. PRADA SPRING/SUMMER 2009
Fashion, 2009

Miuccia Prada's experimental approach has made
her an interdisciplinary fashion designer of our time.
Her often shocking approach, evident in the Prada
Spring/Summer 2009 collection, include extensive
use of latex, inside-outside fabric variations, linen
treated with whitewash, and elastic bands used to
give fabric a wrinkled look. A dry humour pervades
her work, as in her description of a metal chain
skirt as 'a bit of a nuisance'.

289. MAISON MARGIELA
SPRING/SUMMER 2009,
TWENTIETH ANNIVERSARY
COLLECTION
Fashion, 2009

For his twentieth anniversary year, Maison Margiela
reminded us how many of the design innovations
we have enjoyed over the years were originally his:
from the 'Ming the Merciless' pointed shoulders
that were responsible for the revival of shoulder
padding to the much-emulated Edwardian puff-
sleeved jackets from his 1988 show. Though a

'best of' show sounds like nostalgia, this collection was highly modern in execution, so that items that seemed unsettling when first shown appeared entirely natural.

290. BASSO & BROOKE SPRING/SUMMER 2009
Fashion, 2009

The Basso & Brooke aesthetic focuses on highly complex digital prints as opposed to tailoring, although the two always go hand in hand. In this collection, the duo used an increasingly sophisticated approach, combining computer-generated basic patterns with fluid brushstrokes. The two different designs were integrated by classic sportswear garment cuts. The collection was a fabric-based fashion statement that had the unique vibrancy of the designers' different cultural backgrounds.

291. THE THOUGHTFUL DRESSER
Fashion, 2009

The Thoughtful Dresser was a blog that seriously analysed our attire and the significance of clothes in our society. Contributors came from all over the globe to delve into the human psyche or raise awareness of ecological issues linked with the clothing industry. It was set up by writer and journalist Linda Grant, whose objective was to gather research for her Virago book of the same name.

292. DUCKIE BROWN SPRING/SUMMER 2009
Fashion, 2009

Duckie Brown takes risks with proportion, print and accessories within America's traditional menswear market. The label has developed a reputation for well-crafted clothing leavened with touches of whimsy. The designers are committed to creating alternative wardrobe choices for men, but for their Spring/Summer 2009 collection they rejected the brightly coloured palette they have become recognised for, instead subtly integrating electric blue and yellow with predominant blacks and greys.

293. 'A BLACK ISSUE', JULY 2008
Fashion, 2009

In July 2008, Italian *Vogue* dedicated its issue to black models, accompanied by an editorial on black women in the arts industries. The issue propelled a debate around the absence of black models on magazine covers and in advertising into the public arena, challenging the notion that covers featuring black faces do not sell.

294. LOUISE GOLDIN SPRING/SUMMER 2009
Fashion, 2009

Since graduating from Central Saint Martins in 2005, Louise Goldin has reinterpreted the role of knitwear, making it relevant to the way we dress now. Goldin's Spring/Summer 2009 collection developed her vision for knitwear as an essential, year-round component of the modern wardrobe. Her accomplished use of colours and print, along with her layering of gossamer fine and solid fabrics, resulted in distinctive but wearable pieces.

295. LANVIN SPRING/SUMMER 2009
Fashion, 2009

Alber Elbaz has turned the traditional French house of Lanvin, founded in 1889, into one of the most-desired labels of the twenty-first century. Key to Elbaz's success are bias-cut dresses that exploit satin, lace and the other materials of traditional seductive French dress in a totally modern spirit. The result is cutting edge clothing that appeals to women of all ages.

296. TREMBLED BLOSSOMS
Fashion, 2009

Trembled Blossoms is an animated four-minute short video that worked both as an artistic expression and as an advertisement. It depicts a lush, slightly scandalous landscape of flowers and nymphs that evokes Prada's vision, blending suggestions of Art Nouveau, Liberty and Aubrey Beardsley. Aside from the references to earlier artistic movements and aesthetics, the ink-like drawings incorporate Prada's accessories from their Spring/Summer 2008 collection.

297. THE HOUSE OF VIKTOR&ROLF RETROSPECTIVE
Fashion, 2009

In 2008, the Dutch design duo Viktor&Rolf were invited by the Barbican Art Gallery to present their first UK retrospective. The exhibition design replicated the theatricality of their catwalk shows while seamlessly communicating the story of how their partnership habitually combines craftsmanship with commercial ambition. The exhibition dressed meticulously detailed dolls in perfect scaled-down versions of Viktor&Rolf clothes, pushing beyond the traditional retrospective format.

298. WONDERLAND
Fashion, 2009

The collaboration between Helen Storey and Tony Ryan, a polymer chemist at the University of Sheffield, resulted in the creation of biodegradable dresses that disappear once submerged in water. Wonderland highlighted the wider and much greater issues of sustainability and ethical living. It demanded and suggested intelligent change through brave collaboration and experiment in the realm of science but also in the world of fashion.

299. CHRISTOPHER KANE SPRING/SUMMER 2009
Fashion, 2010

Christopher Kane's Spring/Summer 2009 collection brought his talents for detail, colour and intricate construction methods to the fore. Taking *Planet of the Apes* and prehistoric animal scales as starting points, Kane's entire line used half circle three-dimensional geometric forms in monochromatic shades of bright colours and more muted tones, paired with animal-print elements. The scalloped edges worked best when fanning out from a skirt, framing at the shoulder or running down the arms.

300. COMME DES GARÇONS
AUTUMN/WINTER 2009/2010
Fashion, 2010

Rei Kawakubo's Autumn/Winter 2009/2010 collection had a profound influence throughout fashion. Featuring pyramidal pile-ups of army-like jackets, constructed from blankets and tent-canvas, juxtaposed with a flesh-coloured multi-layered tulle-world, this collection was initially deemed odd and avant-garde. Yet, in the subsequent season, army-like and delicate flesh-to-beige styles recurred in many other designers' works and were replicated up and down every high street.

301. ALEXANDER MCQUEEN
SPRING/SUMMER 2010 AND
SPRING/SUMMER 2010 'PLATO'S
ATLANTIS' CATWALK PRESENTATION
Fashion, 2010

McQueen is known for embracing radical silhouettes, collaborating with ground-breaking artists and producing remarkable catwalk presentations. His Spring/Summer 2010 collection combined all of these elements. Hinting at a futuristic underwater world, the forty-five striking ensembles gently blossomed around the shoulders and hips, suggesting carapaces; the startling, monstrously sculptural shoes provided dramatic punctuation. Two giant robotic film cameras rolled along the catwalk, streaming the show live to an estimated audience of forty million.

302. BOUDICCA SPRING/SUMMER 2010
'REAL GIRL' LOOKBOOK
Fashion, 2010

In 2010, Zowie Broach and Brian Kirkby came up with an inventive way to show the Boudicca collection: a digital lookbook. Mashing-up the trade standard of a photographic top-to-toe 'line up' with time-lapse photography, they conveyed three-dimensional views of each outfit in the collection. The jerky, almost robotic rotation showed the clothes from a variety of angles, replacing the need for a catwalk show.

303. BETH DITTO AT EVANS
Fashion, 2010

Plus-size fashion has traditionally disguised generous proportions through dark colours and long, loose silhouettes. In 2009, Evans – producer of affordable fashion for full-figured women – introduced Beth Ditto at Evans. Collaboratively conceived by Ditto, audacious lead singer of the Gossip, and Lisa Marie Peacock of Evans, the

collection included sharp curve-enhancing cuts and bold patterns. The biker jacket was cropped close to the body; the dresses all featured thigh-grazing hemlines.

304. BALMAIN JACKET
Fashion, 2010

Designed by Christophe Decarnin and first shown at Balmain's Spring/Summer show, this jacket was indisputably one of the most influential items of womenswear in 2009: the sculpted Balmain shoulder had been seen on Rihanna, Kate Moss and Beyoncé. Endorsements by celebrity clients undeniably boosted its popularity, but the elegant styling of the pointed and highly padded shoulders, military overtones and a Michael Jackson-esque 1980s nostalgia all contributed to the design being emulated on the high street.

305. GOGGLE JACKET '989–'009
Fashion, 2010

A 2006 graduate of the Royal College of Art, Aitor Throup grew up in Burnley where C.P. Company garments were cult objects. Throup, an artist and designer of extraordinary rigour, was commissioned to adapt the infamous C.P. Company Goggle Jacket for its twentieth anniversary. Throup's design uniquely used *TintoTerra* GORE-TEX materials, and was constructed around a human form in a driving position concentrating on functionality and postural anatomy, making it even more focused on driving than the original.

306. HATS: AN ANTHOLOGY
BY STEPHEN JONES
Fashion, 2010

Two years in the making, this V&A blockbuster exhibition proved fascinating and timely. It revealed Stephen Jones' design inspiration, the creation process and the fashion secrets of famous clients, including Isabella Blow and *Vogue Italia's* Anna Piaggi. Margot Fonteyn's favourite Dior cloche and Marlene Dietrich's signature beret were among the 300 hats exhibited.

307. MADELEINE VIONNET,
PURISTE DE LA MODE EXHIBITION
Fashion, 2010

Pamela Golbin curates fashion with skill and erudition. In 2010, she exhibited the dresses donated by Madeleine Vionnet in 1952 on simple mannequins in mirrored vitrines without sets or unnecessary interventions. This retrospective was the first time Vionnet's dresses had been assembled for the public and showed just how influential and forward-thinking the 'designer of designers' was.

308. ACCESSOIRES ET OBJETS,
TÉMOIGNAGES DE VIES DE
FEMMES À PARIS 1940–1944
Fashion, 2010

This exhibition of 1940s wartime fashion offered a clear reminder of the ingenuity encouraged by fashion's great motivator: hope. In association with Palais Galliera, the Musée Jean Moulin presented this display of several hundred fashion accessories created during the Occupation. These objects showed the Parisian determination, despite wartime privations, to continue dressing well as a point of both professional pride and patriotism. The exhibits included wooden-soled shoes, hats accented with wood shavings and bags with document-concealing compartments.

309. COMME DES GARÇONS
TRADING MUSEUM
Fashion, 2011

Rei Kawakubo has continually pushed the boundaries of retail, most notably as protagonist of the pop-up shop revolution. In 2011, she expanded her ground-breaking retail empire with the Trading Museum. In the Gyre Building, a Tokyo shopping centre designed by Dutch architects MVRDV, the Trading Museum is part shop and part exhibition space. Antique display cases contain vintage Comme des Garçons pieces alongside its new collection and a selection of works by emerging and established designers.

310. LANVIN SPRING/SUMMER 2011
Fashion, 2011

Despite respecting traditional techniques, Albar Elbaz produces modern clothing stripped of fussy structure, decoration and weight. The Spring/Summer 2011 collection kicked off with flowing dresses and wide belts, each accentuating the waist and emphasising the body. Full-length dresses gave way to elegant businesswear, which morphed into evening dresses. The collection culminated in a series of sophisticated looks incorporating metallic and tribal prints.

311. OHNE TITEL SPRING/SUMMER 2011
Fashion, 2011

After an apprenticeship with Karl Lagerfeld, designers Flora Gill and Alexa Adams founded Ohne Titel in 2007. Their garments are feats of design and manufacture intended to enhance the female body with punk grace and well-constructed comfort. For the Spring/Summer 2011 collection, the designers took inspiration from the prints of Japanese artist Utagawa Kuniyoshi. Adapting linear shapes, colour blocking and open volumes into a modern silhouette, they experimented with striated sheer cottons combined with slick neoprene.

312. MELONIA SHOE
Fashion, 2011

Fashion designer Naim Josefi designed an accompanying shoe for the Melonia 2010 collection, which industrial designer Souzan Youssouf rendered using 3D software. The shoes were then 3D-printed, the first haute-couture shoes in the world to use this process. They were inspired by the ecological concept 'no material waste', since the homogenous nylon material is easy to recycle, creating a tight manufacturing and disposal loop.

313. GARETH PUGH SPRING/SUMMER 2011
Fashion, 2011

In September 2010, Gareth Pugh showed an important collection that confirmed his reputation for creations that are part theatre and part fantasy, connecting him to London's long tradition of fashion experimentation and iconoclasm. Softer and more wearable, these clothes retain the designer's tendency toward the fantastical: tunics of silvery armour and garments with a scale-like construction. Fabrics such as aluminium-coated nylon acted as a two-way mirror and super-reflective silver delivered a modern take on camouflage.

314. ORGANIC JEWELLERY COLLECTION
Fashion, 2011

Flavia Amadeu's Organic Jewellery Collection is made from Tecbor, an eco-friendly rubber produced by micro latex-processing plants in the Brazilian Amazon and operated by local rubber tappers and their families. While Amadeu's innovative bracelets and necklaces benefit from the flexibility and lightness of the material, the project is also a good example of how design can empower forest inhabitants and workers, adding value without contributing to deforestation.

315. UNIQLO +J AUTUMN/WINTER 2010/2011
Fashion, 2011

Jil Sander's initial collaboration with UNIQLO gained worldwide recognition. The designs explored the territory between couture and sportswear. Emphasising the silhouette, easy and gracious movement, practicality and the perfect fit, +J was characterised by pure tailoring and avant-garde textiles. Arctic blues, tempestuous greys and warm foliage colours were complemented with fine wools, cashmere and flannel.

316. TESS GIBERSON
SPRING/SUMMER 2011, SHIFT
Fashion, 2011

After several years in hiatus, Tess Giberson relaunched her clothing line for Autumn/Winter 2010/2011, but it was her Spring/Summer 2011 that enhanced her reputation for thoughtful and poetic clothing designed around a central theme. Called Shift, it criticised the wastefulness of the fashion industry by transferring details, rearranging material and repositioning the balance of garments. Shift included asymmetric shirt dresses, double-layered tank dresses and the occasional tailored jacket.

317. MARGARET HOWELL PLUS SHIRT
Fashion, 2011

Featuring a button-fly front and an unique pocket specifically designed for pens, Margaret Howell's Plus Shirt was designed in collaboration with industrial designer Kenneth Grange. The Plus Shirt is collarless, with a generous fit and minimal styling. The shirt comes in a classic slate-grey cotton fabric with a paler grey on the inner collar band and cuffs.

318. FILM FOR GARETH PUGH
SPRING/SUMMER 2012
Fashion, 2012

Ruth Hogben is a fashion film-making authority with a great understanding of Pugh's aesthetics. This film introduced Pugh's Spring/Summer 2012 catwalk show, using layered flashing images to represent the designer's geometric intensity. The film was not just an illustration of Pugh's work, but an original and inspiring interpretation of his oeuvre.

319. ALEXANDER MCQUEEN:
SAVAGE BEAUTY
Fashion, 2012

In 2012, the Metropolitan Museum translated McQueen's genius into a ground-breaking show. Featuring some 100 ensembles and 70 accessories, Savage Beauty focused on McQueen's engagement with romanticism, individualism, historicism, nationalism, exoticism, primitivism and naturalism. In each gallery, materials such as concrete, aged mirrors and glossy white acrylic were used to represent the themes and to create an immersive environment.

320. CÉLINE CROMBIE
Fashion, 2012

As creative director of the French house Céline, Phoebe Philo brought credibility back to the label. Producing garments for sophisticated women that transcend time, Philo makes daytime dresses desirable for women of all ages. Among Philo's most acclaimed pieces was the boyish overcoat with a buttonless front; hanging slightly forward from the shoulder, it never flies open.

321. 132.5
Fashion, 2012

Issey Miyake's 132.5 collection was inspired by mathematics. Its title was chosen to explain the concept: one piece of fabric, a three-dimensional shape reduced to two, plus the fifth dimension – which Miyake described as the moment the garment is worn and comes to life. To make the garment sustainable, Miyake's Reality Lab developed a fabric made of melted plastic bottles,

spinning threads from polyethylene terephthalate (PET). Balancing the practical and the beautiful, 132.5 demonstrated how an original idea can take years of thought.

322. VIVIENNE WESTWOOD ETHICAL
FASHION AFRICA COLLECTION
Fashion, 2012

For this collection, British fashion designer Vivienne Westwood joined the International Trade Centre to provide long-term work for marginalised women in Nairobi. She produced a range of bags made from recycled materials, including tent canvas, PVC and plastic off-cuts, to which skilled local craftspeople added appliqué, braiding, screen-printing, crocheting and Masai bead embroidery.

323. SUNO SPRING/SUMMER 2011
Fashion, 2012

With their 2009 debut collection Suno addressed the crisis of sustainability in the fashion industry without compromising on aesthetics. Maintaining their socially responsible ethos, the Spring/Summer 2011 collection evoked traditional Korean and Kenyan design, with subtle colours inspired by early twentieth-century French illustrator Georges Lepape. The feminine silhouettes were carefully combined with geometric circles, transparent zebra prints, stripes and laser-cut leather.

324. MARY KATRANTZOU
AUTUMN/WINTER 2011/2012
Fashion, 2012

Mary Katrantzou's Autumn/Winter 2011/2012 collection was a piece of daring imagination that confirmed her status as one of the most original designers working today. The concept involved transferring images of objets d'art collected by wealthy and influential women on to clothing. Inspired by coromandel screens, Fabergé eggs, Meissen porcelain and Qianlong china, her collection deserves to be recognised as the high-water mark of fashion in 2012.

325. THE DUCHESS OF CAMBRIDGE'S
WEDDING DRESS
Fashion, 2012

Designed by Sarah Burton of Alexander McQueen, the Duchess of Cambridge's dress was made of satin gazar – a stiff, gauzy silk fabric that ensures the gown holds its shape. A tight bodice, cinched-in waist, slightly padded hips and floor-length skirt recalled Dior's late 1940s 'New Look'. The three-metre train was attached to the waist by a gathered bustle, and exquisite and understated lace appliqué added a sense of modesty to the Duchess's otherwise bare shoulders and arms.

326. MELISSA AND GAETANO
PESCE BOOT AND FLIP FLOP
Fashion, 2012

In 2012, Brazilian brand Melissa reinvented itself by commissioning international designers to reposition ordinary plastic footwear as high design. Italian designer Gaetano Pesce produced a flip flop and ankle boot formed from a series of plastic discs connected only by their edges. This structure, made of the extremely elastic patented MeliFlex plastic, is breathable yet covers the foot completely, and the wearer can cut discs away to customise their footwear.

327. LATE NIGHT CHAMELEON CAFÉ
Fashion, 2012

This east London shop is the whimsical physical home for online fashion retailer LN-CC. It shows garments from established international designers and new talent in a 557-square-metre basement. Seven different spaces represent each of LN-CC's product areas, with interior treatments ranging from highly finished to raw: the 'warmroom' is coated with a cement finish, the 'lightroom' features waxed plywood and the 'forest area' has reclaimed wooden 'trees'.

328. ORATORY CYCLING JACKET
Fashion, 2012

The Oratory jacket was made to be suitable for formal occasions as for cycling. It resembles a classic, two-button unstructured cord jacket, but has numerous hidden functions. The silicone-coated cotton fabric is highly water-resistant, while a concealed back pleat allows freedom of movement even when the wearer adopts a riding position. Reflective panels under the lapel and fold-down cuffs, and a pull-out high-visibility rear panel, help keep the wearer safe.

329. CRAIG GREEN AUTUMN/WINTER
2012/2013 COLLECTION
Fashion, 2013

Craig Green's MA collection was presented on the catwalk during London Fashion Week as part of the Central Saint Martins show. It showed not only Green's passion but also his willingness to create something new. The collection, evidently influenced by his degree programme in textile design, combined two key points of fashion: vision and result. It provided a fresh take on menswear and proved that the coming generation has something new to say.

330. I WANT MUSCLE
Fashion, 2013

Paying homage to the glamour of the late 1970s and early 1980s with this film about the golden age of female bodybuilding, Smith-Leverock challenged the conventions of fashion film-making. It features bodybuilder Kizzy Vaines styled in the theatrical jewellery of Fred Butler. With film becoming an increasingly important medium for

fashion content, *I Want Muscle* was provocative for its visuals, its highly charged soundtrack and as a challenge to our perceptions of this rapidly emerging discipline.

331. LOUIS VUITTON
SUMMER 2012 COLLECTION
Fashion, 2013

Yayoi Kusama is one of the most prominent contemporary artists. In 2012, her polka-dot patterns were picked up by Louis Vuitton for a line of leather goods: a ready-to-wear collection, shoes and accessories. The Japanese artist's collaboration with the French fashion house included a commission for a 'worldwide window': London's Selfridges dedicated all twenty-four of its windows to the project, as well as a concept store. This dotty assault proved Vuitton's ability to converse with the art world.

332. GILES DEACON AUTUMN/WINTER
2012/2013 COLLECTION
Fashion, 2013

Since its debut in 2004, Deacon's Giles label has consistently proposed clothes for the elegant urbanite. His Autumn/Winter 2012/2013 collection combined the theatricality of the grand gown with the delicacy of fine detail, presented as a dramatic catwalk with a romantic sensibility. Giles's constructions were consistently well executed, both in tailored pieces and full-length, formal gowns. Burnt textiles were the collection's leitmotif, with invitations to the catwalk show similarly singed.

333. PRADA SPRING/SUMMER 2012
READY-TO-WEAR COLLECTION
Fashion, 2013

Miuccia Prada intended this collection to be about 'sweetness', traditionally a taboo in fashion. Textiles are particularly important for the Milan-based Prada, who works with a variety of producers to secure fabrics. The choice of retro textile prints featuring vintage cars was the stand-out success of this collection – along with inventive accessories, at which Prada excels, here including shoes with tailpipe flames bursting from the heels. It was all extremely successful at conveying 'sweetness' without being saccharine.

334. ANNA KARENINA COSTUMES
Fashion, 2013

Jacqueline Durran's costumes for Anna Karenina made a significant contribution to the beautiful and highly theatrical mise en scène. Suggestive of imperial Russia in the 1870s, the elegant designs made clever reference to succeeding interpretations of luxury, desire and control. Durran had created distinguished work for Atonement (2007), Vera Drake (2004) and Young Adam (2003), but Anna Karenina established her as one of the most innovative and thoughtful designers in the film industry.

335. DIANA VREELAND:
THE EYE HAS TO TRAVEL
Fashion, 2013

This 2011 film traced Vreeland's life and career using insightful interviews and seductive imagery in a neat, three-act structure. First, as fashion stylist at *Harper's Bazaar*, Vreeland elevated her profession to a new prominence. Then, as *Vogue*'s editor, she moved the magazine from its conservative origin to showcase contemporary culture and avant-garde fashion, inventing supermodels, celebrity models and super-photographers on the way. Finally, as chief curator of New York's Costume Institute, she created blockbuster fashion exhibitions.

336. PROENZA SCHOULER AUTUMN/WINTER
2012/2013 COLLECTION
Fashion, 2013

McCollough and Hernandez started Proenza Schouler in 2002. Graduates of New York's Fashion Institute of Technology, their designs promote the American tradition of wardrobe components that can be mixed and matched. Building on their reputation for slick city dressing, Proenza Schouler's strong Autumn/Winter 2012/2013 collection combined an interest in oversized pieces – including boxy jackets and layered pieces – with delicate woven leatherwork, quilting and embroidery. Such well-crafted, technically accomplished designs set Proenza Schouler apart from their ready-to-wear collections.

337. COMME DES GARÇONS
AUTUMN/WINTER 2012/2013
READY-TO-WEAR COLLECTION
Fashion, 2013

Rei Kawakubo has consistently pushed the boundaries of fashion. Her Autumn/Winter 2012/2013 collection featured oversized cartoon silhouettes of garments that looked like flat pattern pieces stitched together. They were minimalist garments, but bold in terms of colour. The coat is one highlight: it uses an exaggerated flower print but remains powerfully simple in its design. Overall, this was a rebellious, inspirational and challenging collection.

338. RICK OWENS SPRING/SUMMER 2014
COLLECTION PRESENTATION
Fashion, 2014

Rick Owens's Vicious presentation took the form of a riotous and combative dance routine by four step troupes from American college fraternities. It was filled with strong thighs, big frizzy hair and ferocious women, celebrating everything absent from the dominant high-fashion aesthetic. The show represented five months' work by choreographers Lauretta Malloy Noble and her daughter LeeAnét. The clothing was customised to allow for energetic movement and athletic body shapes.

339. PRADA SPRING/SUMMER
2014 COLLECTION
Fashion, 2014

Shown in Milan against a backdrop of large murals by artists and illustrators, Prada's rainbow-coloured collection featured vivid, block-colour dresses and coats, embellished and textured by jewels and embroidered and printed images of painted female faces. Themes of 'femininity, representation, power and multiplicity' were demonstrated by the use of the bra as a graphic form, applied to the surface of garments with sequins or contrasting colour prints.

340. DAS COLLECTION
AUTUMN/WINTER 2013/2014
Fashion, 2014

Responding to the theme of the winter forest, this abaya collection, from sisters Reem and Hind Beljafla, combined complex, cut and draped forms with intricate embroidery and beading. Covering the whole body except the face, feet and hands, the abaya is worn by some Muslim women in the Middle East. DAS Collection designed abayas for special occasions and social gatherings, combining tradition, quality and attention to detail in clothes with a sense of fashion and elegance.

341. A MAGAZINE CURATED
BY STEPHEN JONES
Fashion, 2014

Steven Jones considers drawing to be a designer's signature way of distilling an idea, and hoped to fight its decline through this publication. His edition of A Magazine was a love poem to the fashion sketch and to fashion illustration, drawing contributions from a vast list of former creative partnerships, from Raf Simons to Rei Kawakubo. Among several insights into his own working method, the magazine featured faxed correspondence between Jones and fashion houses for which he sketched hat designs.

342. THE HINTERLAND OF RONALDO FRAGA
Fashion, 2014

Fashion designer Ronaldo Fraga reinvents vernacular Brazilian design into contemporary clothes and accessories. He stimulates knowledge exchanges with craft communities, creating jobs and adding value to the traditions of different regions. Fraga's 2014 Autumn/Winter collection took inspiration from the north-east of Brazil, the poorest region of the country, but also the area with the strongest craft work. The collection used leather in various textures, combined with silk, cotton and jacquards; crochet, knitting and embroidery were also present.

343. TOTEMIC COLLECTION
Fashion, 2014

For her graduation collection from the MA in Textiles for Fashion at Central Saint Martins, Sadie Williams made full-length, stiff A-line dresses from 'jumbo-lurex', a textile she developed herself. Williams transformed the usually flimsy lurex by heating, printing and embossing it to create geometric graphic patterns in shimmering metallic reds, blues and silvers. Her inspiration came from old-fashioned Harley Davidson motorcyclists and Japanese biker gangs.

344. DIOR READY-TO-WEAR
SPRING/SUMMER 2013 COLLECTION
Fashion, 2014

In his first ready-to-wear collection for Dior, Raf Simons was faced with the legacy of some of the best-known silhouettes from recent fashion history. The Belgian designer looked back to Dior's post-war work and softened the lines of such classics as the ballgown skirt with iridescent organza fabric. His take on the Dior Bar jacket of 1947, which symbolises the end of wartime austerity, was also less tapered and elongated.

345. TRACEY NEULS GEEK
REFLECTIVE BIKE SHOES
Fashion, 2014

Tracey Neuls' rubber-soled Geek shoe was always hugely popular with female cyclists, but in 2013 Neuls designed a new rubber heel. This simple, brilliant idea transformed a smart and beautiful shoe into one that is practical and comfortable for cycling. The heel is moulded in a single piece that will never come off or need to be repaired. Reflective piping, or 'cat's eyes', on the back of the shoe is another touch that's both decorative and functional.

346. BACK SPRING/SUMMER
2015 COLLECTION
Fashion, 2015

This collection featured several of Back's signature elements: stripes, safety-pin detailing, bare shoulders. These often asymmetric garments were made in familiar materials – checked fleece, jerseys and wool suiting, corduroy and fringed denim – that were given new appeal. With a style rooted in Scandinavian aesthetics, Back designs clothes that question conventional beauty and traditional feminine forms, with humour and intelligence.

347. CATEGORY WINNER
THOMAS TAIT
AUTUMN/WINTER 2013/2014
Fashion, 2015

Thomas Tait's exceptional skill in tailoring and precision is evident in the multi-panelled garments of this collection. It features a lightweight pleated skirt, where panels of leather, printed silk and contemporary woven textile move and drape as if a single piece of cloth. Another garment, which appears to be simple striped trousers, is constructed as a three-dimensional jigsaw, with two tones of suede stitched in deep chevrons that create a crisply geometric, fitted garment without side-seams.

348. SATU MAARANEN SPRING/SUMMER
2015 COLLECTION, GEOMETRY
OF FUTUFOLK
Fashion, 2015

Satu Maaranen's Spring/Summer 2015 collection combined folk craft techniques, a space age aesthetic and ornamental Baroque. Its hand-made prints were coated with silkscreen and digital prints drawn from Finnish natural elements such as birch bark, granite and wooden planks. Having hand-painted and embroidered on those prints, she printed on top of the embroidery to create a fascinating layered effect.

349. FAUSTO PUGLISI AUTUMN/WINTER
2014/2015 COLLECTION
Fashion, 2015

This ready-to-wear collection from Fausto Puglisi combined irregular blocks and triangular shards of strong contrasting colours. The harlequin effect came from mixed fabrics in silk, crêpe wool and soft leather. These garments – short and pleated skirts, loosely fitting knitwear and structured jackets and trousers – were inspired by the movement, speed, colour and strength found in the fragmented forms of early twentieth-century abstract art.

350. RODARTE AUTUMN/WINTER 2014/2015,
COLLECTION FINALE
Fashion, 2015

The couture dresses that Kate and Laura Mulleavy, designers of the Los Angeles-based fashion house Rodarte, conceived as the finale of their Autumn/Winter 2014/2015 collection paid tribute to the enduring legacy of George Lucas and Star Wars. Digitally printed images of R2-D2 and C-3PO, along with the Death Star and Luke Skywalker, enlivened silk gowns cascading from hand-draped bodices adorned with Swarovski crystal.

351. RAF SIMONS/STERLING RUBY
AUTUMN/WINTER 2014/2015
Fashion, 2015

Belgian designer Raf Simons and American artist Sterling Ruby presented this menswear collection in Paris in January 2014. It was shown under the 'Raf Simons/Sterling Ruby' label for one season only. This unique collaboration was born from mutual admiration, and prompted by the desire of both to experience a creative process together. The result was a complete men's wardrobe that combined Simons' constant search for innovation with Ruby's aggressive formal aesthetics.

352. J.W. ANDERSON SPRING/SUMMER 2015
WOMEN'S CATWALK SHOW
Fashion, 2015

This ready-to-wear Spring/Summer collection was an homage to a type of French femininity inspired by the seaside and the comedies of French director Jacques Tati. A relaxed formality was presented with loosely tailored jackets and geometric leather dresses, short A-line wrap-over skirts, camisoles and chunky heeled moccasins. The oversized leatherette sun hats were made by milliner Noel Stewart, featuring exaggerated, floppy brims that obscure the wearer's face and hair.

353. ARCHIVIST – THREE FACES, ARCHIVE CHALAYAN
Fashion, 2015

Archivist was launched in 2012 as a curated journal to explore designers' archives, important personal collections and emerging talent. It focuses on clothes that are not for sale, rejecting the assumptions that a 'fashion magazine' should be a seasonal showcase. This issue featured three different fashion archetypes: a young face, a supermodel, and an older face, all wearing clothes from designer Hussein Chalayan's archive.

354. CHROMAT AUTUMN/WINTER 2015/2016, LUMINA COLLECTION
Fashion, 2016

Architecture-trained Becca McCharen-Tran creates garments that she describes as 'structural experiments for the human body'. For the February 2016 runway show of her brand Chromat, she designed body-conscious garments with viscose bandage knit, featuring zips, corset boning and electroluminescent strip lighting. McCharen-Tran embraces innovative technologies, and for Lumina she collaborated with Intel Innovation and StretchSense to create accessories that can sense the wearer and are able to adapt and respond accordingly.

355. AGI AND SAM AUTUMN/WINTER 2015/2016, THE COOLMAN COLLECTION
Fashion, 2016

Agi Mdumulla and Sam Cotton's Coolman Collection was inspired by a clothing range Mdumulla had designed aged four. Believing that fashion shouldn't be taken too seriously, the duo asked primary-school children what they would like to see in a fashion collection. The result was deconstructed coats fastened with velcro, oversized broad-shouldered jackets, and cropped trousers, predominantly in black with cutouts, panelling, colour-blocking and Agi and Sam's trademark surface-pattern prints.

356. RICHARD MALONE SPRING/SUMMER 2016
Fashion, 2016

Graduating from Central Saint Martins in 2014, Malone has rapidly established himself as a vital young designer. His observations of working-class Irish life and the role of Irish stereotypes provide the inspirational framework for playful structural forms. This collection featured woven striped dresses that twist and turn in giddy combination with skirts and dresses in coral nylons, hand-embroidered T-shirts and knee-high socks.

357. KIDS VS FASHION
Fashion, 2016

Kids vs Fashion was an astute and powerful comment on the fashion industry, made with the kind of wit that made it seem effortless. Domínguez asked a group of eight-year-olds from CEIP La Rioja School in Madrid to describe what they saw in recent fashion campaigns. The results were revealing: children saw women as sick and dead drunk and men as heroes, leaders and entrepreneurs. Using humour and knowing naïvety as a mask, Domínguez raised some heavy-hitting questions about the ethics of fashion.

358. YAKAMPOT AUTUMN/WINTER 2015/2016 COLECCIÓN 7
Fashion, 2016

The Mexican fashion brand Yakampot aims to preserve the country's cultural heritage and traditional manufacturing methods by creating clothes that are at once contemporary and time-less. Their garments are hand-made by artisans from forty-five Mexican indigenous communities, promoting socially responsible design. For Colección 7 in Autumn/Winter 2015/2016, Yakampot took its inspiration from Mexican succulent plants and the wardrobe of photographer and social activist Gertrude Duby Blom, who herself spent fifty years working with Mayan cultures in Mexico.

359. CRAIG GREEN SPRING/SUMMER 2015
Fashion, 2016

From the restrained blue, black and white palette to the padding and the peepholes, this collection marked a definitive coming of age for Craig Green. It is Green's interest in the menswear aesthetic of cultures beyond Europe and North America that sets him apart. The confidence with which he presented what might be considered 'difficult' shapes – panelled, martial arts-inspired jackets and loose pants and robes – proved persuasive within a conservative market.

360. NIKE PRO HIJAB
Fashion, 2017

Nike Pro Hijab is a performance garment for Muslim women. Working alongside athletes such as figure skater Zahra Lari, Nike developed a lightweight hijab made of a single layer of polyester mesh. The soft and stretchy material incorporates tiny opaque holes for optimal breathability, as well as an elongated back to ensure it stays in position. This design thus provides culturally appropriate and comfortable attire for professional Muslim athletes, as well as eliminating one of the barriers that stops Muslim girls participating in sport.

361. ECOALF
Fashion, 2017

Ecoalf is an upcycling project based in Spain, a country whose extensive coastline is exposed to sea pollution. Ecoalf removes waste from the sea and transforms it into new materials from which the Madrid-based studio creates a selection of wearable goods, all with a very contemporary design and look. Involving local fishermen but reaching out to consumers worldwide, this project considers the full design process, from initial idea to final products.

362. PUSSYHAT PROJECT
Fashion, 2017

The simplicity of the Pussyhat Project belies its audaciousness. From the outrage that followed President Donald Trump's toxic and aggressively sexist admission of 'grabbing 'em by the pussy' came the most visually effective and internationally recognised symbol of protest this century – the pink pussyhat. The vision of co-founders Krista Suh and Jayna Zweiman, the project was launched ahead of the Women's March on Washington in January 2017, as hundreds of thousands of people were encouraged to download a rudimentary, open-source pattern to knit a pink hat.

363. LEVI'S COMMUTER TRUCKER JACKET
WITH GOOGLE JACQUARD
Fashion, 2017

Project Jacquard, conceived and created by Google, makes it possible to incorporate interactivity into any textile. Any garment can be lined with this connective fabric, transforming it into a surface that is sensitive to touch and gesture. Jacquard yarns, which combine thin metallic alloys with natural and synthetic materials such as cotton, silk or polyester, are visually indistinguishable from normal contemporary yarns, and can be woven on standard industrial looms.

364. 'THE RITE OF SPRING/SUMMER/
AUTUMN/WINTER' NEW
OBJECT RESEARCH
Fashion, 2017

Aitor Throup presented his highly-anticipated New Object Research collection, titled The Rite of Spring/Summer/Autumn/Winter, on six life-size articulated sculptures. The articulated sculptures - acting as performing puppets during the show, aided by a team of puppeteers - were executed to Throup's exact measurements and physically expressed the emotion and energy in his autobiographical narrative. Presented in three acts, the show was set in the Holy Trinity Church in London.

365. LIFE OF PABLO POP-UP STORE
Fashion, 2017

Coinciding with his album *The Life of Pablo* and Saint Pablo tour, Kanye West launched pop-up stores across twenty-one international cities. The store locations were revealed on Twitter twenty-four hours before they opened, resulting in customers lining up for hours to get branded T-shirts and hoodies. Musicians have long made more money from merchandise than by selling music, but West has explicitly inverted this by holding a big launch for the merchandise while quietly streaming the album for free.

370. HELVETICA
Graphics, 2008

Helvetica is a feature-length independent film directed and produced by Gary Hustwit. It invites some of the most eminent figures in design to discuss typography, graphic design and visual culture, specifically examining the Helvetica typeface, which was developed by Max Miedinger with Eduard Hoffman in 1957. The film surveys the influence of Helvetica on design, advertising, psychology and communication. The film was screened worldwide and inspired special events to celebrate the typeface's fiftieth anniversary.

371. MONOGRAPH DECEMBER ISSUE '07
Graphics, 2008

Launched in September 2007, *Monograph* is a monthly publication from *Creative Review*. Available exclusively to subscribers of the magazine, each issue is a twenty-page A5 booklet showcasing a personal project or body of work. The December issue explored Daniel Mason's archive of materials, books, posters and processes, collected over fifteen years. Each item opens a space in which to question practice and processes, presenting ideas that can be explored by graphic designers to push and challenge current systems.

372. PRADA PROTOTYPES
AUCTION WEBSITE
Graphics, 2008

AMO, the think tank of Rem Koolhaas's OMA practice, has collaborated with Prada to create an online auction site. Prada.com gave visitors the opportunity to bid for unique items of clothing from the Prada Autumn/Winter 2007 collection. The auction featured twenty-four one-offs, some never seen before and some specifically made for the auction. Not surprisingly, these pieces proved highly desirable, especially for collectors, and attracted high bids. Profits were then donated to an Italian charity.

373. MUSEUM FÜR GESTALTUNG
EXHIBITION POSTERS
Graphics, 2008

Since the 1980s, Zürich's Museum für Gestaltung has commissioned leading designers to produce artwork for posters to accompany and promote their exhibitions, some of whom, among them Cornel Windlin and Lars Müller, represent the finest in Swiss graphic design. The range of posters, which have won several international awards, show the museum's commitment to commissioning original and stimulating work. Designers for the 2007 series include Norm, Bonbon, Leander Eisenmann, Martin Woodtli and Ralph Schraivogel.

374. MAGCULTURE WEBSITE
Graphics, 2008

magCulture is a blog that offers the opportunity for people to discuss and contribute to the conversations surrounding editorial design.

Edited by Jeremy Leslie, who originally wrote the book *magCulture* back in 2003, the blog was derived from a website that supported the publication. It draws on issues raised in the book and examines the latest in innovative editorial design. This platform proves that newspapers and magazines have maintained their appeal and authority within an emergent digital age.

375. GRETA TYPEFACE FAMILY
Graphics, 2008

The Greta typeface was designed for text and display. It consists of four text weights, specifically to meet the needs of newspapers. A brochure demonstrates its versatility: while Greta Text is optimised for small sizes, Greta Display has increased contrast, tighter spacing and more refined details, ideal for headline typography and nameplates. Besides all the Latin-based languages, Greta also supports Greek and Cyrillic scripts, altogether including over 2,000 glyphs per font.

376. THE GRAND TOUR
Graphics, 2008

In summer 2007, the National Gallery in London wanted to promote its permanent collection and highlight its relationship with technology partner Hewlett-Packard. The Partners – a London-based design agency – conceived the Grand Tour. Forty-four exact replica framed paintings were hung in the bustling West End for twelve weeks, supported by a website, featuring maps, downloadable tours and audio, from Digit. Viewers were thus encouraged to visit the originals in the gallery, where they could dial up expert commentary recorded by Antenna Audio.

377. BUTT BOOK: THE BEST OF THE FIRST 5 YEARS OF BUTT MAGAZINE – ADVENTURES IN 21ST CENTURY GAY SUBCULTURE
Graphics, 2008

The *BUTT BOOK* celebrates *BUTT*, an international quarterly magazine designed to bring together gay men worldwide. Since 2001, Jop van Bennekom has created and produced *BUTT* with Gert Jonkers. It encompasses fashion, sex and art, with photo essays and interviews. Avoiding the customary full-colour glossy magazine style, Bennekom and Jonkers collaborate with the likes of photographer Wolfgang Tillmans, integrating striking imagery with a black and pink aesthetic.

378. CLEAN CITY LAW
Graphics, 2008

In 2007, under the terms of São Paulo's Lei Cidade Limpa ('Clean City Law'), mayor Gilberto Kassab enforced a radical ban on outdoor advertising within this commercial capital. The objective was to combat visual pollution in the world's fourth-largest metropolis, removing billboards, neon signs and public transport advertising to transform the urban backdrop. The results were widely welcomed by residents, with more than seventy per cent showing their approval. Artist Tony de Marco documented the cityscape with the bare billboards and painted shopfronts.

379. 'SILENTLY' MUSIC VIDEO
Graphics, 2008

Mike Mills is a film-maker, graphic designer and artist, who has directed videos for bands including Air, Pulp and Moby. The video accompanying the Blonde Redhead song 'Silently' puts on a black background white text describing, sentence by sentence, the video for the Madonna song 'Like a Prayer'. Mills initially worked on CD cover artwork, but transferred his two-dimensional design skills to create experimental pop videos.

380. NASSIM TYPEFACE
Graphics, 2008

Nassim was a new typeface for Arabic and Latin script, designed and developed by the Austrian designer Titus Nemeth while studying typeface design at the University of Reading. The typeface family covers a range of weights and versions, giving flexibility for various typographic problems. The principle is to pull two writing systems, Arabic and Latin, effectively together, resulting in independent and accurate designs. It was conceived as a clearly readable, economical and sturdy newspaper typeface.

381. PENGUIN CLASSICS DELUXE EDITIONS
Graphics, 2008

The Penguin Classics Deluxe Editions featured one-of-a-kind book covers by a number of leading and internationally renowned cartoonists and illustrators. The graphic artists involved produced wraparound pieces for the front and back covers, as well as French flaps. The Creative Director of the series was Paul Buckley, who was also responsible for the designs of some of the titles. Artists and illustrators featured in the series include Frank Miller, Julie Doucet and Dan Clowes.

382. PERFORMA 07: PERFORMA ART BIENNIAL IDENTITY AND GRAPHICS
Graphics, 2008

Founded by Kirsty Carter and Emma Thomas in 2003, APFEL's work for Performa began in 2005 with the identity for the arts organisation, after which they developed the identity and marketing materials for Performa's New York biennial. This included stationery, invitations, programmes, posters and bags. The use of arrows within the identity reflects the flow of people who attend art festivals, illustrating the various routes and directions.

383. 'ADIDAS ORIGINALS' FOOTWEAR CATALOGUE
Graphics, 2008

Printed specifically for the Chinese market, this catalogue revealed the adidas Originals Sleek Series. Only 800 copies made, using a light, thin, semi-transparent paper (65gsm stock), the catalogue integrates photographs, text and graphics associated with the adidas brand, including their three stripes, and the edge of the paper echoes the saw-tooth line of the stripes. The full-colour die-cut printing technique brings an unusual, eye-catching finish, enhanced by gold foil stamping that had been applied by hand.

384. SELFRIDGES WAYFINDING AND SIGNAGE
Graphics, 2008

Selfridges commissioned Cartlidge Levene to create a wayfinding strategy and signage system for the flagship store on London's Oxford Street. Collaborating with product designer Julian Brown to create a totem and a hanging directional sign, Cartlidge Levene created a calm, stylish and simple solution. Along with the three-dimensional signage, there are maps and guides to meet the needs of different customers: those in a hurry and those with more time to browse.

385. KATE MOSS IDENTITY
Graphics, 2008

Peter Saville collaborated with typographer Paul Barnes to form the brand identity for Kate Moss. The logo was based on a typeface designed by legendary art director Alexey Brodovitch. Described as sophisticated and modern, it embodies the spirit of Moss herself, the geometric forms achieving a quirky contemporaneity. The logo had to be versatile, since it would be used for a range of products, including a clothing line available through Topshop and fragrances from Coty.

386. SWISS NATIONAL BANK BANKNOTES
Graphics, 2008

In 2005, the Swiss National Bank ran a competition for the development of a new series of banknotes, inviting twelve artists to design six denominations on the theme 'Switzerland: Open to the World'. They were to encourage contemplation of Swiss national identity. Pfrunder's design was chosen. The Swiss graphic designer focused on economics, education, research and development, human rights, tourism and recreation, culture and, lastly, sport.

387. VAROOM! THE ILLUSTRATION REPORT
Graphics, 2008

Varoom! is a platform for contemporary illustration that celebrates the art of image-making. The journal looks at practitioners and features highly visual essays that discuss contemporary illustration within a wider context. It also critically explores the genre through interviews, reviews and profiles. The magazine is designed and art directed by Kjell Ekhorn and Jon Forss, who together make up the award-winning creative team Non-Format. The editor, Adrian Shaughnessy, is an art director and writer.

388. YOUR HOUSE
Graphics, 2008

Likening the experience of reading a book to walking through his house, *Your House* was conceived and designed by the artist Olafur Eliasson. The final publication was realised by Michael Heimann and Claudia Baulesch and produced by Kremo, who laser-cut two pages to create a negative-space rendering of Eliasson's house in 8:1 scale. The hand-bound book has a series of shapes cut into every page, each presenting a vertical cross-section of the building and forming a reverse to the conventional three-dimensional architectural model.

389. THIS IS NOT A BROTHEL... STICKER
Graphics, 2008

Peter Saville was asked to produce work on the theme of 'selling out' for the February 2007 issue of *Creative Review*. Saville was inspired by a sign he saw in London's Soho. His sticker was distributed in the issue, which discussed the extent to which those working in visual communications 'prostitute' themselves. Unbeknownst to Saville, the original sign was the work of artist Sebastian Horsley.

390. UNREST
Graphics, 2008

Unrest showcased the thoughts and work of Jonathan Ellery. The exhibition was made up of three projects: *13 Points of Reference* (2005), *8 Ellery* (2006) and *Works in Brass* (2007). The nominated and perhaps dominant part of the show was Works in Brass: two striking, large-scale, sculptural machined brass objects, displayed in juxtaposition to form new and subtle meanings. They were suspended in the cavernous, dark space using carbon-fibre wire and lit to create an atmosphere reminiscent of a Byzantine church.

391. LETMAN
Graphics, 2009

Working under the pseudonym Letman, Job Wouters' passion for typography is evident from his prolific body of work. Described as 'colourful craft', his handmade style rejects the computerised, refined typography that is prominent today. His work spans the disciplines of illustration and graphic design, creating typographic forms that simulate eloquent graffiti tags, while also communicating their message effectively, presenting information in distinctive layouts through the application of visually striking type and bold use of colour.

392. PROJECT VITRA
Graphics, 2009

Project Vitra is a comprehensive publication about the furniture company's past, present and future. The copiously illustrated chapters tell stories about the places, products and people connected with Vitra, as well as featuring extensive unpublished material from the Vitra archives. The typography is strong, the text clear and opinionated, the choice of images judicious.

393. AESOP RETAIL STORES AND BRANDING
Graphics, 2009

Impressed by their socially incisive 'Pen Plan' art-based projects, Aesop founder Dennis Paphitis approached March Studio to collaborate on the design of the retail stores and graphic identity for Aesop body products. The store interiors are inspired by packaging for Aesop products. For example, the Adelaide shop was transformed by an impressive wavy ceiling material made entirely from glass bottles.

394. DESIGNING DESIGN
Graphics, 2009

In *Designing Design*, Japanese graphic designer and curator Kenya Hara discusses the process and ethos of design. He impresses on the reader the importance of 'emptiness' in the visual and philosophical traditions of Japan, and the concept's application to design, using numerous examples from his own work and the projects of others through exhibitions, contests and even the work of his students.

395. IS NOT MAGAZINE: ISSUE ELEVEN – ALL THAT GLITTERS IS/NOT GOLD
Graphics, 2009

First appearing in April 2005 as a two-sheet bill poster, *Is Not Magazine* inverted the traditional typology of a cultural magazine. Published every two months and distributed across Melbourne and Sydney, the magazine covers fiction, non-fiction, reviews, comics, illustrations, lists, letters, diary entries and a variety of uncategorisable contributions. The final issue ('All That Glitters Is/Not Gold', July 2008) extended to three sheets and 8,000 words.

396. BIG BROTHER LOGO
Graphics, 2009

With each passing season, the Channel 4 reality television show *Big Brother* commissions designer Daniel Eatock to develop a new identity for the show. Eatock was asked to develop the logo for the first season in 2000, and responded to the brief by adapting the form of the human eye into something reflecting the Orwellian idea of surveillance. Although every manifestation of the show's identity is different, they share a common lineage.

397. THE SOCIAL INNOVATION LAB FOR KENT (SILK)
Graphics, 2009

SILK challenges the way the design process is led by sharing ideas with users and providers of public services to the benefit of all. One project, Engaging Fathers, looks at how the county can support fathers to make them feel as important as mothers in

bringing up their children. Engine Service Design, together with Kent County Council, created a set of services and tools that enable fathers to get more involved in their children's lives.

398. BARACK OBAMA POSTER
Graphics, 2009

Shepard Fairey is a street artist renowned for propaganda-style artwork, whose Obey images attract a large international following. He was commissioned to create limited edition work for sale to raise money and awareness for Obama's 2008 presidential campaign. Based on the image taken by photographer Mannie Garcia, the initial Obama posters by Fairey were PROGRESS and HOPE. Then, on his own initiative, Fairey used both these images as part of an unofficial viral poster campaign. The posters demonstrated the cultural momentum surrounding Obama.

400. ALL THE TIME IN THE WORLD
Graphics, 2009

As part of a programme of art installations for the new Heathrow Terminal 5, Troika was commissioned to create a twenty-two-metre-long electro-luminescent wall. It extends the conventional idea of a world clock, linking real time to places with exciting and romantic associations. The animated letters and numbers can be shown in up to five different fonts, and the screen does not cast light and disturbing shadow on its surroundings.

401. STATISTICAL REPRESENTATION OF THE ECONOMIC SITUATION
Graphics, 2009

The *Guardian* presents statistical data in a simple format, using graphs and charts to represent the economic crisis and the global financial situation. Geometric shapes of proportional sizes show the value of objects past and present, or convey the undulating markets with simple clarity. The *Guardian*'s design team has consistently covered the financial news using this approach in order to make the information accessible to a broad readership.

402. BAGHDAD CALLING
Graphics, 2009

In the book *Baghdad Calling*, photojournalist Geert van Kesteren shows how Iraqi refugees live in Jordan, Syria and Turkey. Alongside his professionally shot images, the book reveals everyday life in Iraq during 2006 and 2007 through the eyes of ordinary Iraqis, using hundreds of photos they took on their mobile phones and digital cameras, revealing places where journalists dare not tread.

403. MARTIN KIPPENBERGER: THE PROBLEM
PERSPECTIVE EXHIBITION CATALOGUE
Graphics, 2009

Martin Kippenberger (1953-97) is one of the
most significant artists of our time. This catalogue,
which accompanied his first major retrospective
in the United States, was designed by award-winning graphic designer Lorraine Wild. Wild has
been creating publications for some of the most
prestigious figures within contemporary art for
over twenty years. She likes to collaborate with
the artists or curators, reinforcing her designs
by fully understanding the theoretical basis
of the work.

404. BARACK OBAMA OFFICIAL
ELECTION CAMPAIGN LOGO
Graphics, 2009

In contrast to the simple typography often
associated with political logos, the brand identity
for Barack Obama's 2008 presidential campaign
stands up against some of the most recognisable
corporate logos. The white space inside the
'O' merges into the other graphical elements,
conveying the sun rising over the American plains
–suggestive of the hope and anticipation associated
with Obama's campaign.

405. OASE 74 – JOURNAL FOR
ARCHITECTURE: INVENTION
Graphics, 2009

OASE looks at the developments and influences
from the post-1945 history of architecture. Issue
74 investigated specific moments when designers
discover new forms of expression. It examined architectural projects by Hans Scharoun, Norman Foster,
Alejandro de la Sota and Fernand Pouillon, and
presented a series of interviews with contemporary
architects (Annette Gigon/Mike Guyer Architekten,
XDGA, Neutelings Riedijk Architects) who place
the invention of new solutions at the heart of
their practice.

406. JAN BONS: A DESIGNER'S FREEDOM
Graphics, 2009

In contrast to the usual oversized monograph,
this combined book and DVD modestly presents
the work of Dutch designer Jan Bons. The bilingual
publication is accompanied by a short biography
by Paul Hefting, with a catalogue of posters bound
into the covers. The DVD – a fifty-three-minute
film by Lex Reitsma – is presented in a die-cut
pulpboard container. From the mix of coated and
uncoated stock to the overall layout, the design
of every page is carefully considered.

407. CAFE OF EQUIVALENT$
Graphics, 2010

Playing with the notion of value under global
capitalism, Cafe of Equivalent$ engaged City
workers with some simple 'truth derivatives'
during their lunch. Located at the heart of London's
financial district in Leadenhall Market, the Cafe

sold soup and bread at a cost equivalent with
food affordability in producing countries. For
a Mozambican worker earning $2 a day, a 20¢
lunch accounts for ten per cent of their wage –
the Cafe applied the same percentage to the
average bonus-earning banker: their bread and
soup cost £111.20.

408. IT'S NICE THAT
Graphics, 2010

It's Nice That is the printed publication from the
design blog of the same name. Founded in April
2007, the online platform covers a wide range of
work from across the creative industry. Directors
Will Hudson and Alex Bec launched their printed
incarnation two years later, allowing the blog's
audience to engage with their content away from
a computer screen.

409. THE HAPPY HYPOCRITE
Graphics, 2010

The Happy Hypocrite is a biannual journal of new
writing and research-based projects from artists,
writers and theorists. It is a testing ground for
experimental ideas, which might not otherwise be
realised or published. APFEL's design for the journal reflects the written nature of the contributions.
Each section has a different typographic language,
illustrating the diversity of the work included.

410. THE NEW YORKER COVER,
2 NOVEMBER 2009
Graphics, 2010

Since 1999, the cartoonist Chris Ware had
produced several celebrated covers for *The New
Yorker*. The cover for the cartoon issue featured
a group of distracted parents whose faces, illuminated by the glow from their iPhones, match the
ghostly masks worn by their children. The cover is
actually the first panel of a four-page comic about
a woman who visits her widowed mother after an
angry dispute with her husband, only to learn that
her father once committed adultery.

411. 032C MAGAZINE
Graphics, 2010

Under the art direction of Mike Meiré, *032c* became
a contemporary culture magazine that stood out
from the crowd in a busy market. The use of clashing colours, demanding page layouts and mixed
types of paper generates a feeling of disorientation
and spontaneity. On closer inspection, however,
these combinations are far from rash. Rather, they
are the result of considered and rigorous experiments that challenge the perceived principles of
graphic and editorial publishing.

412. ALTERMODERN: TATE TRIENNIAL
CATALOGUE AND POSTER DESIGN
Graphics, 2010

When curator Nicolas Bourriaud commissioned
M/M (Paris) to design the exhibition identity and
catalogue for *Altermodern* at Tate Britain, they

developed a strong visual language, the centre-piece of which was a typically challenging logo. Using numerous typefaces separated over multiple lines, the logo has an almost baroque feel, forcing the viewer to concentrate hard in order to decipher the text. The logo was also used as the main image for the accompanying poster and catalogue.

413. THE NEWSPAPER CLUB
Graphics, 2010

The Newspaper Club solves several problems to do with printing small runs of publications. Taking advantage of downtime at newspaper printers, the company takes care of the print and production side of things, providing online templated designs for amateur publishers or accepting bespoke designs from professionals. The result is an easy-to-use process providing relatively cheap but high-quality colour newsprint printing, ideal for newsletters, one-off special events, special reports or regularly published projects.

414. RUSSIAN CRIMINAL TATTOO ENCYCLOPAEDIA VOLUME III
Graphics, 2010

Now in its third volume, the *Russian Criminal Tattoo Encyclopaedia* brings to a close the fascinating ethnographic study of over 3,000 unpublished drawings and photographs of tattoos. FUEL have illuminated this previously closed world of criminal iconography, compiled by Danzig Baldaev during a lifetime working as a prison guard. Through the publication of this rarefied collection, the reader is encouraged to create narratives to fit imagery that is darkly comic, surreal, disturbing and sometimes vulgar.

415. VOLTAÏC: SONGS FROM THE VOLTA TOUR
Graphics, 2010

M/M (Paris) consistently create inventive and eye-catching graphic solutions. Working with Björk on a limited edition version of her live album, M/M determined that a bold approach was needed for a world where music is more often downloaded than bought over the counter. Collaborating with photographers Nick Knight and the duo Inez and Vinoodh, they created a visual language combining photography and graphic elements – such as original typography.

416. WAR MEMORIAL
Graphics, 2010

Harry Pearce's wall-mounted memorial is a reverential tribute to the London Science Museum's employees who fell in the First and Second World Wars. Made from a single piece of cast iron, the plaque is layered with typographic interventions. A cross is de-embossed through both sections, while raised and polished Raleigh lettering speaks of permanence and respect.

417. YES
Graphics, 2010

The cover design for the 2009 limited edition vinyl version of Yes consists of a simple tick made from eleven coloured squares, one for each track on the album. Reducing the title to a symbol deliberately creates more of an identity: simple, memorable and 'pop'. The album is split over eleven vinyl records, each in a coloured sleeve. When correctly arranged, these form the tick symbol at a much larger scale.

418. CORPORATE DIVERSITY: SWISS GRAPHIC DESIGN AND ADVERTISING BY GEIGY 1940–1970
Graphics, 2010

Corporate Diversity is the first comprehensive look at the design studio of chemical and pharaceutical company JR Geigy AG, one of the most impressive bodies of corporate design ever made. During the 1950s and 60s, Geigy became the focus of an influential period in Swiss graphic design. The corporation's design studio produced work across identity, advertising and packaging that combined a formal language with a refreshing approach that chimed perfectly with the second wave of European modernism.

419. TRILLION DOLLAR CAMPAIGN
Graphics, 2010

When *The Zimbabwean* newspaper was driven into exile for attacking the Mugabe regime, it needed to drive sales outside Zimbabwe, South African-based advertising agency TBWA/ Hunt Lascaris conceived a unique solution. A symptom of Zimbabwe's world-record inflation, the trillion-dollar banknote could not buy even a loaf of bread. The campaign turned the money into its own medium by creating posters and flyers from the banknotes themselves. News of the campaign spread globally and sales soared.

420. THE INDIAN TYPE FOUNDRY
Graphics, 2010

Perhaps because of the time it takes to develop a new typeface, or to maximise potential usage and profit, most type design concentrates on creating Latin typefaces. The Indian Type Foundry attempts to give as much attention to non-Latin fonts, with a focus on Indic scripts. Their first typeface, Fedra Hindi, was a Devanagari script, a Brahmi-derived writing system developed to write Sanskrit and now used widely in India and Nepal.

421. DAILY VISUAL COLUMN FOR DE VOLKSKRANT
Graphics, 2010

Six times a week, the Dutch newspaper de Volkskrant gave the Gorilla design collective three hours to create a visual response to the day's news. Gorilla developed its own unique visual identity for the task and a fixed place in the paper's layout, acting not only as designers, but as authors and even opinion-formers. The simple and colourful designs look innocent, but their message is razor-sharp.

422. TYPOGRAPHIC TREES
Graphics, 2010

When artist Gordon Young was asked to design a site-specific artwork for a new library in Crawley, West Sussex, he suggested a 'forest' of floor-to-ceiling typographic columns. Fellow artist Anna Sandberg held workshops with library-users to hear about favourite books, places and memories. Young worked with typographers why not associates to design fourteen solid oak 'trees' from the workshop material. The oak, with all its cracks, was deliberately chosen to contrast with the new interior.

423. PIG 05049
Graphics, 2010

PIG 05049 is the result of a three-year study during which Dutch artist and designer Christien Meindertsma tracked all the products made from 05049, a pig she selected at random from a commercial farm in the Netherlands. The animal was used in 185 different products, all pictured in the book. Aside from the expected foodstuffs, parts of 05049 were used for non-food products including photographic film, toothpaste and even the glue used to bind the pages of Meindertsma's book.

424. THE LIFE AND OPINIONS OF TRISTRAM SHANDY, GENTLEMAN
Graphics, 2011

When APFEL were asked to design a new edition of *Tristram Shandy*, they looked back at Laurence Sterne's first edition from 1759 for inspiration. Sterne subverted the available print and typographic techniques of the day to illustrate his loquacious tale, using different length dashes to denote words too rude to print or printing pages entirely in black or marble effect. These interventions were reimagined by APFEL, restoring something of the original visual experience of reading *Tristram Shandy*.

425. FOUR CORNERS FAMILIARS SERIES
Graphics, 2011

Four Corners Familiars are artists' responses to classic novels and short stories, providing a fresh look at the tradition of the illustrated book. Contributors are encouraged to interpret 'illustration' loosely, and to suggest new ways texts and images can relate to one another. The result is magazine adverts appearing in *The Picture of Dorian Gray* and images of 1930s Hollywood within *Vanity Fair*.

426. IRMA BOOM: BIOGRAPHY IN BOOKS
Graphics, 2011

Irma Boom is one of the world's most renowned book designers but this 'biography' of her work measures just five centimetres high. The size reflects Boom's own working practice: she makes tiny models of all her books, often creating six or seven for each. *Irma Boom: Biography in Books* accompanied the designer's retrospective at the University of Amsterdam Library, and is a refreshing antidote to the usual coffee-table design book.

427. UNIT EDITIONS
Graphics, 2011

Unit Editions is a progressive publishing venture producing high-quality, affordable books on graphic design and visual culture. A collaboration between self-confessed book lovers Tony Brook and Adrian Shaughnessy, Unit Editions combines impeccable design and production standards with insightful texts and informative commentaries on a wide range of subjects.

428. A LOVE LETTER FOR YOU
Graphics, 2011

As a young graffiti artist, Stephen Powers spent many hours clambering over buildings to paint his tag, ESPO. Twenty-five years later, he returned to West Philadelphia to organise an unprecedented community arts project. A series of murals containing hopeful messages were painted across rooftops spread along an elevated train route. The resulting love letter, meant for one but with meaning for all, encompasses fifty walls facing the Market–Frankford train line and used 1,200 cans of spray paint.

429. HOMEMADE IS BEST
Graphics, 2011

When developing an IKEA marketing campaign, Forsman & Bodenfors realised that the best way to get people excited about microwave ovens, fridges and fans is to talk about the delicious things you can make with them. *Homemade is Best* is a 140-page book of classic Swedish recipes. The recipes are depicted as colourful graphic still-life portraits, with all the ingredients laid out in carefully composed photographs.

430. I WONDER
Graphics, 2011

Marian Bantjes' densely decorated book is a treat for the senses and the mind. The cover is hardbound with a black satin finish, foil stamped on front and back in gold and silver. Inside, ornamented pages examine the role of wonder in design. Bantjes' writing is accessible and at times teasing, inspiring the reader to contemplate the world in an unorthodox way and fostering leaps of the imagination.

431. COALITION OF THE WILLING
Graphics, 2011

Coalition of the Willing is a animated film dedicated to the fight against global warming. Written in the immediate aftermath of the 2009 Copenhagen Climate Summit, the animator, Simon Robson, realised his chosen in-camera animation route would take forever to complete. He then invited a network of artists to collaborate. The intense fourteen-month production period involved seventeen animation units and seventy-eight individuals. The finished film is optimistic exploration about using new internet technologies to empower of activists, experts and ordinary citizens.

432. LONDON COLLEGE OF
    COMMUNICATION, POWER OF
    TEN SUMMER SHOW '10
    Graphics, 2011

Morag Myerscough/Studio Myerscough has brought the indistinct internal architecture of the London College of Communication (LCC) to life. The latest phase of the project transformed the campus' triangular 'piazza' for its summer degree show. Shipping container galleries, carnivalesque spaces and colourful seating areas bridged the gap between the college and its uncompromising urban location.

433. DESIGN CRIMINALS
    EDIBLE CATALOGUE
    Graphics, 2011

Produced as a catalogue to accompany Sam Jacob's *Design Criminals* exhibition at the Vienna MAK, this book is entirely edible. Its typographic slipcase is made of pastillage – effectively, shaped sugar. Individual pages are made from wafer printed with coloured vegetable ink. Some of the books were created on site at the MAK with the help of visitors, and attendees at an evening event were invited to eat the printed wafer pages and pastillage ornaments.

434. AA FILES
    Graphics, 2012

The *AA Files* is an academic journal produced twice a year by the Architectural Association School of Architecture. Redesigned by John Morgan Studio in 2008, the issues show confident graphic design that engages the reader while still reflecting the seriousness of the journal. For the display type, John Morgan worked with font designer Paul Barnes to develop heavy relief forms with bold shadows, informed by lettering by eighteenth- and nineteenth-century signwriters and gravestone engravers.

435. PHOTO-LETTERING
    Graphics, 2012

Photo-Lettering is an online service that allows users to buy, modify and create typeset letters in vintage American fonts. Founded in 1936, Photo-Lettering, Inc., was one of New York's most successful type houses. The company closed in 1985 but, in 2003, House Industries purchased its remaining assets. It has since been working to digitise – and make available once more – the thousands of original Photo-Lettering fonts, one character at a time.

436. GF SMITH 10,000 DIGITAL
    PAINTINGS CAMPAIGN
    Graphics, 2012

When GF Smith wanted to promote their digital papers, SEA Design produced a series of 10,000 generative prints inspired by the microscopic detail of paper fibres. The designers wanted to show how revolutionary digital technology currently was, and were inspired by the fact that variable imaging enables each print to be unique. Digital artists FIELD created a series of 10,000 images that draw on the same intense colour palette, while completely different from each other.

437. BEAUTY IS IN THE STREET:
    A VISUAL RECORD
    OF THE MAY '68 PARIS UPRISING
    Graphics, 2012

This book gathers for the first time a complete visual history of the uprisings that took place in Paris during 1968. That May, demonstrations against the French government spread from Parisian universities into a general worker's strike. Among the students, the Atelier Populaire produced hundreds of screen-printed posters, which have become landmarks in political art and graphic design. *Beauty is in the Street* reproduces more than 200 posters alongside first-hand accounts and photographs of the clashes.

438. JOIN US COVER ARTWORK AND VIDEO
    Graphics, 2012

The cover artwork for the They Might Be Giants album *Join Us* depicts the unlikely fusion of a monster truck chassis with a pink funeral hearse. Its designer Paul Sahre is known for his memorable work. In addition to the striking image of a mutated funeral hearse, Sahre made a downloadable file of a cut-out hearse/monster truck, complete with instructions to print it out life-size by typing 3,400 per cent in the printer dialogue box.

439. THE COMEDY CARPET BLACKPOOL
    Graphics, 2012

Designed by Gordon Young and why not associates, the Comedy Carpet is a unique celebration of Blackpool. The 2,200-square-metre granite and concrete artwork is made up of jokes, songs and catchphrases from notable British comedians and comedy writers, including Morecambe and Wise, Tony Hancock, Tommy Cooper and Monty Python. The Carpet was installed as part of the regeneration of the sea defences on the seafront promenade at the foot of Blackpool Tower.

440. ONE THOUSAND CRANES FOR JAPAN
    Graphics, 2012

Following the devastating Japanese earthquake and tsunami in March 2011, a group of designers collaborated to raise funds to help those affected. Inspired by the Japanese fable that a wish is granted to anyone with the devotion to fold 1,000 origami cranes, Anomaly and UNIT9 designed a website selling specially created crane designs for downloading and folding. The aim was to raise awareness of those affected by the tragedy.

441. MATTHEW HILTON IDENTITY AND WEBSITE
Graphics, 2012

Asked to design a new logo for furniture designer Matthew Hilton, Spin developed a new identity derived from Hilton's initials. Inspired by the forms that Hilton uses in his work, the new identity's bold yet subtle appearance reflects the designer's idiosyncratic vision. The accompanying website is a well-crafted visual experience, demonstrating that digital design no longer needs to be the poor relation of the printed form.

442. WHAT DESIGN CAN DO
Graphics, 2012

Not only did De Designpolitie create the identity for What Design Can Do, but they also initiated an annual two-day conference with some like-minded designers. The strong and direct visual identity features a yellow background with the title printed in red, followed by a bold black subtitle. An energetic felt-tip squiggle underlines the word 'design'. The subtitle changes to announce different speakers or subjects – sometimes subtitles can be humorously juxtaposed.

443. CUT IT OUT
Graphics, 2012

Artist and illustrator Noma Bar's fascination with negative space – the space around the subject in an image – fuelled his development of an art-making machine in the form of a dog. The dog's teeth control a hole-puncher hidden within its head. To operate the machine, the relevant die-cut mould is inserted into the dog's mouth. When the jaws of the dog clamp down, twenty tonnes of pressure cuts out a bespoke Noma Bar artwork.

444. BLOOMBERG BUSINESSWEEK
Graphics, 2012

A redesign of the popular New York monthly business magazine *Bloomberg Businessweek* introduced arresting front covers, tightly formatted interior pages and an abundance of intelligent photography, illustrations and infographics. The aim of the new design was to create a surprising and original front cover each week that would encourage a range of people to pick up the magazine. The magazine's font is a restoration of the original Helvetica, the most familiar of sans serif fonts.

445. YOUR BROWSER SENT A REQUEST THAT THIS SERVER COULD NOT UNDERSTAND
Graphics, 2012

In this fantastically detailed portrait of the internet, Koen Taselaar comments light-heartedly and engagingly on the relentless advertising and technological problems that the web can bring.

Painstakingly drawn with black fine-liner pen, it shows hundreds of connected computers, servers, keyboards and other imaginable computer components. The screens display error messages or witty interpretations of websites, blogs and pop-ups.

446. SELF SERVICE
Graphics, 2012

Self Service is a Paris-based fashion magazine available in both traditional print and digital formats. With an adventurous approach to fashion, it directs innovatively styled fashion shoots by leading photographers including Alasdair McLellan, Glen Luchford and Ezra Petronio. Sophisticated styling is combined with clean, simple layouts and typography. Viewed on a digital format, photographs are unadorned with text or captions – only by a touch of the screen do the captions appear.

447. NOKIA PURE
Graphics, 2012

A new font family for Finnish mobile phone manufacturer Nokia, Nokia Pure's sans serif characters are easy to read in print, on screen and on the small displays of mobile handsets. Deceptively simple in appearance, every stroke of each letter swells and narrows as if drawn by a calligrapher. Dalton Maag's design is pioneering in that they created Latin, Greek, Cyrillic, Arabic and Hebrew alphabets for the typeface, as well as Devanagari and Thai scripts.

448. STOCKMANN PACKAGING
Graphics, 2012

Approached by Stockmann to refresh the packaging for its department store division, Kokoro & Moi redesigned everything from wrapping paper to shopping bags and food packets. The designers started by conducting extensive research into the Stockmann archive, studying the development of the brand identity over the past 100 years. They increased the ratio of white in the updated logo to allow the brand colour to stand out, and introduced a range of patterns inspired by the archive.

449. DEKHO: CONVERSATIONS ON DESIGN IN INDIA
Graphics, 2013

Dekho is an anthology of Indian contemporary design writing, one of the first such local publications and a beautiful visual platform. The title, which means 'take a look' in Hindi, invites readers to discover the new vernacular of India and consider possible future directions. The illustrations reflect the commentators' voices – respected figures from the Indian design community such as M.P. Ranjan and Amardeep Behl.

450. AUSTRIA SOLAR 2011 ANNUAL REPORT
Graphics, 2013

The 2011 financial report for Austria Solar is printed using a light-sensitive ink. Financial statistics and infographics printed within the document only become visible when sunlight falls on its pages. In order to render the report completely white under artificial light, the printers needed to carefully mix the correct ratio of light-sensitive ink colours. Once completed, the report was sent out inside a light-proof foil packet.

451. ZUMTOBEL 2011/12 ANNUAL REPORT
Graphics, 2013

Zumtobel's 2011/12 financial report was in two parts: first, the lighting company's business accounts; second, a powerful exploration of pure colour that represents Anish Kapoor's video installation *Wounds* and *Absent Objects* in print. Using tactile, uncoated paper, the designers worked closely with printers to experiment with deep saturated pigments. The final design pushed the printing process to its limits and used up to ten neon hues.

452. BAUHAUS: ART AS LIFE
EXHIBITION IDENTITY
Graphics, 2013

The graphic design identity for the *Bauhaus: Art as Life* exhibition at London's Barbican Art Gallery was a contemporary demonstration of the Bauhaus principles of form, scale and colour, created following careful study of the design principles of the Bauhaus School of Art, founded in 1919. APFEL's large-scale images and colour panels recall Bauhaus colour theory, and text was printed in Breite Grotesk, a new version of the Bauhaus typeface.

453. KAPOW!
Graphics, 2013

Kapow! is a novel set during the Arab Spring. The book creates a uniquely immersive experience that invites readers to open and unfold hidden pages and follow multiple texts flowing across and through other passages. The narrative takes place in London and Egypt, as the unnamed protagonist tries to make sense of chaotic and fast-moving events across North Africa. Designed by Studio Frith, the layout was created in close collaboration with the author while the novel was still being written.

454. DOCLISBOA '12 IDENTITY
Graphics, 2013

Commissioned to create the graphic design for the tenth annual Lisbon documentary film festival, local designer Pedro Nora delivered a political statement about the importance of independent arts events at a time of state funding cuts. Nora's design used images of black rocks against vivid yellow backgrounds, photographed to give the appearance of islands. These represent individual directors and their work, forming a metaphorical archipelago that signifies the plurality of ideas shared through the festival.

455. RIJKSMUSEUM IDENTITY
Graphics, 2013

For the new visual identity of Amsterdam's Rijksmuseum, Irma Boom developed a unique palette of 600 colours based on highlights from the museum's collection. The new logo incorporates a specially designed font (called, appropriately, Rijksmuseum) by typographer Paul van der Laan. The logo is a great example of a symbol whose very neutrality invites people to come and see what is behind it – an immense and rich collection of more than a million artefacts.

456. STRELKA INSTITUTE IDENTITY
Graphics, 2013

The non-profit Strelka Institute was set up to 'transform Russia's physical and social environment'. OK-RM's rebranding is based on a grid system reflecting the 'development of public space in Moscow'. Used for Strelka's website, signage and marketing materials, the identity is most effective on the covers of Strelka Press's digital books, where the basic grid is transformed into a new language of shapes in a distinctive yellow.

457. ORGANIC
Graphics, 2013

Organic is a unique pattern-resource book, which demonstrates how programming can help typography evolve in ever more innovative ways. It collects experimental pattern designs inspired by forms found in nature, such as flowers and foliage. Despite their abstract appearance, each of these patterns is a font that can be used to create new designs. The designers carefully evolved these forms in sets, subtly altering their positioning and dimensions to create full fonts.

458. THE OCCUPIED TIMES OF LONDON
Graphics, 2013

The launch issue of *The Occupied Times of London*, published during the 2012 Occupy London protests, was written, designed and printed in just forty hours. Designers Lazaros Kakoulidis and Tzortzis Rallis created a complete visual identity, a twelve-page layout and the entire first issue using volunteers and a £200 budget. Set in contrasting fonts, Jonathan Barnbrook's punk-infused Bastard and Panos Vassiliou's corporate-style PF DIN Mono, the newspaper has back pages that can be used as protest placards.

459. VENICE ARCHITECTURE
BIENNALE IDENTITY
Graphics, 2013

John Morgan Studio's graphic identity for the thirteenth Venice Architecture Biennale was a literal interpretation of its theme 'Common Ground', drawing on Venetian stencil street signs (*nizioleti*, 'white sheets') for inspiration. Morgan and his team not only digitised and updated the original *nizioleti* typeface, but also used local methods for the identity's signage, such as paint and stamps. Their pared-down colour and imagery, applied to exhibition graphics, posters, and banners for bridges, gave rise to an identity that is bold in its quietness.

460. MADE IN L.A.:
WORK BY COLBY POSTER PRINTING CO.
Graphics, 2013

Made in L.A. was a collaborative exhibition featuring old and new work by the Colby Poster Printing Co. The contemporary pieces were created by the show's curator, graphic designer Anthony Burrill, and exhibited at London's KK Outlet. The Colby Poster Printing Co., a family-run company founded in 1946, still prints posters using traditional silkscreen, woodblock and letterpress typesetting methods. Its work demonstrates a distinct West Coast vernacular, with a 1960s-influenced acid palette.

461. THE GENTLEWOMAN MAGAZINE,
ISSUE #6
Graphics, 2013

Edited by Penny Martin, *The Gentlewoman* was founded in 2010 by Jop van Bennekom and Gert Jonkers as a sister title to their men's magazine *Fantastic Man*. Since its creation, the publication's cover designs have strengthened its identity within a highly competitive market. For its sixth issue, the women's fashion magazine featured a startling portrait of the American TV actress Angela Lansbury, shot by controversial fashion photographer Terry Richardson.

462. AUSTRALIAN CIGARETTE PACKAGING
Graphics, 2013

In 2013, the Australian government made it a compulsory requirement for all cigarette packaging to conform to a strict template. Logos and branding are not allowed and seventy-five per cent of the package is covered by an image of a smoking-related illness. The legislation was aimed at preventing the development of brand loyalty. Now every brand must use olive-green Pantone 448c, identified as the least attractive colour for packaging.

463. RALPH ELLISON SERIES
Graphics, 2013

This series of book covers is for the reissued novels of author Ralph Ellison, one of the most important African-American writers of the twentieth century. Researching the project, designer Cardon Webb discovered Ellison's lifelong passion for music. Using the visual imagery of 1940s and '50s jazz records to evoke the era when Ellison's books were written, Webb's bold typography references the Harlem music scene to create book jackets that could just as easily be record sleeves.

464. GRAND-CENTRAL
Graphics, 2014

This graduation project by ECAL student Thibault Brevet is an experiment that creates a physical presence for a digital message. Grand-Central allows people to connect freely, but also to broadcast their conversations or comments in the familiar format of marker pens on paper. At its core is a machine connected to a website where people leave messages. The machine 'writes' these communications on reams of surplus paper, sourced from newspaper offset printing.

465. DRONE SHADOWS
Graphics, 2014

London-based writer, publisher, artist and technologist James Bridle brings attention to the presence of unmanned aerial vehicles (drones) by drawing them in public. On a 1:1 scale, Bridle outlines these aircraft on city pavements. They have appeared in the UK, Turkey, the US and Brazil. By putting the drawings in peaceful, everyday settings, Bridle's quietly potent work prompts contemplation about the ethics of using remote-controlled surveillance devices and the effect these might have on our communities.

466. SERPENTINE GALLERIES IDENTITY
Graphics, 2014

The launch of the Serpentine Gallery's new identity coincided with the opening of a gallery by architect Zaha Hadid and aims visually to unite the two Hyde Park spaces. In this fresh typology with bold geometry, the main visual device is an aperture or peephole on the page, which reveals a view on to another image, artwork or colour. This alludes both to the Serpentine's open parkland location and its approach to programming.

467. FRAC PROVENCE-ALPES-CÔTE-D'AZUR
IDENTITY AND SIGNAGE
Graphics, 2014

Located in Marseille, the FRAC centre for the south opened a new building by Japanese architect Kengo Kuma in 2013. As part of the '1% artistique' rule that new state-funded buildings must spend one per cent of their budget on artworks, Courant and Proyart were commissioned to create a new identity, the first time this rule had been applied to graphic design. The identity featured the typefaces Graphik and Steinschrift and a limited white-to-grey colour palette, with red accents.

468. ESCUYER IDENTITY
Graphics, 2014

Known for their quality underwear, Escuyer's name comes from the Old French word for squire, which, in turn, comes from the Latin for 'shield bearer'. When developing Escuyer's visual identity, Belgian graphic designers Modern Practice delved into heraldry, responding not only to the name but also to the brand's quiet, confident masculinity. In place of the colour and patterns of heraldic shields, the company name is used to create different geometric forms.

469. WORKS THAT WORK: A MAGAZINE
OF UNEXPECTED CREATIVITY
Graphics, 2014

A new international magazine that hopes to surprise the reader with a mix of features exploring creativity, *Works That Work* was founded by Peter Bil'ak of the Typotheque type foundry. Labelled 'the *National Geographic* of design', the biannual magazine includes in-depth essays and stories on refugee-camp gardens, improvised furniture, the shipping container, intercontinental aircraft and globalisation in the developing world, making it both a visual and an intellectual journey.

470. CHINEASY
Graphics, 2014

Chineasy is an illustrated learning method to help people learn Chinese, a language with an intimidating 20,000 characters. Illustrator Noma Bar opted to use the characters themselves as illustrations for the book, setting himself a rule that the character should form no less than eighty per cent of each image. These building blocks can be combined to form complex compounds and phrases.

471. M TO M OF M/M (PARIS)
Graphics, 2014

This monograph marks the twentieth anniversary of influential design studio M/M (Paris), founded by Michael Amzalag and Mathias Augustyniak. The alphabet is a recurring theme in their work, prompting Graphic Thought Facility and Emily King to organise the book alphabetically, but starting and finishing with 'M'. The large-format publication is framed by images of the studio's two 'M's on the front and back.

472. WHITNEY MUSEUM OF
AMERICAN ART IDENTITY
Graphics, 2014

For its move to a new building designed by Renzo Piano, the Whitney Museum commissioned Dutch graphic design studio Experimental Jetset to develop a 'graphic toolbox' for the Whitney's in-house design team. They used a zigzag line as a metaphor for the Whitney's complex approach to art history and to represent the initial 'W' of the museum's name. Their flexible identity uses the space carved out by differently proportioned formats to determine the positioning of this 'responsive W'.

473. ART DIRECTORS ANNUAL: 91
Graphics, 2014

For the ninety-first *Art Directors Annual*, Rami Niemi's illustrations combined simple, thick black outlines, soft sweet-like colours, stylised people and facial features with insightful wit,

honesty and a degree of naughtiness. Each year the Art Directors Club (ADC) in New York, a group of creatives in visual communication, celebrates with an annual awards competition. All the industry winners are featured in the *Art Directors Annual*.

474. BUILDING STORIES
Graphics, 2014

Made up of fourteen separate, differently sized books and pamphlets, *Building Stories* is a graphic novel about the lives of the inhabitants of a single Chicago apartment block. It includes intimate depictions of the lonely old lady who owns the building, an unhappy young couple on the first floor and a young art student who lost her left leg as a child. Chris Ware's drawings are economical, yet capable of capturing every emotion, with an impressive attention to detail.

475. CASTLEDOWN PRIMARY
SCHOOL TYPE FAMILY
Graphics, 2014

Neil Small, an East Sussex primary school headmaster, commissioned Colophon Foundry to design a font that was easy to read for dyslexic children. After carrying out workshops to teach the children about fonts, sizing, capital letters and lower-case letters, the designers developed a family of fonts that could work in different formats across the school. Castledown Primary School now uses these fonts for all correspondence, letters and signage, along with another font developed as a handwriting tool.

476. THE GOURMAND
Graphics, 2014

The Gourmand is a new high-quality, biannual magazine about food, the arts and culture that includes a broad range of writing, photography, illustration, interviews and criticism. Founded by David Lane and Marina Tweed, the magazine responds to the growing interest in food. Lane and Tweed's approach is creative, intelligent, unusual and engaging, favouring extreme styles of photography from Gustav Almestål's glossy tribute to gluttony and lust to Paolo Di Lucente's shadowy shots of New York diners.

477. MODERN DESIGN REVIEW
Graphics, 2015

This new biannual review of furniture and product design takes a creative approach to design journalism, with heavy emphasis on art direction and photography. The photographic still-life on the cover of the first issue, for instance, referred to the Japanese art of *ikebana* ('flower-arranging') by showing elements from the articles inside artfully arranged around a flower-arranger's foam brick.

478. JURRIAAN SCHROFER (1926–1990)
    Graphics, 2015
This is a thoroughly researched and comprehensive monograph on Jurriaan Schrofer, one of the most important Dutch graphic designers since the Second World War. Schrofer's career as a graphic designer, art director and environmental artist is fully explored, with more than 1,000 images of Schrofer's work. The sewn binding is laid bare to let the colour of the pages within show through, and Schrofer's typefaces have been adapted for the book by Radim Peško.

479. BANKNOTE DESIGN FOR NORGES BANK
    Graphics, 2015
After holding a competition, Norges Bank decided to develop their new Norwegian bank-notes by combining two designs from the eight-strong shortlist. On the front are Metric Design's illustrations, inspired by Norway's bond with the sea. The back design, a series of pixellated views of the coast, is by Snøhetta Design. The stylistic differences between these designs – between representation and abstraction – introduce a tone of modernity without losing the narrative tradition of banknote design.

480. MIT MEDIA LAB IDENTITY
    Graphics, 2015
The MIT Media Lab is an interdisciplinary research laboratory, where projects combine technology, science, art and design. The new identity took its cues from previous MIT identities, most recently Richard The and E Roon Kang's system from 2010 that could generate 40,000 permutations of the logo. Bierut and Fay's new logo is an 'ML' Helvetica monogram that uses the seven-by-seven grid of The's logo to create a network of glyphs to represent each of the Media Lab's twenty-three research groups.

481. WIRED CUSTOM TYPEFACE
    Graphics, 2015
When the technology magazine *WIRED* redesigned their identity, they commissioned new typographic section openers. The brief from Andrew Diprose, the magazine's creative director, was to create a sense of dimension, but within 'an ethe-real environment'. After designing the typeface, designers Sawdust created the 3D effect using Photoshop, with the light and shadows manually drawn using brushes.

482. DESIGNING FOR THE
    SIXTH EXTINCTION
    Graphics, 2015
A thought experiment in synthetic biology, *Designing for the Sixth Extinction* explores how new organisms might help to maintain biodiversity if we cannot conserve the planet's 'natural' species. Fungus, bacteria, invertebrates and mammals, made from non-biodegradable proteins, would be designed to replace extinct organisms or to protect against harmful invasive species, diseases andpollution. Ginsberg considers what the impact of this 'rewilding' would be on the environment, expressing her vision with graphics, photography and design patents.

483. THE WAY OF THE SHOVEL:
    ART AS ARCHAEOLOGY
    Graphics, 2015
This advertising campaign for the *The Way of the Shovel*, an exhibition at the Museum of Contemporary Art Chicago which explores contemporary artists' interest in history and archaeology, aims to make the show appealing to the general public. Newspaper inserts gave users the opportunity to become archaeologists through the familiar language of the lottery scratch-card: visitors could scratch off an image of a silver shovel (by artist Mark Dion) to reveal the offer of two-for-one admission.

484. KENZOPEDIA
    Graphics, 2015
Featuring strong graphic images with an intriguing, witty and sexy narrative, *Kenzopedia* was a series of illustrated blogs published on the website of the Paris-based fashion designer Kenzo through spring 2014. The images were created by Helsinki-based illustrator Toni Halonen, who produced twenty-six drawings to support Kenzo's spring collection using a bright, simplified colour palette. Each insightful post had a different letter of the alphabet: 'Z… is for Zips', 'U… is for Underground' and so on.

485. RIPOSTE MAGAZINE
    Graphics, 2015
Riposte is a new magazine for women. Each issue features five ideas, four meetings, three features, two essays and one icon. The aim is to cover a broader range of subjects, eschewing the dominant focus on fashion and celebrity found in other women's magazines. *Riposte* provides candid interviews with women whose achievements are self-evident. This honesty also transfers to the photographs of the women featured, which are not airbrushed.

486. 100 YEARS OF SWISS GRAPHIC DESIGN
    Graphics, 2015
100 Years of Swiss Graphic Design is a survey of a century of Swiss graphic design: typography, posters, corporate image design, book design, journalism and typefaces. Its images and essays cover a period when Switzerland emerged as a centre of graphic excellence with a focus on legibility and clarity. The design by Zürich-based NORM came about as a result of the Museum of Design Zürich's 2012 exhibition of the same name.

487. FRANCHISE ANIMATED
Graphics, 2015

When Amsterdam-based type foundry Animography came up with the concept of moving type, they asked 109 animators to animate a glyph using Adobe After Effects. The massive variations in style and technique hang together thanks to the classic but characterful letterforms designed by Derek Weathersby. A Vimeo 'trailer' leads to social-media showcases and segues to Animography's webshop, where the typeface can be downloaded for 'the price of a tweet'.

488. NO.5 CULTURE CHANEL
Graphics, 2015

To accompany an exhibition at the Palais de Tokyo in Paris on the history of Chanel No.5, Irma Boom created an all-white book that uses no ink, but is instead embossed with images and quotes from the scent's creator, fashion designer Coco Chanel. Boom wanted the book to evoke the essence of perfume: something that is strongly present yet cannot be seen. Without ink, the book becomes mysterious, light and airy.

489. INGLORIOUS FRUITS AND VEGETABLES
Graphics, 2015

Each year 300 million tonnes of fruit and vegetables are thrown away, with fifty-seven per cent of this due solely to the produce's irregular appearance. In response, French supermarket chain Intermarché launched a campaign that promoted produce that was misshapen, showing people it was just as tasty as 'better looking' food, but thirty per cent cheaper.

490. GLASGOW INTERNATIONAL 2014 IDENTITY
Graphics, 2015

Kellenberger–White's identity for the 2014 Glasgow International is a typeface inspired by the hand-painted lettering on the warehouses, docks and ships of Glasgow and nearby Faslane. Kellenberger–White used a roller to hand-paint each letter. This process dictated the weight of each letter and lent the digital typeface a direct, free and painterly quality that fitted perfectly with the festival's programme.

491. P98A PAPER
Graphics, 2016

P98a is an experimental workshop and gallery in Berlin, where multidisciplinary designers aim to rethink letterpress printing for the digital age. Mixing analogue and digital technology, they create new type using techniques such as 3D printing, computer-controlled routing and laser cutting, as well as reproducing old type cut from pear wood. Their findings are presented in *P98a Paper*, a risograph-printed publication with a letterpress cover.

492. CUYPERSPASSAGE TILE MURAL
Graphics, 2016

The Cuyperspassage is a 110-metre-long tunnel in Amsterdam, connecting the city with its ferry terminals on the IJ river. The design emphasises safety by clearly dividing pedestrians and cycle traffic, and the brightly lit raised footpath is lined with light, reflecting off hand-painted blue-and-white Dutch tiles. These make up a mural, designed by graphic designer Irma Boom using nearly 80,000 hand-painted tiles.

493. SHOT ON IPHONE: WORLD GALLERY
Graphics, 2016

The Shot on iPhone campaign celebrates the photos people capture every day on their iPhones, using examples of these non-commissioned images to advertise the latest model of the phone. The images were selected from online photo-sharing platforms and then presented in a white border with a simple tagline and the name of the photographer. The campaign embraced the rise of amateur photographers, and celebrated the way in which the iPhone has opened up access to world-class image-making.

494. BOTTOM ASH OBSERVATORY
Graphics, 2016

This 160-page book by designer Christien Meindertsma explores the waste material that is left after our waste has been burnt: bottom ash. By repeatedly sieving, analysing and separating tens of thousands of pieces by hand, she succeeded in extracting numerous materials. Meindertsma melted down the twelve most valuable – including zinc, aluminium and silver – and cast them as pure cylinders to show how much bottom ash could be worth.

495. ★
Graphics, 2016

The design and marketing campaign for David Bowie's last album was launched on his sixty-ninth birthday, just days before his death. It uses the simplicity of black, both matt and glossy, as a representation of Bowie's mortality. The unicode black star symbol (★) selected for the title also inspired the font. The design's poignant simplicity perfectly matches the album's reflective content.

496. THE NORWEGIAN LANDSCAPE PASSPORT DESIGN
Graphics, 2016

When the design of Norway's new passports was put out to tender in February 2014, Oslo-based Neue Design Studio won the contract with a concept they called 'Norwegian Landscapes'. The new design comprises a reduced version of a familiar theme: the beauty of the nation's natural and open landscapes. A particularly intriguing feature reveals itself when the passport is held under UV lights: the Northern Lights appear suddenly as part of the landscape illustration.

497. WE LISTEN
Graphics, 2016

We Listen is a campaign for the Samaritans, repositioning the charity as 'expert listeners' for people struggling to cope with a variety of issues and not exclusively for people who feel suicidal. Designed to be eye-catching even in busy transport hubs, the campaign uses unusual rear-view portraits by photographer Nadav Kander. The sparse, emotionally charged text exposes people's hidden feelings, while the use of attractive pastel colours, not normally associated with suicide-prevention advertising, help the posters stand out.

498. FIRST AID KIT FOR REFUGEES & NGOS
Graphics, 2016

Based on pictograms, this signage provides clear, easily understandable information to refugees in situations where they need help. It was developed to support and improve the communication process between refugees and NGOs in Vienna, providing some structure to often chaotic places. The project was initiated by designers who wanted to develop a tool to help refugees integrate in Europe. It also stands as a striking political state-ment following the European refugee crisis in the autumn of 2015.

499. CHANNEL 4 REBRAND
Graphics, 2016

Channel 4 was set up in 1982 as a UK public service broadcaster. When tasked with the channel's rebrand, the designers returned to the iconic 3D logo, designed by Lambie-Nairn. Instead of copying or aping the original, however, they broke it into individual blocks – emblematic of the channel's remit to be original and innovative. The associated films, directed by Jonathan Glazer, present the blocks as elemental forms born of nature.

500. HELLO RUBY
Graphics, 2016

Started as a Kickstarter campaign, *Hello Ruby* is part children's story and part activity book. It aims to introduce children to fundamental programming skills and computational thinking. Finnish designer Linda Liukas's book tells a story about Ruby finding gems, introducing concepts such as sequencing along the way. A glossary at the back explains some key terms and there are puzzles and fun activities to extend the ideas presented in the story.

501. DEAR DATA
Graphics, 2016

Dear Data is the unusual correspondence between two friends, Giorgia Lupi and Stefanie Posavec, one living in the US and the other in the UK. In place of email or social media updates, each week, for one year, they sent each other a hand-drawn postcard with data representing what had happened to them during the week: for example, how many times they had complained or smiled at people, or occasions when their partners had inspired their love or provoked annoyance.

502. ALMADÍA BOOKS COVER DESIGN
Graphics, 2016

After working with Almadía, an innovative Mexican publishing house based in Oaxaca, for more than ten years, graphic designer Alejandro Magallanes was given the freedom to build a distinctive identity for the publisher. He uses a combination of draw-ing, type style and flat colour to create a visual narrative that captures the specific character of each book's content, and employs visual and tactile surprises, such as cut-outs, to shock or amuse prospective readers.

503. GRUPA PROTEST POSTERS
AND PLACARDS
Graphics, 2016

GRUPA is an anonymous collective of graphic designers calling for political reform in Malaysia. Five days before the Bersih 4 protest march on 24 August 2015 (*bersih* is Malay for 'clean'), GRUPA – noting an absence of banners and placards – put out an open call to designers for protest materials. In just three days, they had released 110 posters online for free download. These raw illustrations and slogans draw on the designers' understanding of the power of the visual medium to communicate Malaysians' anger.

504. DIKKE VAN DALE DUTCH
LANGUAGE DICTIONARY
Graphics, 2016

Studio Joost Grootens designed the fifteenth edition of the oldest and most extensive Dutch dictionary, Dikke Van Dale. The designers took the radical step of reinterpreting the well-es-tablished existing format to make it easier and more inviting to use. Navigational elements were introduced, such as colour and the use of symbols and illustrations. For optimal readability, they designed a new typeface that took a year and a half to develop and test.

505. 'FRACTURED LANDS', THE NEW YORK
TIMES MAGAZINE, 14 AUGUST 2016
Graphics, 2017

Under editor Jake Silverstein and design director Gail Bichler, the weekly *New York Times Magazine* has been experimenting with special issues where it steps away from its regular design. The 'Frac-tured Lands' issue, designed by art director Matt Willey, is dramatically austere and book-like, with monochrome typography and bold chapter openers. It is an appropriate design for a 40,000-word piece of journalism about the recent history of the Arab world. The issue ran with no advertis-ing to interrupt the feature.

506. PRO-EU ANTI-BREXIT
POSTER CAMPAIGN
(VOTE REMAIN 23 JUNE), 2016
Graphics, 2017

Standing out in the noise created by both sides of the June 2016 European Union Referendum campaign, Wolfgang Tillmans' impassioned pro-European Union initiative exhorted the UK to vote Remain. Available to download for free from his website, the striking posters combined emotive statements with abstract landscape imagery that urged people to reject today's escalating extremism in favour of the Union's values.

507. THE REFUGEE NATION FLAG
Graphics, 2017

Yara Said is an artist who graduated in 2014 from the University of Damascus. What should have been a time of creative development was instead defined by civil war: she fled Syria in a refugee boat. Approached by The Refugee Nation organisation, she created a flag to represent refugee athletes at the 2016 Rio Olympics. Yara's simple and striking design became an act of hope, and an emblem for refugee athletes who marched to a new anthem, watched by millions globally.

508. FINDING HER
Graphics, 2017

Finding Her is a campaign that mimics the maddeningly labyrinthine scenes of *Where's Wally?*, but asks the viewer to find a lone woman among crowds of male workers. It is a creative way to show just how seriously underrepresented women are in Egypt's labour market: only twenty-three per cent of the workforce, among the lowest rates in the world, according to UN Women. Three Finding Her ads appeared in Egyptian magazines at the end of 2016.

509. WALES NATION BRAND
Graphics, 2017

Dylan Griffith and his team at Smörgåsbord have given Wales a comprehensive rebrand. Addressing every brand touchpoint, including core marque, bespoke typeface, tone of voice, photography guidelines and experiential initiatives, they have created a compelling and visually consistent approach to help reveal new and engaging stories about the nation. What began essentially as a tourism campaign had swelled into a nation-wide revamp, providing the whole country with a unifying visual identity.

510. IBIZA MYKONOS JEREMY CORBYN
(POLITICAL POSTERS)
Graphics, 2017

While not affiliated to any particular UK political party, designer Michael Oswell uses tropes of modernism to poke fun at the gap between political rhetoric and how people speak on the internet. Out of necessity, Oswell's posters exist as pre-print screenshots. They were rapidly assembled, then sent into the wilds of the internet to sink or swim. The result is a sense of pace and optimism, similar to the groundswell that allowed web-based groups like Momentum to gain traction.

511. REAL REVIEW
Graphics, 2017

Real Review is a quarterly contemporary culture magazine with the strapline 'what it means to live today'. Its agenda focuses on the politics of space, and how power relations are enforced and reinforced through everyday design conditions. To avoid advertising and to maximise editorial autonomy, *Real Review* was launched using crowd-sourced funding, and is now a membership-based model. Its distinctive vertical fold format responds to the functional and economic requirements of the post, while celebrating the ephemerality and anonymity of print in a digital age.

512. N.A.A.F.I
Graphics, 2017

Founded in 2010, the genre-bending underground record label N.A.A.F.I has a radical and political approach that dramatically changed the nightlife landscape of Mexico. In its early days, the label's eclectic sound was understood as a confrontational stance against the country's drug-related insecurity. Now it sounds like the soundtrack of a growing non-conformist generation, which has slowly infiltrated mainstream culture through the bold use of design as a communication tool.

513. UNIT EDITIONS
Graphics, 2017

Frustrated with contemporary publishers, Tony Brook, his wife Patricia Finegan and his friend Adrian Shaughnessy founded Unit Editions to make new books as well as they can possibly be made. Their mantra is: design books that no one else would think to publish. They operate out of the studio of Spin – Brook and Finegan's design group – and using Kickstarter projects, social media launches and sales on their website to create their audience.

514. ME & EU
Graphics, 2017

ME & EU is a collection of postcards written by British creatives and designed to be sent across Europe, with the aim of remaining connected after the Brexit referendum. The project is a reflection of how political engagement can be extended through design. ME & EU encourages people to become part of this movement, with a design that shows great aesthetic variation and makes clever graphic statements.

515. PROTEST BANNER LENDING LIBRARY
Graphics, 2017
This innovative library provides workshops for
people to make protest banners and is a resource
for those who want to borrow and use them.
The project enables protest against Trump's
political agenda in a number of meaningful ways.
First, by providing a communal space where
people can see, talk and sense solidarity. Second,
the concept of a library holding banners that will
be used and re-used recognises there are no quick
fixes to the political struggles we face today.

516. REYKJAVIK ART MUSEUM
VISUAL IDENTITY
Graphics, 2017
The most striking characteristic of the new
Reykjavik Art Museum's logo is that it never looks
the same. This is a sensible way to represent the
institution, since it exists in three locations: the
main complex, a modern art museum in a city park,
and an artist's former home. Given that visitors to
Iceland didn't realise these three sites comprised
a single museum, karlssonwilker's solution was
to create a rotating triangular logo, with each side
identifying the three locations.

520. NOBODY CHAIR
Product, 2008
Originating in a loose brief from a Swedish
prison, the Nobody was designed to be a light,
comfortable, stackable and noiseless chair that
could not be easily used as a weapon. The chair
uses industrial PET felt, largely from recycled
plastic bottles. This is thermo-pressed into rigid
upholstery. Supported by the inherent strength
of the textile alone, the chair has no structural
frame – 'no body'.

521. NEO COUNTRY COLLECTION
Product, 2008
Drawing on Dutch folklore for inspiration,
designer Ineke Hans creates wooden furniture
that combines rural vernacular elements with a
modern approach. With its simple, joyful forms and
intricately crafted joints, the almost toy-like quality
of the furniture gains an unexpected contrast
through the juxtaposition of artificial and natural
wood grains. The wood-grain-on-wood-grain
effect along the curved back of the chairs is
a decorative motif that is subtle without losing
any visual impact.

522. ANGLEPOISE FIFTY TABLE LIGHT
Product, 2008
Inspired by George Carwardine's original
Anglepoise lamp of 1932, the designer Anthony
Dickens gave the Fifty lamp a very different treat-
ment. The injection-moulded polycarbonate design
is disarmingly simple: a transparent shade with
a lamp fitting. The cable threads through the arm,
retracing the path travelled by its predecessors.
However, in contrast to the complex engineering

and flexibility of the original Anglepoise lamp,
the Fifty is frozen at a permanent angle of fifty
degrees in an irreverent homage.

523. FACETT SOFA AND CHAIRS
Product, 2008
Invited by French furniture manufacturer Ligne
Roset to create furniture that considers form
as its guiding principle, the Bouroullec brothers
responded by developing a compact and comfortable range. In Facett, the internal structure is
completely hidden in a single snug, fitted, quilted
cover. Cut from a single piece, the origami-inspired
quilting creates a soft, forgiving surface that
moulds to the body of the sitter, while giving a
crisp, geometric 'faceted' surface pattern to
the woollen upholstery.

524. 3W LED TORCH
Product, 2008
The Japanese company MUJI has a philosophy
of developing quality products at a low price by
avoiding the waste typical of many products –
unnecessary functionality, excess decoration and
needless packaging. Yohei Kuwano's three-watt
LED torch is an example of MUJI's principles in
action. The one-piece translucent polycarbonate
device minimises waste through its choice of
materials and limited components, while still
achieving instant recognisability by adopting
the classic shape of a torch.

525. PANNA CHAIR
Product, 2008
Japanese designer Tokujin Yoshioka developed
the Panna Chair as part of his ongoing research on
the potential of ordinary materials. 'Panna' comes
from the Japanese word for bread – the raw materials of this prototype are baked in a mould. The
design was taken into production by Moroso, who
used a similar concept but produced by more practical means. The final version is usually formed by
covering it in a white quilted industrial fabric.

526. MAKE/SHIFT SHELVING
Product, 2008
Make/Shift is a system of shelving units with
corrugated edges designed to fill awkward gaps.
The triangular units allow for great flexibility
whether stacked vertically or horizontally, creating
unique structures that provide a solution for
storage and variations for the display of objects.
Its designer, Peter Marigold, has an interest in
the basic qualities of materials. In its rejection
of ostentatious and wasteful ornamentation,
Make/Shift demonstrates an acceptance of
an emerging austerity in design.

527. 100 CHAIRS IN 100 DAYS
Product, 2008
Challenging himself to make 100 chairs in 100
days, Martino Gamper aimed to rethink traditional
notions of chair design. Each chair had to be

created from existing ones, using a stockpile of discarded, dumped or donated furniture. This self-imposed challenge forced Gamper to work and think at speed, akin to sketching in three dimensions. The result represents an unpredictable tonic to the saturation of the 'classic' chair in contemporary design.

528. INFOBAR 2 MOBILE PHONE
Product, 2008

In 2003, the Japanese product designer Naoto Fukasawa designed the original INFOBAR mobile phone for KDDI, a Japanese telecommunications company. The new phone, also designed by Fukasawa, has kept its original shape at heart: a rectangular handset with a single surface interface that is easy to operate thanks to the large gridded buttons. INFOBAR 2 also comes in a range of colours, some with different textures.

529. BAMBU TABLE AND CHAIRS
Product, 2008

The prototype for Bambu, the new line from the Finnish furniture company Artek, was inspired by creative director Tom Dixon's desire to make the furniture industry more sustainable. Bambu retained Artek's well-engineered modernism while incorporating more environmentally friendly materials and manufacturing processes. The furniture is made from pressed bamboo veneer, in a manner similar to Alvar Aalto's pioneering bent plywood of the 1930s.

530. ELECTRONIC CALCULATOR S
Product, 2008

PLUS MINUS ZERO is a product-design company based in Japan that creates electric appliances, such as a humidifier, a coffee and tea maker, and an electric heater. The Electronic Calculator S, designed by Naoto Fukasawa, is a compact device that succeeds in pairing elegance with simplicity and functionality. The clever addition of +TAX and -TAX buttons, for instance, enables the user to work out taxes in a more straightforward manner than traditional calculators.

531. MAYUHANA LAMP SERIES
Product, 2008

As an architect practising in Japan, Toyo Ito is best known for his conceptual yet elegant approach, a principle that also applies to his Mayuhana series of lamp for the lighting manufacturer Yamagiwa. Created by reeling string around a mould, the lamps are made in a manner similar to the way in which thread is spun off a cocoon. The softness of the light is enhanced by the layers of translucent string.

532. ONE LAPTOP PER CHILD
Product, 2008

One Laptop Per Child is a non-profit programme created by the Massachusetts Institute of Technology. The child-size laptop brings learning, information and communication to children where education is needed most: in developing countries. The result is an inexpensive and energy-efficient computer. The machine's reduction in energy use, by ninety per cent, meant it could be charged by hand-cranked power in rural villages. The laptop features Wi-Fi antenna 'rabbit ears' and energy-efficient LCD, digital writing tablet and integrated video camera.

534. SMITHFIELD HANGING LIGHTS
Product, 2008

Jasper Morrison is a designer who prefers to avoid inventing new forms wherever possible, choosing to adapt pre-existing archetypes for contemporary use instead. His range of Smithfield pendant lights is based on the anonymous industrial vernacular lighting that used to be found in London's covered markets. A moulded honeycomb diffuser softens the light, which as a result screens out glare.

535. SKETCH FURNITURE
Product, 2008

Using new three-dimensional technology, the Swedish design duo Front has developed a process that turns 'air' sketches into actual furniture. They filmed themselves creating freehand sketches of chairs, lamps and tables in the air, the movement of which was recorded using motion-capture software. The data was then translated into digital files, ready for three-dimensional fabrication using rapid prototyping technology.

536. EVA SOLO BIN
Product, 2008

Designed by the Danish studio Tools Design, the Eva Solo bin is a contemporary reinterpretation of the dustbin. When opened, the lid balances on the bin's edge and hovers there; only when it is nudged down does the lid shut smoothly. The lid acts as a bowl, which can be filled with refuse and carried to the bin. The rubberised metal ring that holds the bin-liner sinks into place by folding the mouth of the liner around the ring.

537. MOORE ARMCHAIR
Product, 2008

This nylon-lacquered armchair, designed by the French designer Philippe Starck, consists of a rectangular base with a 360-degree swivel seat. The sophisticated simplicity of this chair's form echoes the organic-inspired design of the mid-twentieth century, functioning equally well as a piece of sculpture or garden design. Starck is known for his playful wit and bold use of material, form and colour: Moore seating combines a cool, visual elegance with all the fun of a spinning seat.

538. MEDIA SKIN MOBILE PHONE
Product, 2008
KDDI is one of the largest telecommunications companies in Japan, providing handsets and network connections under its mobile communication branch. For their MEDIA SKIN mobile phone, designer Tokujin Yoshioka emphasised the tactile quality of the handset, using special textured silicon paint for the orange and white versions and smooth urethane for the black version.

539. EL ULTIMO GRITO EN
LA CASA ENCENDIDA:
100M BENCH INSTALLATION
Product, 2008
Commissioned to build public seating at the Casa Encendida in Madrid, Spanish designers El Ultimo Grito responded with a unique construction technique. Created over three days, the 100-metre-long bench began as a basic modular skeleton made from timber. The structure was then covered with bubble wrap and other packaging material and sealed and strengthened with shrink wrap. Every millimetre was then covered with over 90,000 stickers to create what has been described as 'graffiti furniture'.

540. MUON FOUR-WAY LOUDSPEAKERS
Product, 2008
The four-way Muon loudspeakers are limited to only 100 pairs worldwide. Each speaker is made from a six-foot-long block of solid aluminium that is machined in a week-long process to reach the final form, weighing a substantial 253 pounds. The speakers use KEF's Acoustic Compliance Enhancement technology to double the available volume through the absorption of air molecules by activated carbon. The six-millimetre thick enclosures are also heavily dampened to minimise any vibrations.

541. iPHONE
Product, 2008
Launched on 9 November 2007, the iPhone ushered in an era of technological sophistication never seen before. At a time when most mobiles relied on push-buttons, Jonathan Ive introduced an entirely new user interface based on a revolutionary multi-touch display that gives users control with just a tap, flick or pinch of their fingers. More than just a phone, the iPhone brings multiple technologies together to create a truly connected experience.

542. XL X-BEAM RATCHETING WRENCH
Product, 2008
The X-Beam revolutionises the traditional spanner thanks to a subtle but crucial design change. By adding a ninety-degree twist to its centre, the hand contact area is increased by 500 per cent over traditional wrenches, making the X-Beam the first hand-tool to be approved by the American Arthritis Foundation for its ease of use.

543. SATURN COAT STAND
Product, 2008
The Saturn is a visually stunning sculptural piece of furniture. Made from six interlocking geometric arcs, joined centrally to create a complex form, the coat stand is both beautiful and practical. The generous wooden arches provide ideal places to hang garments, while the arch can be utilised to place a hanger.

544. TAB LAMP PROTOTYPE
WITH REFLECTOR
Product, 2008
Edward Barber and Jay Osgerby belong to a generation of British designers that grew up strongly influenced by the restraint of English modernism. The Tab Lamp, available as a desk light, wall light and in a floor-standing version, reflects their simple yet modern approach. The engineered ceramic reflector provides a pleasing light quality, while the shade is adjusted by a subtle yet effective tab that gives the lamp its name.

545. WIND UP RADIO
Product, 2008
The original wind-up radio was designed by Trevor Bayliss for use in situations where the electricity supply was lacking or unreliable. From this idea, MUJI designed a miniaturised, lightweight radio that incorporates a hand-crank generator that, with a couple of turns, provides power for twenty minutes. The simple form reflects MUJI's ethos of quiet, unassertive design.

546. PIGGYBACK TABLE
Product, 2008
Thomas Heatherwick and his team responded to a brief for a dividable table by developing a solution that literally 'piggybacks' on its twin. Rather than adopting a stacking approach, they devised a groove and slot system that allows the two tables to merge seamlessly together. It was put into production by Magis using die-cast aluminium and oak veneer.

547. TRANSPLASTIC SERIES
Product, 2008
TransPlastic is of a collection of lights and chairs that imagines a synthetic world that has been overgrown by natural fibres. Like the body's ability to heal an open wound, the wicker forms grow over plastic structures, creating new hybrid structures. With a bold colour palette and dramatic shapes, the Campana brothers' designs combine the found and the new, and the natural with the artificial, to produce work that addresses social and political issues.

548. SAMSUNG REFRIGERATOR J-SERIES
Product, 2008
The Samsung Refrigerator J-Series is a side-by-side fridge freezer with seamless exterior design, user-friendly screen display and tower lighting. The design incorporates a removable tray that can

be used for serving, along with a 'home bar' that gives easy access to snacks and drinks without opening the entire fridge. Space is maximised by the Z-shelf design and a 'twin-cooling' system keeps temperatures constant.

549. PIZZAKOBRA TABLE LAMP
Product, 2008

PizzaKobra is a conceptually elegant yet technically innovative design: it takes the form of a chrome-finished steel tube with integral state-of-the-art LED light sources fitted into its tip and powered by a transparent cable. A series of invisible swivelling knuckle joints within the tube make it possible endlessly to reshape the lamp from a flat coil – its 'pizza' incarnation – to a serpentine task light.

550. TENORI-ON DIGITAL MUSICAL INSTRUMENT
Product, 2008

Tenori-On is a digital musical instrument with a 16x16 matrix of LED switches, any of which can be activated to create an evolving musical soundscape. A collaboration between Japanese media artist Toshio Iwai and Yu Nishibori of Yamaha's Center for Advanced Sound Technology, Tenori-On brings fresh elements to the more traditional musical experience. It provides six different performance and sound/light modes for versatility and these can be combined and used simultaneously for rich, complex musical expression.

551. TEN KEY CALCULATOR
Product, 2008

With its prominent buttons, the Ten Key Calculator is a tactile pleasure to use in comparison with the flush and unresponsive surfaces of digital calculators. However, rather than harking back to a comfortable bygone age, the Ten Key Calculator belongs to the modern world through the addition of an in-built USB cable. By connecting the calculator to a laptop, number-crunching becomes much easier than tapping buttons on the top row of a laptop keyboard.

552. VOLANT ARMCHAIR
Product, 2008

Patricia Urquiola's Volant system of seating combines a flamboyant and colourful upholstery seat with a slender, simple steel base-structure. With its soft textures, inviting colours and blousy form of layered fabric, the seat becomes the focus of attention. Floaty, rough edges recall the processes of dressmaking or tailoring. This unfinished look gives the chair an informal, relaxed and inviting quality.

553. WAVY CHAIR
Product, 2008

Ron Arad tends to challenge a material to its limits to create a completely new form. The design of this lightweight, stackable chair uses thermo-formed plastic (ABS) to create a moulded seat that captures the appearance of a piece of fabric in motion. The texture and shape of the chair both form part of the chair's structure. The seat, though fluid in appearance, is firm, with the armrests acting as structural supports, while the ribbed textured surface gives further solidity.

554. NINTENDO WII
Product, 2008

Wii was the fifth home-video game console from Nintendo. The way players interact with Wii was innovative in that its wireless remote controls are used as handheld pointing devices, detecting acceleration and orientation in three dimensions. Players thus play tennis or box as if they were actually on court or in the ring.

555. JAR TOPS
Product, 2009

Jar Tops are a simple yet ingenious way of making empty jars useful. There are five variations, allowing ordinary jam jars to be transformed into a milk jug, sauce jug, sugar shaker, oil/vinegar pourer or chocolate/herb shaker. The tops are made to fit 'twist off' jars, an international standard that is used for food jars with metal or plastic screw caps.

556. STACK CHEST OF DRAWERS
Product, 2009

Challenging our perception of what a chest of drawers can be, Stack is a 'floating' unit of drawers that can be pushed and pulled in either direction. A smart piece of thinking was required to figure out how the drawers could sit on each other. The result is a surprising and original alternative to a product that hardly ever changes.

557. LOVER'S CHAIR FROM THE EVOLUTION SERIES
Product, 2009

The Evolution Series presents a range of furniture that provides a refuge and a space to reflect, either by yourself or in the company of others. Designed in response to the uncontrolled and chaotic rhythms of everyday life, designer Nacho Carbonell demonstrates a striking understanding of intimacy in this age of heightened personal exposure.

558. COMPOSITE BENCH SYSTEM
Product, 2009

A modular system of cushions and bench elements, Composite is designed to work within a corporate environment while still rethinking conventional furniture design. Effectively, it deconstructs the sofa, rearranging its components on a purpose-built platform. As well as offering comfortable seating, there are handy surfaces to place books or bags. The effect is akin to an upholstered Japanese garden, with serene chiselled structural cushions.

559. FIG LEAF WARDROBE
Product, 2009

Highly ornate and impossibly romantic, Tord Boontje's Fig Leaf wardrobe is made of 616 hand-painted enamel leaves, in ten basic shapes. The complicated tangle of hand-formed supporting vines was made by an iron foundry in rural France, while the life-like tree and matching hangers used a casting process that is now almost obsolete.

560. CLEAN
Product, 2009

CLEAN is a series of brushes and dust collectors: a feather duster, a dustbin, a brush and brooms in two different sizes. Instead of being made through conventional industrial processes, each piece is individually hand-crafted. The handles are made from raw chestnut, which is steam-bent to form the desired curve to fit the brush attachment, an elegant alternative to the plastic dustpan and brush.

561. HOMEHERO FIRE EXTINGUISHER
Product, 2009

Technically, there is little wrong with standard fire extinguishers. However, they tend to end up hidden in a cupboard or out of reach when a fire starts. The HomeHero could thus help save your house, simply because it looks good enough to stay on a worktop in full view.

562. IPOGEO TASKLIGHT
Product, 2009

The design of the Ipogeo Tasklight was inspired by the undelivered promise of many tasklights, which often drift after they have been repositioned. Ipogeo's delicate and friction-free engineering means it can be positioned using little more than a finger, while its bold counterweights allow an astonishing reach of four metres.

563. CABBAGE CHAIR
Product, 2009

When Japanese fashion designer Issey Miyake was invited to curate the exhibition *XXIst Century Man*, he commissioned designers Nendo to create furniture from pleated paper – an unwanted by-product of making pleating fabric. Nendo's solution is disarmingly simple: they individually peeled back the outside layers of a roll of paper back, in the same manner as peeling cabbage.

564. SURFACE TABLE
Product, 2009

The Surface Table is a limited edition experiment by industrial designer Terence Woodgate and racing-car engineer John Barnard that aimed to push the design, materials and manufacturing of a table as far as possible. The result is a super-slim composite table. By exploiting the inherent rigidity of layered carbon fibre, Woodgate and Barnard have created a three-metre long table with a barely-conceivable thinness of just two millimetres at its edges.

565. THE MACGUFFIN LIBRARY
Product, 2009

A 'MacGuffin' is a term used by filmmaker Alfred Hitchcock to describe a filmic object that lacks intrinsic importance but keeps a cinematic plot in motion (such as the titular statue from *The Maltese Falcon*). This project proposes the foundations for a fictional library of MacGuffins, made using rapid-prototyping processes. The resulting object encourages viewers to imagine what the plot of the otherwise fictional film might be. This is design as a prop for storytelling and flights of imagination.

566. PIXEL CLOCK
Product, 2009

The Pixel Clock's face is made of honeycomb-effect fibreglass with 300 LEDs, which simulate the movement of hands on an analogue clock. The effect is paradoxical; the clock is clearly electronic, yet the illusion of moving parts persists.

567. MYTO CHAIR
Product, 2009

MYTO started as a project by chemical company BASF, who had developed a new high-tech plastic called Ultradur High Speed. Designer Konstantin Grcic was invited to create a new chair using the material. He discovered that the material contained nanoparticles which make it extremely fast-flowing in liquid form, so that even a complicated form can be created rapidly in a single mould with a single injection point. The resulting cantilevered form is a breakthrough in chair design.

568. ARMADILLO VEST WITH FACE MASK
Product, 2009

The Armadillo improves personal protection equipment for mine-clearing. Kode Design completely redesigned the face mask by introducing a new protective material that reduced its weight by fifty per cent, while integrated protective goggles are closer to the head, reducing visual distortion. The vest has a raised chest-cum-neckpiece that enables the overlapping shells of the face mask to fit into the vest when the wearer crouches to remove mines.

569. WORKIT OFFICE SYSTEM
Product, 2009

Vitra's office furniture system WorKit is based on a single small detail with a big impact; a cube-shaped connector unit named Pinbox. The Pinbox unit serves to secure and connect the tabletops while also defining the legs and providing holders for IT equipment and cable management. Individual workstations can be expanded and combined with each other.

570. STITCH CHAIR
Product, 2009
The Stitch Chair demonstrates an immediately obvious yet elegant mechanism for fold-away furniture. The hinges (or 'stitch') allow the chair to be easily folded open or closed in a swift single movement. As well as being clever engineering, the hinges lend the chair a certain aesthetic appeal.

571. MAGNO WOODEN RADIO
Product, 2009
A small and simple radio encased in a shell of wood, the Magno Wooden Radio is an example of entrepreneurship through design. Singgih Susilo Kartono is the creative brain behind Magno, designing the radio to help improve economic conditions and employment prospects for villagers in Kandangan, central Java. The radio is made from local, sustainable materials and uses local labour, with new employees learning the basic carpentry skills required in less than a week, despite having no craft tradition.

572. WITNESS FLAT
Product, 2009
Designer Jurgen Bey is regarded as a major exponent of narrative design. Invited to hold a show at Pierre Bergé's exhibition space in Brussels, Bey transformed the gallery into a show flat. The studio designed new furniture in wood and felt, referring to the building's history as a centre for fur trade. The furniture's pixelated form and materials refer to packaging used in the fur trade, acting as silent 'witnesses' to the building's invisible past.

573. LIGHT WIND
Product, 2009
Due to the oversized span of Light Wind's propeller, the energy generated by even a slight breeze converts wind power into light. The pleasing presence of this street lamp has the combined charm of Dutch windmills and the idea of self-sufficiency.

574. GREEN FELT PROTEST SUIT
Product, 2009
When the Serious Organised Crime and Police Act of 2005 threatened to make it an offence to stage a spontaneous protest within one kilometre of London's Houses of Parliament, designer Tony Mullin decided to stage a subversive protest in favour of free speech. His Green Felt Protest Suit imagines a world in which protestors can use Hollywood's green-screen digital technology to display on-screen political messages outside the Houses of Parliament while still technically complying with the letter of the law.

575. SENZ XL STORM UMBRELLA
Product, 2009
Due to its asymmetric design, the Senz XL Storm Umbrella always finds the best position in the wind. The form resists inversion and allows a good view out of the front, making it very comfortable to use even in strong gusts of up to seventy miles per hour.

576. ROTATIONAL MOULDED SHOE
Product, 2009
The Rotational Moulded Shoe explores the possibilities of using rotational moulding to make footwear. The process involves filling a negative mould with a small amount of liquid, which is then rotated at high speed. As the mould spins, the liquid solidifies against its inner walls. Ten Böhmer created a machine specifically for shoe production. The result is technically innovative and sculpturally beautiful.

577. CLOAKROOM AT THE MUSEUM
BOIJMANS VAN BEUNINGEN
Product, 2009
Commissioned to create a new cloakroom for the foyer of the Boijmans van Beuningen Museum in the Netherlands, Wieki Somers created something that falls between furniture, architecture and sculpture. Inspired by Jiska Rickels' film *4 Elements*, which shows mineworkers hoisting coats up and down a mineshaft, Somers produced a joyously ingenious carousel of levers and pulleys which is operated by members of the public.

578. VENUS NATURAL CRYSTAL CHAIR
Product, 2009
Japanese designer Tokujin Yoshioka describes the Venus Natural Crystal Chair as a message for the future. To make the chair, a fibre structure is submerged in a water tank to create ideal conditions for crystals to grow on to the structure. The shape of the chair evolves as the crystals multiply. At a time when making objects tends to be reliant on man-made applications and processes, the Venus Chair relies instead on nature.

579. STEELWOOD FAMILY
Product, 2009
The Magis Steelwood Family is built around the unexpected juxtaposition of steel and wood. Cut and pressed steel plates are simply connected with visible joints to wooden parts to build objects with formal autonomy but a familiar touch. This use of expressive materials with visible connections evokes a sense of the 'ready-made', and the furniture is designed to acquire a patina over time.

580. 3D STENCIL
Product, 2009
Like its two-dimensional counterpart, the 3D Stencil is subversive in its approach to product design. A cardboard mould in the form of a lampshade is attached to a wall and filled with

expanding foam. Once the foam has hardened the mould is removed, leaving the lampshade on the wall. A battery and LED provide a small light source, giving previously bleak surroundings unexpected domestic warmth.

581. PLANTLOCK
Product, 2010

PlantLock was conceived as a means of moving bicycles out of domestic hallways and stairwells by providing a secure means of locking them in front yards or gardens. Kept in place by sheer weight, PlantLock's appeal has spread to shops, restaurants, cafés, community gardens, parks, workplaces, schools and local authority street-use. The containers have been used to grow a wide variety of plants, flowers, hardy shrubs, vegetables and fruit – all while providing excellent security for bikes.

582. BLOWN-FABRIC LANTERNS
Product, 2010

The traditional Japanese chochin lantern is made of bamboo and paper. Nendo has reinterpreted the chochin by adopting blow-moulding technology and a special kind of non-woven fabric. Since the manufacturing process is impossible to completely control, each lantern takes a unique form, resulting in a collection of objects whose infinitely varied imperfections are reminiscent of the mutations of viruses and bacteria.

583. SKI HELMET FOR GIRLS
Product, 2010

Addressing the disparity between the number of girls and boys wearing ski helmets, Per Finne created a product just for girls. The result is narrower, lighter and smaller than other helmets, but not at the cost of safety. A curved shape around the neck leaves room for a ponytail and removable ear flaps make the helmet suitable for summer skiing.

584. GRASSWORKS
Product, 2010

One of the fastest growing plants on earth, bamboo is a grass that can be harvested again and again from the same stalk. Grassworks is a furniture collection of flat-pack, self-assembly structures made from bamboo sheet laminates. The designer Jair Straschnow wished to avoid the use of screws and glue, which led him to develop a new version of the traditional woodworking technique of the dovetail joint.

585. THE PALLET PROJECT FURNITURE
Product, 2010

The Pallet Project consists of chairs, lighting and even toys made from reclaimed materials. Products can be ordered online or, for a much reduced price, purchasers can download DIY instructions and make their own, bypassing costly

and unsound supply chains and enabling furniture to be created from reclaimed pallets anywhere in the world.

586. MU FOLDING PLUG
Product, 2010

Min-Kyu Choi's folding plug revisits the design of the standard UK electrical plug, which has remained largely unchanged since its introduction in 1947. Infuriated by having to carry around a plug that was thicker than his laptop, Choi developed a system that folds down to a width of just ten millimetres. The concept has since been expanded to include a multi-plug and a USB charger, allowing for several devices to be plugged in without messy cables and bulky multiple sockets.

588. CARBON FIBRE CHAIR
Product, 2010

Setting out to make the lightest chair in the world, Japanese architect Shigeru Ban turned to carbon fibre. While carbon fibre has extremely high tensile strength, it performs less well under compression. To exploit the material's advantages while avoiding its disadvantages, Ban sandwiched aluminium between thin layers of carbon fibre to create a new composite. The result is a wafer-thin super-light material able to withstand the pressures needed for a chair.

589. EXTRUSIONS
Product, 2010

Designer Thomas Heatherwick is known for his fascination with materials and manufacturing processes. Extrusions is an experiment in producing a potentially infinite chair using an extrusion process that squeezes aluminium through a chair-shaped die. With this specialist technology, traditionally used in the aerospace industry, Heatherwick Studio created the world's largest extruded piece of metal. While the benches were produced as limited-edition pieces, it is how this technique might be used to create architectural cladding or mass seating that really matters.

590. SETU OFFICE CHAIR
Product, 2010

Setu is the epitome of a task chair – designed and built to support and offer comfort to the user every day for hours at a time. The flexible bone-like ribs at the rear have a mimetic quality, seeming to reflect the sitter's spine. The form was inspired by the contours of the nautilus shell.

591. REPAIR PROJECT
Product, 2010

British designer Linda Brothwell uses traditional craft techniques to repair everyday objects within the public realm. As part of the British Council's contribution to Experimenta Design in Lisbon, she learnt traditional wood-inlay techniques. Using her new skills, she repaired local park benches by replacing broken oak slats with 1950s Portuguese domestic patterns and personal maps of the area.

592. THE IDEA OF A TREE
Product, 2010

The Idea of a Tree combines a freely available natural resource – light from the sun – with a mechanical process. Driven by solar energy, a machine creates one object each day. It starts producing when the sun rises, growing the object by pulling threads through a basin of glue and winding them around a mould. It stops when the sun sets, and the product is ready to be 'harvested'. Like the rings of a tree, the produced object is a record of its process.

593. CASE ABYSS
Product, 2010

CASE Abyss is an advanced data-logger for deep- and shallow-water oil and gas exploration. The device is stored on board a ship before being lowered 3,000 metres under water to collect data. Devices can be stacked, allowing ships to take more than twice as many as previously, resulting in faster and better data collection. The project is an example of how industrial design can be used as an analytical tool from concept through to the engineering phase.

594. 360° WORK CHAIR
Product, 2010

Konstantin Grcic's 360° family brings a playful edge to the potentially dull subject of office furniture. At first glance, the chair appears confusing. Do you sit on it sideways or straight? Do you use the upright as an armrest or backrest? Yet this flexibility is central to the chair's design, providing dynamic furniture for people who like to constantly change positions while they work.

595. KYOTO BOX
Product, 2010

The Kyoto Box is an oven powered by solar energy. The simple design is created from just two boxes, with an acrylic cover. The outer box is lined with silver foil, which reflects the sun's rays towards an inner box, painted black to absorb as much heat as possible. The cooker costs just £3.50 to manufacture and quickly reaches a temperature of 80°C, hot enough to boil water, cook dinner or bake bread.

596. HOUDINI CHAIR
Product, 2010

The pared-down proportions of the Houdini chair are made from a production method inspired by aeroplane model-making, which uses no nails or screws. Two flat plywood slabs are stretched by hand around a solid wood ring to form the back and part of the seat. The slabs are then glued to the base, producing the shape of the chair.

597. BREATHE FURNITURE
Product, 2010

Helen Kontouris's Breathe furniture family is designed for outdoor furniture manufacturer SunWeave. Breathe is enduring in two senses. Physically, it is strong, lightweight and resistant to indoor and outdoor elements. Stylistically, its unobtrusive form is designed with the hope that it will prevent the chair from becoming part of the culture of 'throwawayism'.

598. DESIGN BUGS OUT COMMODE
Product, 2010

Redesigning a commode for hospital patients may not be sexy, but it saves lives. PearsonLloyd's improved commode was a result of the Design Council's Design Bugs Out challenge, which asked designers and manufacturers to unite in the fight against superbugs like MRSA and C. difficile. A detachable plastic shell and robust stainless-steel frame make this commode easy to clean and store, while fewer touchpoints between patient and commode reduce cross-infection.

599. BEEHAUS
Product, 2010

Beehaus is a radical new design for an urban beehive. Traditional beehives, which date to the 1920s, tend to be unsuitable to the needs of hobby beekeepers, many of whom want rooftop hives. Made from easy-to-clean plastic and available in five colours, Beehaus has a sheltered landing area for easy access, a wasp guard to keep out unwanted visitors and triple-pocket insulation that keeps bees warm in winter and cool in summer.

600. CLOUDS
Product, 2010

A modular system of triangular textiles, Clouds fits somewhere between curtains, furniture and installation. Each tile is joined with elastic bands, allowing the user to sculpt their own three-dimensional forms by adding or removing elements over time. Users are provided with a kit of parts from which they can create a unique arrangement to suit a particular space.

601. PACT UNDERWEAR
Product, 2010

PACT takes underwear design into new realms of sustainability. Made of 100 per cent sustainable organic cotton, grown within a 100-mile radius of production, the garments feature patterns promoting different environmental charities and are shipped in compostable bags.

602. PARCS FURNITURE
Product, 2010

Parcs is an innovative new programme that challenges the design of workplace furniture. A hybrid between architecture and furniture-making, Parcs offers a range of spaces where staff can work away from their desks in informal and collaborative settings. The management of acoustics and privacy, and the appropriate provision of technology, help to deliver a new type of workplace, which challenges traditional archetypes.

603. DESIGN AND DEMOCRACY:
   BLANKE ARK
   Product, 2010

To cast a vote is a fundamental democratic right, yet many voting systems make it difficult for people to do so. Blanke Ark is an entire product system for democratic elections in Norway, encompassing the voting booth, ballot box, signage and the ballot paper itself. The entire system was designed to make the act of voting accessible and welcoming to everyone, including wheelchair users, the visually impaired and those who cannot read.

604. WORLDMADE SPORT WHEELCHAIR
   Product, 2010

The Worldmade Sport is a low-cost sports wheelchair designed to help grassroots pro-grammes in low-income countries. Motivation's £150 solution is a tenth of the price of many other sports wheelchairs, yet doesn't compromise on quality or adjustability. The lightweight steel frame meets international regulations for wheelchair basketball and tennis, while differently sized wheelchairs can be purchased and adjusted to the needs of individual athletes.

605. SUGRU
   Product, 2010

Sugru is a silicone-based putty that hardens over a couple of hours. Fresh from the pack, it is like modelling clay. Leave it overnight, it forms a durable and flexible material that is dishwash-er-safe and heatproof. It can be used to mend things, stick things together, patch up holes, and create any number of add-ons to existing products.

606. REAL TIME
   Product, 2010

Real Time replaces the mechanisms of analogue clocks with human performances. In one project a person appears to live inside a grandfather clock, perpetually drawing the time on the face minute by minute. In another, two men sweep lines of rubbish around a public square, mimicking the hour and minute hand. For a third project, two assistants stand behind a giant 'digital' timepiece and change the digits manually using squeegees, brushes and a bucket of black latex. The project is a subtle commentary about commodified time and human labour.

607. THE STORY OF STUFF
   Product, 2010

The Story of Stuff is a twenty-minute film presenting a critical vision of American consumer society. Presented in an engaging and simple format, the film tackles complex issues, including the notion of built-in obsolescence. The film also offers impassioned suggestions about possible solutions and points of intervention. Criticised and celebrated in equal measure, *The Story of Stuff* has been seen by an estimated eight million people.

608. SOMA
   Product, 2010

Soma (meaning 'body' in Greek) is an atmospheric light installation, created from intertwining forms of two-millimetre-wide tinted glass filaments. The filaments are woven together to produce spatial structures, sprayed with polymer to generate a skin-like crust. The lights are akin to illuminated coral, transforming their immediate environment into an underwater landscape.

609. HOPE CHANDELIER
   Product, 2010

Hope is a modern interpretation of the traditional chandelier. Utilising the principles of a Fresnel lens, designers Francisco Gomez Paz and Paolo Rizzatto have created a high-quality plastic that they refer to as 'meta-crystal' due to its capacity to capture and refract light. Delicately moulded polycarbonate leaves are carefully arranged around a light source to avoid glare and ensure a perfect diffusion of light.

610. POLYTOPIA
   Product, 2010

Cutting-edge contemporary furniture is difficult to pull off, frequently delivering an imbalance between aesthetics, comfort and concept. Lucas Chirnside's Polytopia seating system strikes a balance between the three issues. Conceived as communal seating, Polytopia examines how people interact and communicate while sharing a space. The cascading geometry can be arranged in multiple configurations.

611. SAMSUNG N310 MINI NOTEBOOK
   Product, 2010

Naoto Fukasawa's N310 laptop has many of the qualities of a portable, well-proportioned notebook. Fukasawa's design exploits a tendency to favour physically pleasing objects, as smooth corners combine with a tactile rubberised casing to produce a product just begging to be picked up and used.

612. L'EAU D'ISSEY
   ETTORE SOTTSASS EDITION
   Product, 2010

In 1997, the Italian architect Ettore Sottsass produced three drawings for Issey Miyake's new perfume bottle. The sketches lay on Miyake's desk for a decade. When Sottsass died in 2007, Miyake developed his design as a tribute. Normally left invisible, the delicate polypropylene tubes that carry the perfume to the spray are transformed into the bottle's defining decorative feature.

613. PALINDROME SERIES
Product, 2010

Peter Marigold's Palindrome Series explores symmetry in furniture. A reinforced composite casting material is layered into a simple wooden mould, which is then opened up, turned inside out and used to create the opposing side to the cast. The form, textures and details on one side are mirrored on the other. Imperfections and damage become complementary features, circular saw marks become symmetrical decorative swirls, knots in the wood become motifs and holes become handles.

614. IN-BETWEENING CLOCK
Product, 2011

The In-Betweening Clock displays time as a continuous, fluid entity by melting digital digits together. While the sweeping arms of an analogue clock suggest the flow of time, this is not the case with digital displays, which switch crisply from digit to digit. Taking its name from an animation technique that creates the necessary 'in-between' frames when given a starting and end image, Park's clock generates frames between the fixed moments of displayed time.

615. FREECOM MOBILE DRIVE CLS
Product, 2011

Organising and managing data is one of the biggest challenges of our time. On an individual level, the data problem can seem overwhelming. The Freecom CLS allows users to create a digital storage library in the old-fashioned, physical mould. Data is stored, organised and labelled on any number of cartridge-like drives, any three of which can be connected to a single dock at one time.

616. CONTEMPLATING MONOLITHIC DESIGN
Product, 2011

Launched at the 2010 Salone del Mobile in Milan, Contemplating Monolithic Design presented a future vision of electronics design, merged with furniture and home architecture. Sony designers worked with Barber & Osgerby to create an all-encompassing, fully immersive experience, constructed in a space designed to eliminate superficial sounds and views. Acoustic foam wedges of varying heights formed this anechoic landscape, while the diverse archetypes on display included lighting, furniture and architecture.

617. ACT FIRE EXTINGUISHER
Product, 2011

Most fire extinguishers are visually intrusive for easy identification in an emergency. ACT avoids this by connecting to a wireless fire alarm system and alerting users with sound and light from the extinguisher when the alarm is triggered. And instead of confusing meters and gauges, ACT sends the user a text message when servicing is needed.

618. PLUMEN 001
Product, 2011

An imaginative masterclass in using design to transform something of bland utility into a thing of coveted beauty, Plumen makes the bare bulb chic. Rather than hiding the unappealing low-energy lightbulb behind boring utility, Plumen 001 is designed as an object the owner would want to show off. The glass tubes take an irregular yet harmonious form, the two organic shapes mirror one another to create symmetry, and the silhouette changes from every perspective.

620. PAVEGEN
Product, 2011

Pavegen harness the energy generated from footsteps to power street lighting, signage and information displays. The top rubber panel flexes around five millimetres with each impact, sparking internal components to convert this kinetic movement into electrical energy. Five per cent of the power produced is used to make the slab light up. The remaining ninety-five per cent can run low-power applications, such as streetlights, pedestrian lights and wayfinding solutions. The rubber surface is made from recycled car tyres.

621. PLAYING WITH LEGO
BRICKS AND PAPER
Product, 2011

LEGO Bricks and Paper is a collaboration between Japanese retailer MUJI and Danish manufacturer LEGO. The two organisations explored how various combinations of artistic activities stimulated new forms of creative play, with the aim of developing a product to help parents engage in creative craft play with their children. MUJI's paper puncher enables children and parents to draw, colour in, cut out and put together paper or card creations using LEGO bricks.

622. AMPLIFY CHANDELIER
Product, 2011

Traditional chandeliers are made of numerous lights and crystals. Yves Béhar challenged this by creating a chandelier from a single crystal, one LED light and one faceted paper shade. Six different shapes, each carefully crafted to maximise refractions on the inner surfaces of the shade, mean each light becomes a large glowing paper crystal.

623. PRAMPACK
Product, 2011

PramPack is a wheeled bag designed to protect prams during transportation. Inspired by the repeated damage her seven-month-old son's pram sustained during air travel on a round-the-world trip, inventor Anne Morkemo decided to research the issue. Six prototypes later, PramPack was approved by several airlines. It fits almost all types of prams, and can be rolled up when not in use.

624. DYSON AIR MULTIPLIER
Product, 2011

The blades on a conventional fan chop the air as they spin, causing uneven airflow and constant buffeting. Dyson's Air Multiplier technology amplifies the surrounding air, giving an uninterrupted, smooth stream. Drawn in by an energy-efficient brushless motor, air is accelerated through the circular loop of the fan and passes over an airfoil-shaped ramp that channels and directs its flow. Air behind and around the fan is then pulled into the airflow and amplified.

625. COLLEC+ORS COLLECTION
Product, 2011

Collec+ors is a collaborative and interrelated body of work by Australian furniture designer Khai Liew. Six eminent visual artists were invited to make work illustrative of their current practice, which was then integrated within an individual, one-off design by Liew. Collectively there is a shared aesthetic vision, a common language underpinned by overlapping frames of reference, a rigorousness of process and meticulous attention to detail.

626. DUNE FURNITURE
Product, 2011

Designed as modular lounge furniture for public spaces and outdoor use, Dune is an expandable system with an endless number of combinations. This flexibility guarantees maximum comfort and, when the elements are arranged in a group, multiple opportunities for connection. Manufactured from fully recyclable fibre-cement panels, the units are durable and able to withstand the demands placed on public seating.

627. BRANCA CHAIR
Product, 2011

Branca is a revolution in wood-carving, marrying craft knowledge with industrial routing techniques. Made from a single piece of wood, Branca's back legs support the critical joints of the armrest, seat and back like branches supporting the joints of twigs and leaves. The complexity of its three-dimensional design is belied by the way the armrest seamlessly grows out of the back leg.

628. FLYING FUTURE
Product, 2011

Flying Future uses ninety Novaled OLED (organic light-emitting diode) modules set into a large transparent plastic sheet in a gridded pattern. The modules are created from glass substrates, which render them transparent when switched off, creating the effect of a delicate cloth floating in the air and moving in the wind.

629. BLUEWARE COLLECTION
Product, 2011

With Blueware, Glithero adapted the Victorian technique of blueprinting to capture impressions of botanical specimens on ceramics using light and photosensitive chemicals. Using age-old preserving techniques, humble weeds from inner-London pavements are pressed, dried and then delicately composed on the surface of a vase or tile. Working with light-sensitive chemicals, the objects are exposed for several hours under ultraviolet light, which develops a photogram in intense Prussian blue. What remains is a crisp white silhouette of the specimen.

630. SEE BETTER TO LEARN BETTER
Product, 2011

See Better to Learn Better is a free children's eyeglasses programme developed in partnership with the Mexican government and Augen Optics. The collaboration has led to a collection of customisable and stylish corrective eyewear, specifically designed for six- to eighteen-year-old students whose families are unable to afford the cost of eyecare. Yves Béhar created frames that were durable and ergonomic, and that children could personalise by choosing the style and colour themselves.

631. VIGNA CHAIR
Product, 2011

For the Vigna Chair, Martino Gamper took inspiration from one of the most popular examples of early mass manufacturing: the ubiquitous Thonet bentwood chair. Gamper mimics Thonet's revolutionary use of steam-bent wood by making Vigna's seat element from double-injection plastic moulding, a favoured industrial process of contemporary mass-manufactured furniture. The legs climb like vines – from which the chair gets its name – elegantly entwined around one another to form the main structure on which the seat is fixed.

632. QUARZ SERIES
Product, 2011

Max Lamb's Quarz is a series of crystal tumblers representing perfect mathematical prisms. The shapes mirror the hexagonal prisms formed when quartz – the main raw material for glass production – grows in an uninhibited space. Each tumbler is mouth-blown into the same cylindrical wooden mould, then cut at three assorted heights, providing variation within a manufactured production process.

633. INTIMATERIDER
Product, 2011

IntimateRider is the only product on the market designed to enhance sexual mobility for those with limited or no lower-body muscle control. Originally designed by a C6-7 quadriplegic for his own personal use, the designer wanted to provide a natural fluid motion that would help people with an assortment of physical challenges in their intimate relationships. No motors or springs are used; a gentle movement of the head or upper body is enough to set the swing chair in motion.

634. DROP TABLE
Product, 2011
In this collaboration with furniture company Living Divani, Junya Ishigami exploits manufacturing processes to create something close to a one-off: a transparent table with a top which acts like a kind of magnifying lens. Drop is created from a single piece of Perspex, the lower part of which is curved like a lens, playfully manipulating the sense of depth beneath. The entire production process takes over fifty hours.

635. DIAMANT SERIES COFFINS
Product, 2011
The Diamant Series is a line of universal, timeless coffins and urns, where form and emotion unite to provide a dignified farewell. From concept to production the design process lasted more than two years and involved seventy-five prototypes. The coffins are made by local Danish craftsmen and assembled by hand from Nordic birch ply. They are available in black or white lacquer finish, with a hand-finished interior upholstered in organic cotton.

636. PLYTUBE
Product, 2011
Plytube is made by applying the technologies for making basic cardboard tubes to wood veneer. Royal College of Art graduate Seongyong Lee's process wraps laminates together and hardens them with glue. The resulting material is very light, extremely strong and suitable for different types of tooling and finishes. The resulting series of furniture demonstrates the specialist qualities of Plytube, including structural rigidity and lightness.

637. ENDLESS CHAIR
Product, 2011
Endless is made from pellets of recycled refrigerators, extruded as a single continuous ribbon by a programmed robot. The unusual production technique is, in a sense, itself recycled. Designer Dirk Vander Kooij rescued his robot from a Chinese production line after a 140,000-hour non-stop career and transformed it into a large-scale prototyping machine. For each chair, the production process requires the designer to work in tandem with the robot.

638. iPAD
Product, 2011
Apple's iPad was the first genuinely usable and consumer-facing tablet computer. While previous devices relied on clunky interfaces operated with a stylus, the iPad offers the multi-touch user interface and the operating system used by the iPhone. Unlike the iPhone, the iPad is not successful because it is innovative, but because it performs tasks in a way that is more intuitive, enjoyable and engaging than similar devices.

639. SAYL TASK CHAIR
Product, 2011
The Sayl chair is the lowest-cost task chair Herman Miller has ever produced. It combines ergonomics, material savings, quality, aesthetics and comfort. One of the main distinguishing elements is its full-suspension frameless back. Removing unnecessary elements resulted in the development of the Y-shaped rear tower and the ArcSpan, which allows fine-tuning to mirror spine curvature.

640. WALL PIERCING
Product, 2011
Aptly named, Wall Piercing appears to penetrate the wall from which it hangs, tacked on simply like a piercing. The circular lamp uses composite materials to seamlessly blend its fixtures into its surroundings and become part of the physical structure of a building. Each individual piercing is an austere hoop of LEDs, lodged shallowly into a wall, which diffuses its own shadow to give the appearance of being shrouded in a light tulle fog.

641. YII
Product, 2011
In Taiwanese philosophy, Yii (meaning 'change') is the underlying law of nature. Taking this as inspiration, Yii is an ambitious design project aiming to create strong and sustainable links between local craft traditions and contemporary design practice. The first Yii collection focuses on skilful craftsmanship and manufacturing processes deeply rooted in a harmonious relation between man and nature. The pieces include Starbucks coffee cups made from basketwork, ceramics and blown glass.

642. SPUN CHAIR
Product, 2011
A completely rotational symmetrical form, Spun grew out of Heatherwick Studio's research into simplifying the geometry of familiar objects. Using full-size test pieces, they developed a chair in which the seat, back and arms all share the same profile. At first glance, the result looks more like a sculptural vessel. However, it forms a comfortable and functional chair, in which the sitter can rock from side to side or even spin round in a complete circle.

643. THIN BLACK LINES SERIES
Product, 2011
Designed by the seven-strong Tokyo design team Nendo, the Thin Black Lines series includes furniture, lamps and vases exploring the theme of outlines. Rendered in simple black lines fashioned from bent steel, the forms are inspired by Japanese calligraphy. Their distinct graphic quality creates an illusion of objects cutting through space, simultaneously appearing as two-dimensional shapes and three-dimensional forms.

644. ONE ARM DRIVE WHEELCHAIR SYSTEM
Product, 2011

The One Arm Drive by Nomad is a sleek, compact wheelchair that, as the name suggests, can be moved using one hand. It shows that design for disabled people need not be clunky and ugly. It has got a sense of 'cool' and it is easy to manoeuvre. The wheelchair is lightweight yet strong – made from aircraft-grade aluminium – and designed to be practical, with quick-release wheels.

645. LEVERAGED FREEDOM CHAIR
Product, 2011

The Leveraged Freedom Chair is a mobility aid designed specifically for developing countries, where the only connections to education, employment and community are a long distance over harsh terrain. The LFC has a variable mechanical advantage lever drivetrain that enables its user to travel ten to twenty per cent faster on tarmac than a conventional wheelchair, and off-road like few other mobility aids. All moving parts are made from bicycle components easily found in any developing country.

646. UNIVERSAL GOWN
Product, 2011

Ben de Lisi's radical redesign of the standard NHS gown is designed for comfort and ease of movement while preserving the patient's dignity. The Universal Gown fastens with polymer press-studs that provide access for IV drips and other equipment without exposing the patient's skin. Completely reversible, nursing staff can place the press-stud openings on the side nearest to any bedside equipment, while the polycotton fabric feels soft against the skin.

647. ORIGIN PART I: JOIN
Product, 2011

Join is a series of three space dividers handmade in traditional Japanese wood joinery (known as *tategu*). In each piece, two lined frames are visually merged to create a product that departs from the conventional aesthetic. The intention is, while respecting the traditional core of *tategu*, to raise awareness of and interest in the vanishing craft. The *tategu* technique allows the joining of material through highly precise joints, with minimal glue and no screws or nails.

648. SOLO BENCH
Product, 2011

Solo Bench is part of Domingos Tótora's line of recycled cardboard furniture. Motivated by the huge amount of material discarded by local businesses, the designer began to use cardboard as a source material. Starting with recycled cardboard pulp, Tótora works with local craftsmen to create objects and sculptures where beauty is inseparable from function.

649. EARTHQUAKE TABLE
Product, 2012

At any given time, more than 300 million pupils face danger as their schools are unable to provide adequate protection from earthquakes. This earthquake-proof table is strong enough to withstand a ceiling collapse, yet is still affordable and light enough for two children to lift and move around in everyday use.

650. CARBON BLACK WHEELCHAIR
Product, 2012

Inspired by Formula One techniques and materials, Carbon Black is a high-tech, bespoke carbon-fibre wheelchair. Andrew Slorance, the designer, was inspired to produce a new model that did not look like medical equipment. Carbon fibre is lightweight and strong, but also warm to the touch and can be moulded into attractive ergonomic forms. Carbon Black is full of attractive features, such as inbuilt LED lights that can illuminate dark paths at night.

651. NEST LEARNING THERMOSTAT
Product, 2012

Nest is a high-tech thermostat that learns its user's habits and programmes the household temperature accordingly. During the first week, inbuilt sensors records how the thermostat is used. When the temperature is adjusted, the dial glows orange for heating and blue for cooling, and shows the time it will take to reach the required temperature. The thermostat wirelessly links to the internet, and can be controlled remotely.

652. WHITE COLLECTION LIGHTS
Product, 2012

These high-luminosity lights were designed in Finland where, during the long winter, people can find it hard to get enough light to maintain physical and mental well-being. The collection's central light, Bright White 1, is medically certified for bright light therapy. Elegant frames were created for the lights, using finely crafted birch veneer and plywood that is painted white and fitted with acrylic diffusers.

653. HARBOUR CHAIR
Product, 2012

The Harbour Chair is designed for public and domestic spaces alike. It has been designed specifically to take advantage of recent advances in mechanical tooling processes, which allows the manufacturer to finish the chair by hand and still be able to offer it at an affordable price. The result feels incredibly smooth underhand.

654. THE CRATES SERIES
Product, 2012

Beijing-based Jingjing Naihan Li created The Crates series as a response to the city's warp-speed development, which forced the designer to move four times in one year. The collection includes not only a sofa, desk and bed, but a home cinema and table football. Apart from the collection's comprehensiveness, its pieces are distinguished by how well conceived and detailed they are.

655. 1.3 CHAIR
Product, 2012
Balsa wood has never before been used to make furniture, as it is considered too soft. However, designer Kihyun Kim has developed a process of treating balsa wood that makes it robust enough to be used for furniture. Inspired by the De Havilland DH.98 Mosquito, the wooden British bomber, the lightweight 1.3 Chair is made from compressed balsa wood with a hardwood veneer for extra structural stability.

656. ASCENT
Product, 2012
This collection of lamps is inspired by the structural and engineering form of moving craft, building on Ed Barber and Jay Osgerby's shared passion for planes and boats. Osgerby grew up close to an air base, while Barber developed a fascination with boat design while sailing as a child. Ascent references the duo's love affair with moving craft; for example, by drawing inspiration from the shape of a boat's hull, or the delicate tensile framework of a kite.

657. HERACLEUM LIGHT
Product, 2012
A light that looks like it has been made by nature, this decorative LED lamp was inspired by the Heracleum plant genus. During the day, the lamp looks like a tree in winter. At night, it brings to mind a swarm of fireflies. The white lenses emanate from one branch, creating a technical yet natural structure.

658. NSEPS
(NOT SO EXPANDED POLYSTYRENE)
Product, 2012
Silo reinvents one of the modern world's ubiquitous materials in an unexpected way. After experimenting with EPS (expanded polystyrene) – a material widely used for packaging fragile goods – the chair's designers realised that they could make a chair mould by filling one-off hand-sewn textile moulds with coloured polystyrene granules. The mould is then steamed in order to expand the polystyrene. Inflated and hardened, the fabric mould is removed to reveal NSEPS chair's pixelated form.

659. OAK INSIDE FURNITURE
Product, 2012
Commissioned to produce a contemporary interpretation of the 400-year-old Dutch Hindeloopen furniture, Christien Meindertsma looked back to the early use of decorated oak. This traditional furniture was decorated with colourful flowers, birds and garlands – motifs

influenced by the journeys made to Scandinavia by sailors from Hindeloopen in the seventeenth century. Meindertsma's experiments revealed that oak turns dark blue when it is treated with iron.

660. A-FRAME AND CORB
Product, 2012
After the chair, designing spectacles is a favourite challenge for designers. It is rare to see new ideas in this field, but Ron Arad has done so. The A-Frame's adjustable wire frame is reminiscent of the central hinge of binoculars. The second line, named after the architect Le Corbusier, contains an inventive vertebra-like structure.

661. DEFIBTECH LIFELINE VIEW AED
Product, 2012
Lifeline VIEW is an automated external defibrillator (AED) that can provide a life-saving electric shock to restart or reset the heart rhythm of a cardiac-arrest victim. Through clear, step-by-step video and audio instructions, it guides a rescuer through CPR resuscitation procedures. The interface design is clever enough to allow untrained bystanders to deliver the immediate reaction that is often the key to saving lives.

662. OLYMPIC TORCH 2012
Product, 2012
The torch relay is one of the most iconic and enduring Olympic traditions. The shape of Barber & Osgerby's design for the London 2012 Olympic Torch is made from aluminium alloy, perforated with 8,000 circles (the same number of individuals who took part in the relay) using cutting-edge laser technology. Functionally, the circles reduce the weight and ensure that heat from the flame is quickly dissipated without being conducted down the handle.

664. JAMBOX
Product, 2012
Compact enough to fit in a pocket or small bag, Jambox is a portable Bluetooth wireless audio speaker that generates a sound loud enough to fill a room. Designed by Yves Béhar, it features a smart rubber casing with a faceted metal grill that covers the front, back and sides. The result is a speaker that is satisfyingly robust yet pleasing to the touch.

665. HÖVDING CYCLE HELMET
Product, 2012
The Hövding cycle helmet provides inflatable head protection for cyclists. It takes the form of a folded airbag worn around the neck. If an accident occurs, the airbag inflates into a hood that surrounds and protects the cyclist's skull. The trigger mechanism is controlled by sensors that pick up the abnormal movements that occur during an accident.

666. HEMP CHAIR
Product, 2012
This prototype Hemp Chair is manufactured with a process used in the car industry for door linings and glove compartments. The plant fibres of hemp and kenaf are mixed with a binder that sets at a heat of around 160°C to form a strong and lightweight composite material consisting of seventy per cent natural fibres. The cantilevered chair is moulded as a single piece, with contoured fold lines adding strength to the structure.

667. OSSO CHAIR
Product, 2012
The Osso chair is assembled from geometrical wooden panels that slot perfectly together. The pared-down simplicity of the chair is achieved by using digitally controlled machinery alongside highly skilled handcraft techniques. The high-tech construction gives the chair both strength and lightness of form.

668. MOON ROCK TABLE
Product, 2012
Inspired by the moon's craters, the surfaces of Moon Rock tables are decorated with intricate marquetry made from plastic laminate, a humble material that Bethan Laura Wood elevates to a thing of beauty. The patterns, reminiscent of cut agates or imaginary space landscapes, add value to what is often perceived as a cheap, imitative material.

669. BOTANICA
Product, 2012
Plastic is now so ubiquitous that it has little value. When designing their Botanica collection, Studio Formafantasma decided to approach the project as if oil-based plastics had never been discovered. In their research, the designers discovered unexpected textures, materials and processes offered by natural polymers extracted from plant or animal derivatives. Botanica illustrates Formafantasma's ongoing interest in creating work that reflects the materials from which it is made.

670. LIGHTWOOD CHAIR
Product, 2012
Lightwood uses the least possible amount of wood to achieve a lightweight but strong dining chair. One of the problems of designing a solid wood chair is finding a way to produce the seat. Jasper Morrison's breakthrough was to add a mesh to the frame to create the seat. Superficially, Lightwood looks like a conventional dining chair, but on closer inspection it adds up to more than the sum of its parts.

671. CHASSIS CHAIR
Product, 2012
Using innovative technology from the car industry, Chassis is a multi-purpose chair formed using a sheet steel frame. Stefan Diez's chair is lightweight and covered with a replaceable shell of finely grained four-millimetre-thick polypropylene. The chair's strength and elegance is achieved through thin profiles of pressed sheet steel that are cunningly jointed and robotically welded.

672. ORB-IT VACUUM CLEANER
Product, 2012
The Orb-it is a spherical handheld cordless vacuum cleaner. Small and compact, it is designed for delicate jobs such as dusting a computer keyboard. A button releases the handle and nozzle from inside the circular form, making the cleaner ready for use.

673. THE SOLAR SINTER
Product, 2012
Solar Sinter is a solar-powered machine that prints out glass objects made from desert sand. It was developed by Markus Kayser as part of a project to explore the potential of manufacturing in a desert environment. In a world increasingly concerned with questions of energy production and shortages of industrial raw materials, this experiment explored the potential of desert manufacturing using the abundant resources of sun and sand.

674. TMA-1 HEADPHONES
Product, 2012
Pared down in appearance yet robust in performance, these matt-black headphones were developed and tested by twenty-five professional DJs. The pliant, nylon single-piece headband supports two detachable ABS plastic ear cups. Moving the oversized belt-style notches on the headband adjusts the head size. A bold simplicity of design belies a complex, highly crafted headset that includes injection-moulded nylon and forty-millimetre closed titanium drivers that provide the highest possible sound quality.

675. TIP TON CHAIR
Product, 2012
The Tip Ton is an informal, comfortable chair that transforms into a work chair in one easy, forward-tilting action. The chair then remains stable in its new position. The Tip Ton's name was inspired by the shape of the chair's rocker-style legs, which curve upwards at the front.

676. SHADE
Product, 2012
Simon Heijdens delights in using elements from nature as a starting point to re-evaluate the spaces and places that define daily life. His multimedia installation Shade brings nature indoors by making the weather visible, using a live sensor that tracks the movement of the wind. The wind's movement then manifests itself in the form of a captivating LED light projection on the windows of the building, changing their opacity from transparent to shaded.

677. XXXX_SOFA
        Product, 2012
This is an innovative three-seater sofa that can be compressed into either a two-seater or a chair. Inspired by the repetition of geometric shapes, its designer created a concertina-shaped unit made from a few simple components: joint, ring and straight lengths. When viewed alone, the individual parts do not appear particularly special, but when assembled their beauty becomes clear.

678. TOTEM LIGHTS
        Product, 2012
Totem is inspired by familiar scientific, medical and cooking equipment made from Pyrex. The parts are stacked into spectacular totemic configurations, creating crazy but sparklingly clear chandeliers. Each piece locks to one another along the central core, a delicate balancing act made possible only by the material's extraordinary lightness.

679. WAVER ARMCHAIR
        Product, 2012
Waver is an armchair with a swivel base, featuring materials and structures inspired by windsurfing and paragliding equipment. A lightweight fabric seat hangs snugly over the back of the cantilevered tubular steel frame and is suspended by two straps at the front. The fabric is cut precisely to fit the human form and provides both support and room for movement.

680. THIXOTROPES
        Product, 2012
Thixotropes is a moving sculpture comprising eight illuminated, mechanised structures. Each structure is an arrangement of intersecting geometric profiles, constructed from thin tensed steel banding lined with rows of LEDs. The steel banding spins on its own axis at a bewildering speed, 360 times per minute, creating the illusion of solid cones of alternating warm and cold light.

681. TEXTILE FIELD
        Product, 2012
Textile Field was a thirty-metre-long gently inclining upholstered platform built for the Victoria and Albert Museum's Raphael Gallery. Visitors could sit, lie or walk on the platform as they viewed the Raphael Cartoons. Colour was an important element: thirteen different shades of grey, blue and green fabric, arranged in bands, were carefully chosen to reflect the delicate colours in the Cartoons.

682. MINE KAFON
        Product, 2012
Mine Kafon is a wind-powered landmine-clearance device. The spherical structure rolls with the wind like a huge tumbleweed, its weight detonating any mines in its path. A GPS tracking device sends information to a website that charts the areas that have been cleared. Its designer, Massoud Hassani, was born in Afghanistan, where there are thirty million anti-personnel landmines covering twenty-five per cent of the landmass.

683. LITTLE SUN
        Product, 2013
Olafur Eliasson is known for his all-enveloping art installations such as The Weather Project at Tate Modern in 2003, which placed a giant sun inside the Turbine Hall. With Little Sun, he has designed a solar-powered lamp for the 1.6 billion people worldwide without access to mains electricity. Once charged, a high-end LED emits five hours of light. Importantly, Little Sun was designed to allow local distributors in developing countries to profit from selling it.

684. LIQUID GLACIAL TABLE
        Product, 2013
The Liquid Glacial table plays with the idea of water as structure, capturing its surface tension and fluidity in clear, prismatic acrylic. The smooth, placid tabletop belies the turbulent flow of vortices below, which spiral downward dramatically to form the legs. The complex design was modelled using 3D computer-graphics software that simulates chaotic systems and natural phenomena. A computer-controlled milling machine carved the table from a solid block of acrylic, which was polished by hand.

685. FUTURE PRIMITIVES
        Product, 2013
A table leg turns into a cantilever lamp, a shelf seamlessly merges into a table, and seating blends into a cabinet – the minimal structures and their pure compositions of the Future Primitives furniture series may appear spartan in style, yet it is the playful combination of functions that positions this collection firmly within the contemporary.

686. RE-IMAGINED CHAIRS
        Product, 2013
Born out of a tight project deadline and budget, Studiomama turned to their east London neighbourhood to provide the raw material for their Re-Imagined Chairs. Salvaged metal frames from discarded chairs were collected, cleaned and powder coated in bright colours, and bulbous seats and back rests added. This project is representative of Studiomama's approach, which often explores the reuse of existing and second-hand materials.

687. W127 WINKEL LAMP
        Product, 2013
Berlin-based product designer Dirk Winkel created this slim black desk lamp to show that plastic can be as attractive as metal or wood. The w127 winkel is made from a fibreglass-reinforced bioplastic containing sixty per cent castor oil from

the castor plant, making it recyclable and more environmentally sound than crude oil-based plastics. It also incorporates a new form of adjustment – forty-six miniature gas springs instead of the more conventional metal springs.

688. BEOLIT 12 PORTABLE SPEAKER
Product, 2013
Small and portable, the Beolit 12's progressive design-thinking links Bang & Olufsen's exceptional sound quality to Apple's AirPlay technology and wireless smart devices. The leather strap and perforated aluminium give a handmade feel and suggest a love of craft reminiscent of early industrial equipment.

689. A-COLLECTION FURNITURE
Product, 2013
The A-Collection provides an insight into the Bouroullec brothers' obsession with thoughtful simplicity. The innovative use of the bent-ply strengthening rib linking the centre of the seat pad to the cleverly fabricated equilateral triangle nesting legs is the dominant feature – this looks initially as if it might be irritating, but is in fact quite comfortable.

690. COLOUR PORCELAIN
Product, 2013
By exploiting a legacy of local Japanese master-pieces and colour spectrums – aquarelle blue, light green, red-orange and ochre – Stefan Scholten and Carole Baijings have produced a collection of tableware born of Asian craftsmanship, yet infused with quintessentially Dutch insight. Presenting three editions which feature grids, lines and layered colours, the designers unite distinct visuals in a sleek, tempered synthesis of colour, material and texture.

691. CHILD VISION GLASSES
Product, 2013
An estimated sixty million short-sighted children in the developing world lack access to proper eye care. The Child ViSion project allows young people to adjust the power of their glasses to correct their own vision, using a fluid-filled lens technology. Thin and perfectly round, a rigid front lens and hard-coated back membrane form a cavity for silicone oil, which can be driven in and out of the lens by two simple adjusters.

692. SWITCH AND SOCKET COLLECTION
Product, 2013
Inga Sempé's collection is a radical re-thinking of the humble light switch and electric socket. Longiligne, for example, is easily operated with an elbow if your hands are full. The decorative relief patterns of the Trompe L'Oeil wall sockets disguise their function, which is only revealed when a plug is inserted. The Variateur dimmer switch indicators are hidden behind their knobs until they are turned on, avoiding visual clutter.

693. MEDICI CHAIR
Product, 2013
Most manufacturers outsource production, but the wooden furniture producer Mattiazzi still works with its own machines and artisans. When Konstantin Grcic was invited to produce a new chair, he expressed a wish to return to his roots as a cabinet maker. He set himself an exercise to make a three-dimensional chair using only the two-dimensional form of the plank; the most basic of wooden components. The finished chair is not conventionally attractive, but it is surprisingly comfortable.

694. 100 CHAIRS
Product, 2013
100 Chairs is a charity project, featuring furniture woven in PVC piping by ex-prisoners from Colombia as part of a rehabilitation project. While the furniture follows local forms with tradi-tional patterns, the twenty colours were chosen by the fashion house Marni. All profits went to ICAM, an organisation that allows the infants of female prisoners to grow up with their mothers in domestic surroundings.

695. KIOSK 2.0
Product, 2013
Inspired by Bruce Sterling's science-fiction short story 'Kiosk', Unfold's project explores the possibility of digital fabricators becoming part of everyday life. The designers created a vending rickshaw, just like a fast-food stall, that fixes bro-ken shoes, prints out gifts or manufactures hacked downloads of products. During Milan's Salone del Mobile, Unfold used Kiosk to print 'cover versions' of classic designs. Some designers encouraged them; others considered it illegal. As a provocative talking-point, it certainly succeeded.

696. PALMA KITCHENWARE
Product, 2013
Japan Creative, a non-profit organisation set up to draw attention to Japanese crafts, brings new life to businesses by inviting contemporary designers to collaborate with them. Jasper Morrison's cast-iron pots and pans stand out for their practicality and beauty. Cast iron is an environmentally friendly material for cooking utensils which can last up to 100 years if treated properly. Morrison's design introduces the humble cast-iron pot to a new generation of consumers.

697. FACETURE VASES
Product, 2013
The mould for the Faceture vase series is made from a sheet of folded plastic that can be manually manipulated each time it is used, rendering each vase unique. Although the sharp-lined accuracy of these vases mimics the precision of 3D printing, it comes as a surprise to learn they are entirely handmade. Even the workbench and casting

jig have been hand-constructed, with the low-tech process centre stage in the designer's accompanying video.

698. WELL PROVEN CHAIR
Product, 2013

The Well Proven Chair emerged from research into the re-use of sawdust. Designers James Shaw and Marjan van Aubel discovered a chemical reaction between sawdust and bio-resin, in which the resulting mixture expands up to five times its original volume and sets hard. They developed a moulded chair shell with this new, sustainable composite material. The rawness of the back of the chair tells the story of how it was made.

699. PLUG LAMP
Product, 2013

Too many plugs, not enough sockets. With Plug, design studio Form Us With Love created an ingenious and beautifully designed solution to the frustration of millions of gadget nomads worldwide: a dimmer lamp with the added bonus of an electrical socket for charging laptops or smart devices. Plug's human and humorous qualities may have single-handedly ended domestic quarrels and workplace spats.

700. PIERRE HARDY TRAVEL SPRAYS
Product, 2013

Inspired by accessories designer Pierre Hardy's ability to combine luxury and geometric rigour, perfumer Frédéric Malle invited him to redesign the portable fragrance atomiser. The resulting limited edition run of 1,500 metal cylinders, each hand-sprayed in two high-gloss colours, is a feast for the eyes. Using the existing fragrances, Hardy's handbag sprays add a new dimension to the perfume range's olfactory pleasure.

701. SURFACE TENSION LAMP
Product, 2013

Front has contrasted the extraordinary longevity of the LED bulb, which should last twenty-five to thirty years, with the ephemeral nature of a soap bubble, which gradually expands around the bulb until it bursts. A small container at the top of the metal pipe contains the liquid, which is picked up by a mechanical device and a small fan. These generate air pressure to inflate the liquid.

702. FLYKNIT RACER RUNNING SHOE
Product, 2013

The Flyknit Racer running shoe took Nike more than four years to develop. Wrapping around the runner's foot like tendons, the digitally knit, form-fitting, single-layer upper is made of strong, lightweight fibres that provide maximum support and flexibility at key points. The minimal use of material yields a total weight of 160 grams, making the Flyknit Nike's lightest running shoe.

703. KIT YAMOYA ANTI-DIARRHOEA KIT BY COLALIFE
Product, 2013

ColaLife is an independent non-profit working with Coca-Cola to use their vast distribution channels in developing countries to carry medication to areas that small charities would otherwise find difficult to reach. The AidPod is a clever multi-use container that fits into the unused space between the necks of bottles in a Coca-Cola crate. It also functions as a measuring jug, mixer and cup, for storage and potentially as a water-sterilisation device.

704. THE SEA CHAIR
Product, 2013

The Sea Chair is an example of how design thinking can be applied to social processes beyond the production of objects alone. The designers show how waste plastic picked up by fishing trawlers can be transformed into chairs on board the boat, then sold by the fishermen. The plastic is sorted by colour and chopped into small bits, then melted at 130°C in a DIY furnace. The fishermen can then sell the chair for their own profit.

705. ENGINEERING TEMPORALITY FURNITURE
Product, 2013

Engineering Temporality is a series of objects that seems to defy the concept of furniture: fragile and ephemeral rather than functional and structural. Tuomas Markunpoika Tolvanen enclosed wooden furniture within an irregular framework of small tubular steel rings and lit it on fire, leaving behind a empty reminder of the original. The motivation of the young Finnish designer was personal: the design reflects his grandmother's declining health due to Alzheimer's disease.

706. PAPAFOXTROT TOYS
Product, 2013

PostlerFerguson have been making miniature reproductions for several years, from hyper-realised cardboard replicas of AK-47 rifles to a Boeing 747 engine fabricated out of Styrofoam. While most of their early works were one-to-one scale replicas, their toys for Papafoxtrot are scaled-down toy realities of engineered hardware, from container ships to satellites. These give the impression of future archival artefacts from a modern engineered world.

707. MAGIC ARMS: 3D-PRINTED ROBOTIC EXOSKELETON
Product, 2013

Emma simply called her robotic exoskeleton 'Magic Arms'. Before the idea of using 3D-printed plastic parts, robotic exoskeleton devices were made of metal too heavy for toddlers. For these littlest patients, this often caused extra problems. Emma's medical team saw the potential of 3D-modelling, and can now easily tweak their designs and print new parts immediately.

708. GRAVITY STOOL
Product, 2013
Jólan van der Wiel has harnessed natural phenomena – gravity and magnetism – to invent an entirely new manufacturing process to make a stool. Instead of pushing a material into a preconfigured shape, he built a special machine that uses magnetic fields to draw out a form, dramatically and unequivocally embodying the forces that have configured it. The result is theatrical, spiky and expressive.

709. REPLICATOR 2
Product, 2013
While previous iterations of 3D printers tend to be large and expensive, Replicator 2 is small enough to be used on a table. Not only can it be used to make true-to-life replicas, high-resolution models and functioning prototypes but, in the future, you might buy a digital file and manufacture your own object (and even spare parts), eliminating shipping costs and the whole production line.

710. TIÉ PAPER CHAIR
Product, 2013
Part of a ten-piece collection responding to the materials and crafts of Yuhang, an ancient Chinese district in Zhejiang Province, the Tié chair uses rice paper made from bamboo layered into a mould. The material, usually used to create paper umbrellas, is then fashioned into a one-piece form combining back, arms and legs with a ledge to enable a beechwood seat to be dropped in.

711. LONDON 2012 OLYMPIC CAULDRON
Product, 2013
One of the most abiding memories of the 2012 Games in London was the sight of Thomas Heatherwick's Olympic Cauldron rising from the ground during Danny Boyle's inspiring opening ceremony. Each of the 204 competing teams carried an individually crafted copper object into the stadium, accompanied by up-tempo music. In the end, these copper petals rose together to make one massive flame, representing the joining of sportspeople around the world.

712. ESOURCE
Product, 2013
Seventy per cent of electrical and electronic waste from the United Kingdom is exported to countries like Ghana. There, informal recycling processes, such as burning electrical wires to recover the copper inside, pose significant health risks. Esource is a bicycle-powered cable recycling system that uses water to separate copper and plastic. Unburnt copper can be sold for considerably more than burnt copper, providing a higher income for workers as well as healthier working conditions.

713. TEKIO LIGHTING
Product, 2013
Named after the Japanese word for adaptation, Tekio is a modular lighting system that reappropriates the familiar Japanese paper lantern, the chochin. Reminiscent of flexible ventilation ducting, the tubular concertina form allows sections to be manipulated into limitless shapes for total flexibility within any space. Sections can be made in straight, circular, figure of eight, corkscrew and chain-linked forms.

714. LIQUIGLIDE KETCHUP BOTTLE
Product, 2013
Great design is not always about changing the world through grand, life-altering statements. Sometimes it is just about making something a little bit better. We love the humble glass ketchup bottle for its tasty contents, but hate it for its pouring stubbornness. Engineers Dave Smith and his team at MIT coated the inside of the classic tomato ketchup bottle with a FDA-approved substance, allowing the previously dogged condiment to slide right out.

715. LITTLE PRINTER
Product, 2013
Little Printer is a delightful product that spans the digital and physical worlds. The small printing device sits in your home and brings you information from the web – news, pictures, tweets and calendar notifications – from a range of sources. When you want something to read, just press the button on the box and it prints a personalised newsletter on receipt paper.

716. CORNICHES
Product, 2013
Corniches are a kind of usable sculpture, with a mixture of simplicity and joy that would not be possible without audacity in equal measure from both designer and producer. Normally, shelves are presented in the context only of themselves – rational, ordered and structured. Corniches play a different game – that of asymmetry and randomness – that probably reflects more accurately how we actually live.

717. SIMPLE COLLECTION
Product, 2014
Philippe Malouin's Simple Collection of furniture shows a remarkable sensitivity to materials and details, letting them speak for themselves while revealing the designer's humble rigour. Curated by Maria Cristina Diderot, an exhibition of the collection at Milan's ProjectB gallery included a candle that swung like a pendulum, propelled only by its melting wax.

718. STRING LIGHTS
Product, 2014
Michael Anastassiades's expressive simplicity lies at the heart of String Lights. The chief joy comes from how the electric flex is used to inscribe space. By looping and elongating the cable across a room, the light fitting can be suspended at a precise point. The lighting installation becomes a graphic intervention into the architecture.

719. PET LAMP
Product, 2014
Álvaro Catalán de Ocón's PET Lamp project uses discarded PET bottles to create domestic lights in collaboration with Colombian artisans. Each lamp begins as one PET bottle. The neck provides structure and the bottle is lacerated to form a warp, into which the plastic or natural-fibre weft is woven. Artisans select colours and patterns based on their own weaving traditions.

720. BODLEIAN LIBRARIES CHAIR
Product, 2014
When the University of Oxford's Bodleian Libraries reopened after a lengthy renovation, it seemed right to commission a new chair that respected its venerable surroundings. Barber & Osgerby's three-legged oak chair has a strong contemporary presence, while still respecting the traditions of its surroundings. The vertical wooden back reflects the spines of the books on the shelves, while the upholstered seat and generous arms provide ample support and comfort for scholars.

721. UDUKURI FURNITURE
Product, 2014
Japanese designer Jo Nagasaka uses a traditional Japanese wood-polishing technique called *udukuri* to manipulate the Douglas fir surfaces of his furniture, peeling them to expose the grain and create an uneven face. Brightly coloured epoxy resin treatments are then applied to the surface, delivering a smooth finish that celebrates the natural woodgrain within – albeit through a vibrant, glossy hue.

722. NEST PROTECT SMOKE AND
CARBON MONOXIDE ALARM
Product, 2014
A follow-up to the Nest Thermostat, Nest Protect is a household smoke alarm. Rather than obsessing about the next big idea, Nest's designers focus on refining the small points of interaction 'friction' we quietly accept, but which mess us about. Nest Protect learns from the user, eliminating false alarms at the wave of a hand. In the case of a real fire, it tells you where the blaze is, so you can plan a safe exit.

723. CLEVER CAPS
Product, 2014
Clever Caps is a line of bottle-top building block caps for jars, bottles and tubes. The product has two lives: one as a cap and one as a component for making many kinds of objects (toys, lamps, stools, boxes, wall panels and so on). This transformation occurs without additional energy consumption or industrial manufacturing processes, requiring only the assembly of the individual, LEGO-compatible pieces.

724. GOPRO HERO3 BLACK VIDEO CAMERA
Product, 2014
With the introduction of the GoPro Hero3 Black, the video profession looks set to go the way of photography. The Hero3 Black retains the affordable appeal of earlier models, but adds clarity, colour and professional quality – all conveniently supported by the speedy editing capability of the new MacBook Pro all-flash architecture. This thing is a survivor: its flight-recorder black-box aesthetic is just right.

725. FORM 1 3D PRINTER
Product, 2014
Formlabs was a small start-up by MIT Media Lab veterans that drew in Royal College of Art graduates and engaged directly with major players in the sector. It offers professional quality at a mass-market price and redefines how 3D printers should look: part kitchen appliance and part high-spec record player, with a hint of laboratory equipment.

726. ALBA VASE COLLECTION
Product, 2014
Alba is a collection of polyethylene vases manufactured by Serralunga, a company with long experience in plastics. Despite their archetypal forms, the vases are unique for the gradient that brings the smooth surface of the vases to life. The peculiarity of Alba lies in the process used to produce it, which pushes traditional rotational-moulding technology to the limits of its unexplored aesthetic potential. Rather pleasingly, no two vases are alike.

727. LUNAIRE LAMP
Product, 2014
Lunaire is a wall and ceiling lamp producing lighting effects reminiscent of the phenomenon produced by eclipses. Depending on how the small disk is positioned, two different effects are possible: back-lighting, when the front disk is pushed towards the wall, or from inside the diffuser when the disc is pulled forward. Simply pulling or pushing the rod on the front of the disk changes the effect to suit your mood.

728. PLUME CYCLE MUDGUARD
     Product, 2014
Mudguards spoil the clean, elemental lines of a bike. They cause friction against the wheel, break easily and are frequently stolen. Made out of flexible sheet steel that recoils under the saddle, Plume is barely visible in profile. In its coiled state, it looks like a tight circle, which cleverly incorporates a reflector disc; when extended for rainy days, it floats like a blade above the rear wheel.

729. LUFFA LAB
     Product, 2014
Most of us think of a loofah or luffa as a tool for scrubbing our backs in the shower, with little appreciation of what it is actually made from and what else it might be useful for. Designer Mauricio Affonso has taken the trouble to find out. It turns out that loofahs have amazing material properties and a huge range of potential applications: from acoustic wall tiles and limb splints to toxin-absorbing dyes in manufacturing processes.

730. RIPPLE TABLE
     Product, 2014
This dining table weighs less than 12.5 kilograms and uses eighty per cent less material than solid timber structures. The lower weight also reduces the table's overall carbon footprint through raw material use and transit considerations. Ripple's patented corrugated-plywood construction delivers a very high strength-to-weight ratio and is achieved using Sitka spruce, a natural and sustainable material.

731. A BEHAVIOUR CHANGING
     (ABC) SYRINGE
     Product, 2014
ABC Syringe is designed to deter reuse of non-sterile syringes in the developing world. It addresses the estimated 1.3 million early deaths caused by unsafe needle injections worldwide through the clever combination of a nitrogen-filled pack and a special ink that turns the syringe bright red sixty seconds after use, indicating it should not be used again. The project is a classic demonstration of how design thinking can be brought to bear on an intractable problem.

732. CHAIR4LIFE (C4L)
     MODULAR WHEELCHAIR
     Product, 2014
The Chair4Life team see a wheelchair as a companion that promotes independence and improves quality of life. The demanding brief called for a universal modular platform for children aged four to eighteen, requiring flexibility and adaptability, as well as stability and manoeuvrability in small spaces and across uneven surfaces. C4L is compact and lightweight, and its vertical lift – enabling eye-to-eye interaction with peers – demonstrates that the chair was designed in consultation with children and carers.

733. THE SEABOARD GRAND
     Product, 2014
Seaboard is as much an invitation to experiment with new modes of expression as an instrument. Roland Lamb's conceptual leap was to imagine a responsive and continuous surface instead of separate keys. Surprisingly, Seaboard is not only about redesigning the piano, nor just about music. The development of the ultra-sensitive responsive silicon surface is actually the heart of this venture.

734. THE ALCHEMIST'S DRESSING TABLE
     Product, 2014
The Alchemist's Dressing Table is a clever way to 'go organic' with make-up while retaining that sense of luxury fundamental to the appeal of cosmetics. Women may want to know more about provenance, but if the materials and objects themselves don't embody beauty, they lose their allure. These exquisitely crafted tools for making cosmetics from natural materials at home is far more aesthetically pleasing option than anything else that exists on the market at the moment.

735. PRO CHAIR FAMILY
     Product, 2014
Designing school chairs demands great aptitude. The chair has to be light enough to be moved around, yet strong enough to meet the boisterous energy of children. It also has to be ergonomic and affordable. Konstantin Grcic's Pro incorporates a round seat similar to a stool, so that it does not prescribe a forward sitting position. The slim backrest gives the torso room to move sideways, while the backrest's distinctive S-shape allows freedom of movement and reduces back strain.

736. THE BRADLEY TIMEPIECE
     Product, 2014
The Bradley is a watch for blind people, with touchable ball bearings that travel around the orbit of the face to indicate the time. Beyond its functional value, distinctive looks and affordability, the Bradley illustrates how Kickstarter can be used to support universal design. The designers raised over half a million dollars from prospective users, inviting them into the development process and moving seamlessly from idea to product without taking huge financial risks.

737. PHONEBLOKS
     Product, 2014
The modular smartphone concept Phonebloks suggests a device that adapts to your needs while also fighting against electronic waste. With a simple locking system borrowed from LEGO, the basic mainboard with touch display can carry additional plug-ins, such as your preferred camera, sound or data system. Phonebloks come up against some crucial technical and economic issues, but the project's online followers suggests there is great potential in this open-source idea.

738. SILK PAVILION
    Product, 2014
Silk Pavilion uses 6,500 silkworms as 'biological printers' to make a temporary shelter. It isn't entirely made by silkworms; the animals provide an additional layer of silk over the initial computer-designed and manufactured structure. While the ingenuity of this project is impressive, it is the questions it raises that are most fascinating: as our understanding of nature increases, how far are we prepared to go in the redesign of other life forms to meet our own needs?

739. UN NORTH DELEGATES'
    LOUNGE INTERIOR
    Product, 2014
The renovation of the UN North Delegates' Lounge illustrates Hella Jongerius's ability to move beyond conventional notions of industrial design. Along with her collaborators, Jongerius pioneered an entirely new take on functional meeting spaces. She developed two new furniture designs, the movable UN Lounge Chair and the Sphere Table, both of which can be reconfigured to meet the needs of delegates. She also designed a curtain for the East Facade, created from hand-knotted yarn and 30,000 porcelain beads produced from Dutch clay.

740. RISK CENTRE
    Product, 2014
Onkar Kular's projects ask open-ended questions about the world and the way we understand it. For Risk Centre, Kular and architect Inigo Minns built a 1:1 'experience' in which to explore ideas about risk through self-directed tours, workshops or interactive performances. Entering this mini-city feels like wandering on to a film set: Kular and Minns' re-creation of an actual risk centre creates an uncanny world that takes visitors through a constructed reality.

741. FAIRPHONE
    Product, 2014
Fairphone is an ethically produced smartphone. By building international relationships to ensure conflict-free raw materials and working with manufacturers to encourage the use of recyclable components and cut waste, Fairphone takes a relational approach to the design, manufacture, sale and operation of this most ubiquitous of modern products. Around 25,000 Fairphones were sold before the product was even launched, a testament to the effectiveness of the company's message.

742. MAN MACHINE
    Product, 2015
Glass is not the most obvious material for making furniture; apart from being cold and heavy, it has a reputation for being fragile. Konstantin Grcic's Man Machine is an experiment in making movable glass furniture, named after Kraftwerk's 1978 album.

Instead of hiding the industrial gas pistons, hinges and crank handles that make the glass furniture fold away, Grcic celebrates their utility.

743. ENDGRAIN
    Product, 2015
Attempting to create a coloured wood stain that wouldn't fade, the Israeli duo Yael Mer and Shay Alkalay were inspired by the movement of water through plant tissue. They conducted research to see if a similar uptake process using coloured pigments could be used to permanently dye wood. The furniture is made from dyed timber blocks positioned with their end grain facing upwards, which are then milled into shapes that exploit the technique's graphic and sculptural qualities.

744. DRAGONFLY
    Product, 2015
The asymmetrical shape of the Dragonfly chair was inspired by the insect the chair is named after. The dragonfly's body is characterised by an imbalance in weight distribution between the front legs and its extended tail. Likewise, the chair's four legs are all joined together at the front, giving the impression that it is defying the forces of gravity. This is made possible by means of a U-shaped supporting element hidden under the seat.

745. FIELD EXPERIMENTS: INDONESIA
    Product, 2015
Field Experiments research and develop traditional craft techniques from different parts of the world in order to create objects in close collaboration with local communities. The idea is to combine traditional knowledge with contemporary, creative aesthetics, to update the concept of the conventional souvenir. The project tends to be a cross-cultural exchange between designers and makers to create unique, one-off objects, whose value stands in the quality of the making and in their intelligent design.

746. THE EXTRAPOLATION FACTORY
    Product, 2015
The Extrapolation Factory's product is not a tangible thing that can be made or bought, but a way to bring professional design methods for imagining the future to non-experts. They have developed a highly effective approach to collaborative imagining, where participants translate their ideas, hopes and fears into imaginary products that challenge official futures.

747. MIITO
    Product, 2015
Miito is a radical reimagining of the electric kettle. Using induction technology, it allows users to heat only the water that they need, while bringing a bit of drama and magic to the kitchen. Why struggle to fill the kettle with exactly a cupful of water if you can heat the water in the cup itself? Refreshingly,

this innovation does not come from a large multi-national with a research and development budget, but a tiny Danish design agency.

748. MOOCALL SMS CALVING ALERT SENSOR
Product, 2015

A text-message alert system for birthing calves, Moocall uses gesture recognition technology to monitor cows nearing the end of their gestation. The technology responds to the movement of a cow makes in early labour and sends a text to alert the farmer, avoiding the need to constantly visit calving sheds during the day and night. The sensors are attached to a cow's tail, and one device is more than adequate to monitor a small herd.

749. PROJECT DANIEL
Product, 2015

A South Sudan lab that 3D-prints prosthetics, Project Daniel is an inspiring user-focused application of digitech, enabling amputees to 3D-print their own arms, hands and fingers. Named after Daniel Omar, the programme is a striking example of the winning combination of entrepreneurship, creativity and technology. Through crowdsourcing and sharing both technology and knowledge, the company Not Impossible turned this one-off project into one of the world's first 3D-printing prosthetic lab and training facilities.

750. 10 100 1000
Product, 2015

Developed by the Mexico-based industrial designer Francisco Torres, the brief for 10 100 1000 was simple: design a stool. Ten designers were handed a cardboard box measuring 35cm x 35cm x 35cm and three types of wood, and asked to create one stool in a limited edition of 100 costing 1,000 pesos (£50). Launched during the Abierto Mexicano de Diseño festival in November 2013, the concept was replicated at fairs as far as Dubai and Lebanon.

751. CURRENT TABLE
Product, 2015

Current Table is a continuation of the Energy Collection, an in-depth research project into energy-harvesting solutions. Its technology is based on photosynthesis, using the properties of colour to create an electrical current: the table's surface also collects the energy to power the devices.

752. BLUE DIVERSION TOILET
Product, 2015

Lack of adequate sanitation kills 1.8 million people a year through disease. The Blue Diversion toilet is a synthetic toilet that does not need to be hooked up to a sewerage system or power supply: it is filled just once with water that is then continually recycled into clean water for flushing and hand-washing. A pick-up system treats the faeces and urine for conversion into fertiliser and energy.

753. AIR-PURIFYING BILLBOARD – COMO 1200 ÁRBOLES
Product, 2015

This looks like an ordinary billboard, but it attracts and filters pollution from the sky, returning purified air to the surrounding area at a rate of 100,000 cubic metres per day – equivalent to the work of 1,200 mature trees. As urban populations continue to grow and pollution continues to present major health problems, such a solution could offer tangible improvements to the quality of built-up areas.

754. GROW-IT-YOURSELF MUSHROOM MATERIALS
Product, 2015

If you can bake a cake, you can make structural parts for architecture, furniture or products using Ecovative's Grow-It-Yourself (GIY) Mushroom Materials. The GIY process is easy, takes less than two weeks, uses cheap, reusable moulding tools and only requires standard domestic technology. The material is prepared like dough and placed in the watertight moulds to grow at room temperature for several days, after which the parts are air-dried and then finished in a hot oven.

755. SABI SPACE
Product, 2015

Sabi Space is an easy-to-install range of bathroom products, ranging from shelves to hooks to grab rails. While the original brief from this pioneering Californian brand was to find product opportunities for older users, MAP has created simple, beautiful and easy-to-install products that are multi-generational in appeal. They allow us to adapt bathrooms without making them look like a medical institution.

756. BRYDGEAIR
Product, 2015

The BrydgeAir iPad keyboard is the first wireless keyboard accessory that allows the iPad to replace a laptop. Other keyboard designs concentrate on being a separate item, only to be used when remembered or required. The aluminium BrydgeAir becomes an integral part of your iPad once the tablet is slotted into the casing. As well as protecting the tablet screen, this effectively turns your iPad into a mini MacBook.

757. BRCK
Product, 2015

Statistics show that roughly half of the global population is not yet online. Ushahidi, the non-profit technology company behind BRCK, was set up in Kenya where, during the 2008 elections, the company developed a crowd-sourced mapping platform to alert citizens to protests, violence and election results in real time. Unreliable connectivity in the region limited data flows, and so came BRCK – a robust, portable hub, designed to create internet networks in places where there is little or no basic infrastructure.

758. DIY GAMER KIT
Product, 2015

The founders of start-up Technology Will Save Us describe themselves as a design-led technology business focused on learning. They now have a growing range of DIY gadget kits, aimed at families, teachers and young people. Conceived with a careful eye for user-experience and designed with flair, these kits provide an inspiring example of what a design-driven, knowledge-based economy can achieve.

759. KANO COMPUTER KIT
Product, 2015

Kano is a small computer you can make yourself, even if you're seven years old. It's a series of small parts you connect together like LEGO to make a computer. Powered by a Raspberry Pi Model B, there are simple applications to help kids (and adults) understand code. It comes with everything except a screen, and opens up hardware to a whole new audience at a relatively low cost.

760. STRAP CHAIR
Product, 2015

The Strap Chair is a modern interpretation of the traditional woven chair. The brilliant colours chosen for the matt powder-coated steel frame contrast strikingly with the subtle, elegant tints used for the stripy straps, achieving a very pleasing look. Incredibly lightweight and stackable, the chair can be used both indoors and out, and brings that summer feeling to any interior.

761. TURN ON
Product, 2015

Turn On is a disarmingly simple all-in-one dimmable desklight. Designed by Joel Hoff while still a student at the Royal College of Art, the entire base of the light is a dimmer switch: turn the serrated black tube and the light turns on; keep rotating and the brightness increases. Since the tube is larger than a switch, it is easier to control for young and old alike.

762. HUMAN ORGANS-ON-CHIPS
Product, 2015

A way to research drugs without animal testing, Human Organs-on-Chips was developed by Harvard University's Wyss Institute to replace often expensive and ethically fraught human or animal testing in the medical industries. The 'chips' simulate the functions of human organs, and can be used singly or in combinations to test the effects of drugs on human physiology. For example, the 'lung-on-a-chip' – a clear, flexible polymer lined with bioengineered human airway and capillary cells – is better at predicting outcomes and less expensive than animal testing.

764. QARDIOARM
Product, 2015

An estimated thirty per cent of people in the United Kingdom are at risk from high blood pressure. As it rarely has noticeable symptoms, regular monitoring is important to reduce the risk of a stroke and heart attacks. A discreet personal heart monitor that links to a smartphone app, QardioArm takes its design cues from unobtrusive, portable objects such as sunglasses cases.

765. DOUBLE O BICYCLE LIGHT
Product, 2015

Paul Cocksedge's bicycle light is simple, attractive and solves the problem of theft with a brilliantly easy-to-store solution. The Double O delivers on its primary purpose: a light that is bright enough at night, with a built-in strap that can be attached pretty much anywhere. The genius of Double O is that it can be slid on to any commercial D-lock, with the front and back lamps snapped neatly together by magnets.

766. MUJI KITCHEN APPLIANCES
Product, 2016

Naoto Fukasawa's range of kitchen appliances for MUJI complements the brand's minimal approach to homeware and reinforce its no-logo offering. Fukasawa's intuitive approach favours simplicity of form coupled with comfortable ergonomics and optimum functionality. The all-white designs have soft, rounded edges and the pebble-like form gives them a friendly, tactile quality. Simple controls offer the essential functions and respect the overall elegance of each design.

767. O&G STUDIO DESIGN
AND MANUFACTURING
Product, 2016

O&G Studio is a design firm with a difference: they use design to revitalise traditional manufacturing methods. For the past few years, they have been keeping a declining New England factory alive by creating products that draw on its American Windsor-style heritage. As O&G's order book grew, they took over ownership of the factory's collective knowledge and its machines.

768. ADIDAS X PARLEY RUNNING SHOE
Product, 2016

As initiatives to clear plastic waste from the oceans increase, the question of what to do with the retrieved plastic is another problem. Embracing the challenge, adidas created a trainer with an upper body woven from fibres made of recycled fishing nets and a 3D-printed midsole made of waste plastic. adidas is a partner with Parley for the Oceans, an initiative that encourages creatives to repurpose sea waste and raise awareness of the growing issue.

769. ÎLE/W153 LAMP
Product, 2016

île/w153 is a stylish desk lamp with a versatile clamp. This clamping functionality is familiar from architects' desk lamps, but here Inga Sempé domesticates it to become more friendly and cheerful. With the characterful silhouette of a parasol (provided by its ingenious magnet shade) and available in many different colours, the lamp has a contemporary aesthetic that masks its technical achievements.

770. POST/BIOTICS
Product, 2016

Post/Biotics is a fun kit lab that facilitates the discovery of new antibiotics by allowing citizen scientists of all ages to help identify natural substances with antimicrobial properties. Antibiotic resistance is growing faster than pharmaceutical companies are finding new drugs. This pop-up lab allows anyone to test local plants, vegetables, fruit, fungi and soil. With the help of an app, results are stored online, creating a library of antimicrobials that could be significant for developing new drugs.

771. SPACE CUP
Product, 2016

A cup that works in zero gravity, the Space Cup developed as a result of careful experiments around the calibration of the movement of liquids in low gravity – what Weislogel terms 'space plumbing'. It utilises an interior corner angled to drive fluid upward and into the astronaut's mouth. The tiny cup brilliantly reflects the confluence of science, technology and design, responding to an extremely specific problem.

772. MONO-LIGHTS
Product, 2016

Mono-Lights is a modular LED lighting system that allows users to contort and configure it into any living situation. The idea was to update the old-fashioned uni-body fluorescent tubes familiar from classrooms and civic buildings by making the structural aspects of the light an extension of the tube. Using the latest in LED technology and futuristic materials, Mono-Lights emit little heat and they can bend, be draped or joined together to create longer sections.

773. JOTO
Product, 2016

Joto is an internet-connected drawing system that beautifully brings together doodles, drawings and social media into our homes. It recognises that we need a better way to display digital content in the home than the endless proliferation of screens, a way that does not distract and demand attention. This magical drawing system allows friends and family to share 'Jots': familiar digital content, but drawn with a pen.

774. TOKYO TRIBAL
Product, 2016

Tokyo Tribal is emblematic of the worldwide movement bringing together manufacturing and craftsmanship through mutual collaboration, an important way of improving the incomes of disadvantaged communities. This project features twenty-two items, including stools, chairs, tables and shelves, mainly in compact sizes. The main frames are made from solid oak, while the top board finishes are made from volcanic sand plaster. The bamboo rattan is hand-woven by local artisans in the Philippines.

775. ADAPTIVE MANUFACTURING
Product, 2016

An organic approach to 3D printing ceramics, Adaptive Manufacturing is an ongoing project between Eindhoven-based Sander Wassink and Olivier van Herpt that shows design becoming more intuitive. After using sensors to scan the local environment, organic shapes are formed by dripping material in the same way that Mother Nature has been slowly prototyping stone and wood for millennia.

776. DESIGN MUSEUM DHARAVI
Product, 2016

Design Museum Dharavi is a showcase for local talent in Dharavi, a densely packed neighbourhood of central Mumbai, India. It is a mobile and pop-up museum, supported by a programme of workshops and events, celebrating products that are made in Dharavi and the potential and creativity of their makers. It is an example of design thinking and problem-solving being used as an active agent of social and cultural improvement.

777. THE SMOG FREE PROJECT
Product, 2016

The Smog Free Project tower uses patented ion technology to produce smog-free bubbles of public space. With air pollution frequently reaching hazardous levels in cities across the world, Daan Roosegaarde has dreamt up what is effectively the world's largest smog vacuum cleaner. The project is a collaborative effort between technology, design and desire, between designer Roosegaard, Delft Technology University researcher Bob Ursem, and green tech company European Nano Solutions.

778. ECHO
Product, 2016

The voice-activated Amazon Echo was a first glimpse of mass-market voice computing. From a design perspective, what is significant about it is how Amazon have gone about inventing this interface of the future. It has been created in the round, with developer enthusiasts participating by adding their own applications, and collaboratively discovering new design patterns and best practices. The Echo may not be around forever, but Amazon's pattern of designing in the open is here to stay.

779. LEGO CITY FUN IN THE
PARK – CITY PEOPLE PACK
Product, 2016
Toys play an early and important role in allowing children to negotiate between versions of identity. Having a differently abled LEGO person goes a long way to extending kids' imagination as they explore and rehearse ideas about themselves and others. As LEGO is one of the most popular games ever designed, this reflection of a diverse reality can reach children worldwide.

780. 2016/
Product, 2016
Having worked closely with the Japanese porcelain makers in Arita to create a line of dinnerware, Scholten & Baijings returned to produce their collection 2016/. The project was conceived as a way to support this community of skilled craftspeople and ensure the future of Arita porcelain by combining their talents with those of sixteen international designers. Each collection reinterprets the centuries-old tradition of porcelain-making.

781. DRINKABLE BOOK
Product, 2016
With 3.4 million people dying each year from waterborne diseases, the problem of providing clean water needs to be tackled through cost-effective innovation. The Drinkable Book comprises tear-off paper filter sheets that make contaminated water safe to drink. Each filter is coated with silver nanoparticles, and gives thirty days of clean water.

782. SPECIES II CHAIR
Product, 2016
Taking the form of a polyurethane chair that appears to be hewn from rock, the Species II armchair challenges our expectations about furniture. The Species II chair's texture suggests something that has been roughly hacked from a solid material by brute force, while the denseness of the colour – deep maroon or vermillion red – makes the chair appear as if it is a rendering.

783. WITT – HARVESTING MOTION
INTO ENERGY
Product, 2016
The WITT ('Whatever Input to Torsion Transfer') is an elegantly simple mechanical device that converts motion into power. Essentially, the device harvests kinetic energy and turns it into electricity, so whenever it is shaken, jiggled or rotated, it produces power. This means that it could provide clean, unlimited electricity, for example, in boats, buoys and anything floating on the sea, or carried in a backpack while hiking, or even as a pocket-sized smartphone recharging device.

784. KODAK SUPER 8 CAMERA
Product, 2016
The new Kodak Super 8 is the first new 8mm camera for over thirty years, an analogue camera reworked for a digital generation of film-makers.

Yves Béhar's robust but beautifully crafted design articulates clearly the camera is not a 'digital' product, though it does quietly offer digital recording capabilities. With its material and colour palettes, brown leather and brushed metal, the Super 8 marks out the user as film-maker.

785. THE BBC MICRO:BIT
Product, 2016
The BBC micro:bit is a tiny, free computer designed to encourage children to get involved in writing software and building new things. It is packed with a wide array of technology and works alongside other systems, such as the Raspberry Pi. After noting that the computer had more impact with eleven- to twelve-year-olds, who seemed most interested in using it outside the classroom, the BBC planned to give the micro:bit to every Year 7 child in Britain.

786. ALPHABET OF LIGHT
Product, 2017
BIG's Alphabet lamp is an innovative lighting system consisting of two basic elements: a combination of straight and curved lines of light. It can be manipulated to write any sentence, number or graphic signage. Both an expressive tool and a functional light source, Alphabet can also be seen as a light sculpture. Each light comprises a thin central aluminium core that supports an LED strip on each side. These modular elements are seamlessly fused together with concealed electromagnetic joints.

787. SOLID TEXTILE BOARD BENCHES
Product, 2017
In collaboration with sustainability start-up Really and textile company Kvadrat, Max Lamb has created a new bench collection built from recycled textiles. The benches are produced using solid textile board: a high-density material made from 'end-of-life' fabrics, mostly cotton and wool. Lamb frequently uses overlooked materials to create innovative designs, and here once again demonstrates the enormous potential of a waste product.

788. AVY SEARCH AND RESCUE DRONE
Product, 2017
Those who fled their homelands in recent years had to make a dangerous journey across the Mediterranean: last year alone, 3,500 refugees perished attempting the crossing. The Avy Search and Rescue Drone was specifically designed to help. It is capable of flying long distances and detecting vessels, and can drop life jackets, lifebuoys, food supplies and medication.

789. THE PILOT TRANSLATING EARPIECE
Product, 2017
The Pilot speech translator earpiece is a bit of futuristic wearable technology right out of an Isaac Asimov story, allowing users to speak to each other in foreign languages and have the conversation translated directly and immediately into their

ear. Pilot is being developed by Waverly Labs, an innovative products company created in 2014. They are incorporating the latest technologies in speech recognition, machine translation and wearable tech to allow users to converse without language barriers.

790. SUFFERHEAD ORIGINAL STOUT
Product, 2017

Sufferhead Original is a smart combination of micro-brewing, product design and artistic social practice. It has a strong presence: a matt black 33cl bottle in the imperial stout style and a chic black-on-black label that feels at once medieval and contemporary. The beer tastes of roasted malt, cocoa, coffee and honey, with an unusual highlight flavour: a West African pepper that gives it a fruity taste, heat and originality.

791. WEDGE DOWEL
Product, 2017

This is a really simple design that does away with screws, bolts, screwdrivers and Allen keys when assembling IKEA furniture. Developed in IKEA's prototyping lab, it makes products much easier to put together, and at the same time more stable. While users want furniture that is quicker to put together, they also want to be able to take it apart and reassemble it easily – if they move house, for example.

792. NIMUNO LOOPS
Product, 2017

Nimuno Loops tape has been developed to allow LEGO builders to place their creations on the walls, the ceiling, the furniture – pretty much anywhere. It can be cut to any length, and bends sideways as well. While not developed (or even officially sanctioned) by the LEGO company, it allows for an even more creative engagement with their bricks and other components, already loved for their abundance of possibilities.

793. BUFFALOGRID
Product, 2017

In parts of rural India, power is unreliable. BuffaloGrid distributes electricity, one phone charge at a time. At its core is a luggable battery, kept topped up either by agents who travel village to village or using solar panels. Customers purchase power by sending a premium-rate text message and – using Internet of Things technology – a USB charging port is unlocked for one full charge. The agents get a cut of each purchase, incentivising them to travel further off-grid.

794. DANSBANA! VÅRBY GÅRD
Product, 2017

Dansbana! is a small urban space in Vårby, a southern suburb of Stockholm. It is a terrazzo dancefloor, carefully detailed with a high-quality sound system made of bright

and beautiful metal-clad speakers. Anyone can connect their phone via Bluetooth to the system and dance. Dansbana!, developed through dialogue with local dance groups, is intended to be a rare social space for young girls.

795. FLAX CHAIR
Product, 2017

Christien Meindertsma's Flax Chair shows that it is still possible to make a surprising and radically innovative piece of furniture. The chair is constructed from boards composed of flax and a sustainable glue. After being cut out of this board material, the pieces are bent into their form. The result is a chair that looks wonderfully lightweight and elegant, yet is pared down to the extreme minimum. This look is derived from the chair's innovative material.

796. AIR-INK
Product, 2017

Design often makes the invisible visible, and AIR-INK couldn't be a more literal example. It begins with a filter mounted on the exhaust pipe of a vehicle or diesel generator. This device captures up to ninety-five per cent of the tiny invisible particles in the pollutant, which would otherwise blacken our streets and our lungs. This material is refined and then used as a pigment for ink that can itself be used to communicate.

797. REMOLTEN
Product, 2017

When design studio gt2P began experimenting with lava, they failed to find any relevant scientific and technical information about this highly abundant, native Chilean material. So they designed their own research process and manufacturing method. With funding from the Chilean state and support from New York City-based design gallery Friedman Benda, gt2P have developed a series of objects that include porcelain lamps with melted lava switches, stoneware stools covered with ground lava, and solid lava tiles.

798. SNOO SMART SLEEPER
Product, 2017

In the first year of a child's life, it is estimated that parents lose an average of 1,000 hours of sleep, which can lead to serious health issues. Fuseproject are tackling the issue with the SNOO Smart Sleeper. Based on the methods of world-famous paediatrician Dr Harvey Karp, the Sleeper is a mechanised bassinet that gently rocks babies back to sleep at the push of a button.

802. FIAT 500
Transport, 2008

The original Fiat 500, designed by Dante Giacosa in 1957, was a masterpiece of industrial design born out of post-war austerity. The new, revamped Fiat 500 is a thoroughly practical evocation of the original 1957 car. The car's form is clearly modelled on the original's distinctive silhouette, and the style it exudes on the outside is carried through to the cabin.

803. SKYSAILS
Transport, 2008
SkySails uses wind energy to reduce the fuel consumption for shipping. Modern cargo vessels might be several hundred feet long, so it can be hard to imagine them using sails. SkySails has developed a wind-force system based on large towing kites which, for the first time, meets the requirements of shipping companies. The kites measure up to 320 square metres each, and can reduce fuel consumption by up to fifty per cent.

804. AIRBUS A380
Transport, 2008
The Airbus A380 is the world's largest passenger airliner. Too often, air travellers feel like insignificant cogs in a well-oiled machine, where every seat is identical except for the number. PriestmanGoode aimed to improve the passenger experience in the Airbus by creating clearly defined spaces for relaxation, entertainment, business, sleep and, most importantly, the ability to move around comfortably.

805. TOMTOM PORTABLE GPS CAR NAVIGATION SYSTEM
Transport, 2008
TomTom, a leading manufacturer of automotive navigation systems in Europe, develops compact satellite navigation devices that the driver can operate easily in order to get from A to B without a traditional road map. Its GPS (Global Positioning System) allows the TomTom to show your car's precise whereabouts, as well as a simple-to-operate interface with a bird's-eye view of the road. It also offers visual and spoken directions to your chosen destination.

806. LONDON SERPENTINE SOLARSHUTTLE
Transport, 2008
Powered entirely by the sun, the Serpentine SolarShuttle is an entirely pollution- and noise-free boat on the Serpentine Lake in London's Hyde Park. The innovative curved roof, made up of twenty-seven solar cells, collects all the energy needed to power the boat. SolarShuttle eliminates the production of 4,900lbs of CO2 per year compared with a conventional diesel boat of similar size, and even feeds excess energy into the national grid.

807. MEX-X WHEELCHAIR
Transport, 2008
The Mex-x is a folding wheelchair for children. The seat and frame are constructed independently from each other, combining the advantages of a folding wheelchair with the variability of a regular

wheelchair with fixed frame. This permits the child to grow with the chair. They also have the option of choosing from several different patterns for the wheel guards, which gives the child a sense of individuality.

808. VÉLIB' BICYCLE SERVICE
Transport, 2008
Vélib' (vélo libre; in English, 'free bicycle') is the public self-service bicycle rental system introduced to Paris in July 2007. Cycle racks were set up all over the city to allow subscribers to take a conveniently placed bicycle and leave it at the rack closest to their destination. Subscribers are allowed an unlimited number of rentals, and subscriptions can be purchased by the day, week or year.

809. LONDON CONGESTION CHARGING EXTENSION
Transport, 2008
By charging motorists who drove on London's most crowded roads during the busiest times of day, the London Congestion Charge was introduced in 2003 with the aim of reducing congestion, improving journey times, and making the distribution of goods and services more efficient. In February 2007, the Congestion Charge zone was extended westward – a decision that was reversed in January 2011.

810. STREETCAR
Transport, 2008
Streetcar was a new and innovative alternative to car ownership in the UK. For those who only need a car from time to time, Streetcar provided self-service cars and vans for rent by the hour, day, week or month. Vehicles could be reserved online or by phone, and accessed by a high-tech smart card. In 2010, Streetcar merged with the American company Zipcar.

811. HIGH SPEED 1 AND ST PANCRAS INTERNATIONAL TERMINAL
Transport, 2009
The transformation of St Pancras into a twenty-first-century international rail terminal has been one of the most important restoration projects in Europe. Key to this was the delivery of High Speed 1 (HS1), Britain's first new railway line for over a century. With a maximum operating speed of 300kph, HS1 has sliced the journey time from central London to Paris to only 2 hours and 15 minutes.

812. FLYAK KAYAK
Transport, 2009
Established in 1978, Nelo is one of the world's leading manufacturers for kayaks, canoes and rowing boats, winning more than twenty medals in the 2008 Olympics. The Flyak is the first significant innovation in conventional kayak design

for many years, giving it astonishing increase in performance. This is achieved by the incorporation of two carbon-fibre hydrofoils that lift the hull out of the water at a threshold of around 10kph – more than double that of a conventional kayak.

813. AQUADUCT TRICYCLE
Transport, 2009

Aquaduct is a pedal-powered concept vehicle that transports, filters and stores water. The idea was a response to problems of sanitation and transportation in the developing world, where water sources can be miles from residential areas, resulting in heavy water vessels being carried daily by foot over long distances. Pedalling the bike draws water from a large holding tank through a filter to a smaller, portable tank of clean water.

814. BALANCE SPORT WHEELCHAIR
Transport, 2009

Observing a wheelchair basketball game, it became apparent to the designers of the Balance Sport Wheelchair that hands have two primary roles in the game: propelling, turning or stopping the chair, and shooting, passing, dribbling and blocking. Their wheelchair's hands-free braking and turning system allows athletes to maintain control of the wheelchair without using their hands. When the athlete leans to the left or right, the chair turns accordingly; in order to slow or stop, the athlete simply leans back.

815. LINE-J MEDELLÍN METROCABLE
Transport, 2009

Medellín City in Colombia demonstrates how the cable car, traditionally used in ski resorts, is increasingly used for urban transport. With the introduction of the Line-J MetroCable to the network, the poorer suburban communities of the mountainous hillsides gained convenient and environmentally friendly access to the city. Line-J was accompanied by a series of regeneration programmes on the ground, such as new libraries, public space improvements, and educational and recreational facilities.

816. LÖTSCHBERG BASE TUNNEL
Transport, 2009

At thirty-four kilometres long Lötschberg Base Tunnel is the world's longest land tunnel. The volume of transport crossing the Alps, always significant, has increased at an enormous rate, and the ecologically sensitive terrain has suffered, particularly from heavy road use. Lötschberg Base Tunnel is the first part of Switzerland's Alp Transit programme, Europe's most ambitious attempt to divert passenger and freight traffic from roads to rail.

817. TREK DISTRICT BICYCLE
Transport, 2009

The Trek District is a natural development of the single-speed bicycle. By adopting a Kevlar belt drive, it has eliminated an otherwise noisy, dirty, heavy, rust-prone and easily worn-out chain. In its place is a lighter, stronger, smoother-running system that is considerably quieter, more durable and virtually maintenance-free. As one of the few lubrication-free drive systems on the market, it is the perfect choice for a customer looking for a low-maintenance ride.

818. CHARGE SPOT
Transport, 2009

Charge Spot meets the challenge of 'going green' in the realm of transport by providing accessible top-up points for electrical vehicles. While most users of electrical cars ensure their car is fully charged in the morning, there are few alternatives for topping up the car battery when out and about. Better Place offered a unit that could be accessed in assigned parking spaces and along busy high streets. The first Charge Spots were launched in Israel.

819. CAR2GO
Transport, 2009

car2go provides an alternative to owning a car. Unlike other car sharing schemes, car2go offers the flexibility of pay-as-you-go by the minute. In addition, the fleet of cars is not bound to a particular address or parking space: they can be picked up and dropped off anywhere in the city. The service costs from €0.26 per minute, and can be found and booked online or via mobile phone.

820. KTM 690 STUNT MOTORCYCLE
Transport, 2009

The KTM 690 Stunt is a future-looking freestyle motorcycle. Beautifully made and tuned for maximum torque at low revs rather than speed, the 690 Stunt features a single-sided swing arm, front wheel mounted footrests and a thumb-operated back brake. It has minimal bodywork and light-but-stiff steel-tube trellis frames, and is robustly designed to avoid damage, with crash-bars around the engine and a 'scrape bar' on the tail unit for wheelie specialists.

821. THE GREENBIRD: WIND-POWERED VEHICLES
Transport, 2009

Part aeroplane, part sailing boat and part Formula One car, the Greenbird is powered only by the wind. The project aimed to break the world land- and ice-speed records – and promote zero-carbon transportation. Wind-powered speed records are unlike normal speed records, where more power equals more speed. With wind, the vehicle must maximise lift and minimise drag. On 26 March 2009, the Greenbird smashed the old land record of 116.7mph with a new time of 126.2mph.

822. TH!NK CITY ELECTRIC CAR
  Transport, 2009
Th!nk City is a 100 per cent electric car. The materials are easily maintained and recycled, including plastic bodywork and other plastic panels that are unpainted, reducing energy consumption and toxins. The batteries, which use lithium-ion technology, are returned to the supplier at the end of their useful life. The car itself was produced and assembled in Th!nk's low-carbon emission factory.

823. URBIKES – FOURTH GENERATION URBAN BICYCLE
  Transport, 2010
Urbikes is a bicycle-sharing scheme that works in conjunction with existing public transport networks. The individual components are designed to be hardy but easy to replace, while the non-standard design reduces the likelihood of parts being stolen for use in other bicycles. The unisex frame can accommodate various body types and sizes, and there is a built-in lamp.

824. GINA LIGHT VISIONARY MODEL CAR
  Transport, 2010
Innovative and eye-catching, this one-off concept vehicle was conceived when the BMW design team questioned the purpose of a car's body. Replacing the traditional rigid structure with a high-tech fabric skin stretched over a movable wire frame enables the car to change shape. The headlights are revealed by blinking apertures in the fabric, and the engine is accessed by unzipping a slit in the 'bonnet'.

825. E430 ELECTRIC AIRCRAFT
  Transport, 2010
The Yuneec E430 is the first commercially available electric aircraft. With just two main moving parts in the motor reliability, mechanical safety and maintenance are dramatically improved. With its broad wingspan-to-body ratio, the zero-emissions Yuneec has a particularly elegant dragonfly-like form, which allows quiet take-off and flight or silent gliding.

826. HONDA EV-N CONCEPT CAR
  Transport, 2010
In the male-dominated world of car design, the EV-N Concept is an achievement for Kanna Sumiyoshi, the twenty-nine-year-old who led the Honda development team. The EV-N is a small, four-seater electric battery vehicle. It has solar panels on the roof for recharging, and comes with a door compartment that holds an electric unicycle. As a concept model it will not be built, but it offers intriguing glimpses of what is to come.

827. GOCYCLE ELECTRIC BICYCLE
  Transport, 2010
Gocycle is a lightweight electric two-wheeler that combines power, portability and city-specific design innovations for an easy and no-emission commute.

The frame and wheels are injection-moulded in a high-tech and lightweight magnesium alloy. This delivers the same performance, look and feel as carbon fibre but at significantly lower cost. On release, Gocycle was the world's lightest production electric bicycle, weighing just 16.2kg.

828. MISSION ONE SUPERBIKE
  Transport, 2010
When Yves Béhar was asked to create the world's fastest electric superbike, his design had to be accepted by motorcycle enthusiasts while also appearing instantly recognisable as an alternative energy vehicle. Lacking experience of vehicle design, Béhar didn't fall into the usual design traps: there are no go-faster stripes, nor excessive masculine design cues. Instead, his bold mix of colours and geometric shapes is grouped in a compact form that's like no other.

829. NISSAN LAND GLIDER
  Transport, 2010
Nissan's Land Glider questions the layout, shape and steering mechanism of traditional cars. The driver sits centrally, in a narrow cockpit, just large enough for a passenger seat directly behind. Measuring just one metre wide, the compact car provides urban drivers with the convenience of a motorcycle but with added comfort and safety. The zero-emissions concept car includes an entirely electric drivetrain and leans into corners as it turns, providing added stability for the narrow shape.

830. RIVERSIMPLE CAR
  Transport, 2011
The world's first commercially viable hydrogen car, Riversimple could reduce the environmental impact of personal cars. Vehicles cannot be bought or owned, but are leased for a specific duration. Riversimple has been developed using a whole-system design approach, optimising the entire product and service offer rather than individual elements. This enabled a five-fold increase in efficiency over typical vehicles.

831. FIAT 500 TWINAIR
  Transport, 2011
The retro styling of the Fiat 500 in 2008 earned Roberto Giolito and the Fiat design team a host of awards. The latest model has an engine to match its look: the innovative two-cylinder TwinAir. A two-cylinder engine is unconventional, but has heritage, since the original 500 was also powered by twin cylinders. This radical new 10 engine offers improvements of up to thirty per cent in fuel consumption and CO_2 output.

832. EN-V CONCEPT CAR
  Transport, 2011
The EN-V or Electric-Networked Vehicle is a concept designed to meet the demands of an increasing urban population. Two passengers and

light luggage fit in a vehicle about a third the size of a traditional car, which can turn by rotating on a central point. Drive-by-wire technology with interfaces similar to video games replaces the traditional mechanical control systems, while networked connectivity allows automated and autonomous driving, parking and retrieval.

833. DEZIR CONCEPT CAR
Transport, 2011

The Renault DeZir is a concept car that aims to alter perceptions of electric cars. The shape is reminiscent of a sports car, with a showy pair of reverse-hinged butterfly doors and smoothly sculptural Kevlar body panels. The system generates kinetic energy from deceleration, storing it in the battery for later use.

834. VANMOOF NO.5 BICYCLE
Transport, 2011

VanMoof No.5 is a no-nonsense bicycle. Designed for modern commuters, its frame is made from lightweight, rust-free aluminium and stripped free of all non-essentials. The hollow, slightly oversized top tube hides a multitude of clever ideas. One end features a built-in LED lamp, while the other end contains a hidden high-quality ABUS lock, accessed by turning a key.

835. BARCLAYS CYCLE HIRE
Transport, 2011

Launched in summer 2010, Barclays Cycle Hire (now Santander Cycles) is a user-friendly, robust public bicycle hire scheme in London. The robust bike, built by Cycles Devinci, features dynamo-powered lights that remain on at traffic lights, adjustable saddles, and luggage racks that avoid gathering litter. Docking stations are distinctive enough to be recognisable, yet unobtrusive enough to blend in with the urban landscape.

836. YIKEBIKE
Transport, 2011

Providing city dwellers with a fast, safe and easy way to navigate their environment, YikeBike is the world's smallest and lightest electric folding bike. The carbon-fibre construction means it can be carried on buses and trains, lifted up stairs and easily stored under a desk. YikeBike's design places the handlebars behind the rider, delivering a safe and smooth ride with greater visibility than a traditional bike.

837. TAURUS ELECTRO G4 AIRCRAFT
Transport, 2012

The Taurus Electro G4 offers near-silent flight with no direct emissions. The twin-fuselage aircraft was created by combining two existing Taurus G2 fuselages and wings, connected by a five-metre spar. The lightweight aircraft is made of fibreglass, carbon-fibre and other composite materials, with only five per cent aluminium. This plane points to the future: as battery technology improves, who knows what size and type of aircraft could be developed?

838. BIKE HANGER
Transport, 2012

Bike Hanger is a bicycle storage solution designed for use in dense urban areas. Resembling an elongated Ferris wheel, it uses a vertical rotation system to hang bicycles above ground level. To access their bike, the user pedals the mechanism, rotating the wheel to bring the bike to ground level. The design, which can be installed on the side of a building, aims to reclaim underused urban spaces.

839. EMERGENCY AMBULANCE – REDESIGN
Transport, 2012

It is rare that a redesign can save lives, but the new NHS emergency ambulance does just that. NHS paramedics, clinicians, patients, researchers, engineers and designers worked closely together on the project. The stretcher is moved to the centre of the ambulance to allow 360-degree access to the patient. A digital communications and monitoring system can send information about the patient's condition ahead to the hospital, while the easy-to-clean and unintimidating interior helps to increase patient comfort.

840. MIA ELECTRIC CAR
Transport, 2012

This tiny three-seater zero-emissions electric vehicle is aimed at the urban market. With a no-frills aesthetic, the boxy car features a central driving position and a spacious interior with sliding doors. It comes in three sizes – standard, an extended 12 mia L and a mia box van version. With a range of 80 miles and a top speed of 68mph, it costs about £1.30 per 60 miles to run.

841. 787 DREAMLINER AIRCRAFT
Transport, 2012

The 787 Dreamliner is the first airliner to be made from carbon-fibre reinforced plastic instead of aluminium. Stronger, lighter and more economical, the material has helped reduce the plane's fuel consumption and CO_2 emissions by up to twenty per cent. The slender wings are curved at the tip, enhancing the plane's aerodynamics, and the windows are sixty-five per cent larger than in a 767, which helps reduce air sickness.

842. T27 ELECTRIC CAR
Transport, 2012

The T27 is a small electric city car inspired by Formula One construction techniques. The three-seat layout sets a new standard in passenger compactness, keeping three people warm, safe and comfortable. Sliding the electric motor under the rear seat means the car takes up barely more road than a large motorbike, while the oyster shell-like door emphasises that this is not business as usual.

843. AUTOLIB'
    Transport, 2012
Autolib' is a Parisian public car-hire scheme of a fleet of electric cars that can be picked up and dropped off at various docking stations around the French capital. Operating like the bike-hire schemes in many European cities, this project for electric hire cars seeks to reduce both traffic and pollution. To promote the use of public transport, Autolib' is targeted at weak links in the public transport network.

844. BMW i3
    Transport, 2013
The i3 is BMW's first production electric car. Perhaps uniquely for an electric car, it was developed entirely from the ground up. The i3 features a powerful 167 horsepower electric motor driving its rear axle and the entire thing, with lithium-ion batteries included, weighs just 2,755 pounds. The key to its light weight is the use of carbon fibre-reinforced plastic that has been micro-engineered to balance weight and strength.

845. MORPH WHEEL
    Transport, 2013
Many wheelchair users complain about bulky chairs that sit in the corner of the room, reminding you that you need them. This one can be folded away. In fact, the Morph Wheel is the first time a wheelchair can be folded small enough to go in an overhead locker on a plane or a wardrobe at home.

846. LONDON 2012 OLYMPICS WAYFARING
    Transport, 2013
Even the most implacable detractors of the London 2012 logo could admire the consistency and rigour with which the look of the Games was applied across all the London 2012 Olympic venues. The organisers worked with a wide range of partners, including local authorities, Transport for London, sponsors and all other interested parties to ensure that the 2012 Olympics were represented by a unified look and feel.

847. TOUCH & TRAVEL
    Transport, 2013
Germany's state-owned railway company Deutsche Bahn has been at the forefront of innovating ticketing for urban public transport and national rail services. Its Touch & Travel pilot system enables multi-modal travel for customers without any advance ticket purchasing. Users activate a travel button on their smartphone, which identifies their location across Germany's entire national rail system. While travelling, the mobile phone serves as ticketing proof.

848. DONKY BIKE
    Transport, 2013
Inspired by Dutch 'donkey' bikes, designer Ben Wilson came up with a new take on a familiar form. Available in green or black, the Donky Bike has a long steel beam that balances heavy cargo front and back along its weight. Unlike the Dutch version, however, Donky combines its load-carrying ability with the strength and simplicity of a BMX. The twenty-inch wheels are good for stability and easy handling in urban traffic.

849. EXHIBITION ROAD PROJECT
    Transport, 2013
London's Exhibition Road is an extraordinary proliferation of world-class arts and science institutions. It has long suffered from a 1960s road layout, with congested traffic segregating institutions and people. Dixon Jones's elegant shared-use scheme transforms a cluttered, inaccessible main road into a major European cultural quarter. The newly pedestrianised areas afford time and opportunities to wander, appreciate, sit, eat, watch and hang out, while benches invite loitering.

850. N-ONE CAR
    Transport, 2013
Cars seem to fall into two categories: they are either very serious-looking or friendly and happy. It is the mildly banal that still seems to take up so much of what we see on the streets and, while seriousness has its place, it is the friendly cars that have greater relevance to the city. The Honda N-One is closer to a piece of public design – like a shrunken-down bus – than to a car.

851. AIR ACCESS
    2013
Air Access gives passengers with reduced mobility an easier transition from departure gate to aircraft. The concept consists of two elements: a detachable wheelchair, which transports passengers on and off the plane, and a fixed-frame aisle seat on the aircraft, with which the wheelchair is mated to create a regular airline seat. The design aims to reduce the indignity and discrimination that reduced-mobility passengers face when travelling by air.

852. MANDO: FOOTLOOSE
        CHAINLESS BICYCLE
    Transport, 2013
The Mando: Footloose is a paradigm shift in electric bicycle design. Firstly, it removes the oily chain, chainrings, cogs and derailleurs, and replaces them with an alternator, battery and motor. The motor drive is controllable so you can ride without pedalling, and artificially intelligent gear-shifting changes automatically by detecting slopes. Secondly, the bicycle is foldable. And, just like smart keys for cars, the bike is immobilised when the key is removed.

853. XL1 CONCEPT CAR
    Transport, 2014
Ten years in development, VW's XL1 concept car appears futuristic, stylish and sophisticated, with enclosed rear wheels and sleek silver lines.

To achieve its high level of performance, it combines the lightest possible chassis and body panels with a hybrid power-train. The XL1's aerodynamically optimised shape combined with extremely low drag coefficient means the car can achieve an impressive 261 miles per gallon.

854. ME.WE CONCEPT CAR
Transport, 2014

Designed by French architect and designer Jean-Marie Massaud and the Toyota ED2 design studio, the ME.WE concept elevates Toyota's vision for electric transport. In ME.WE, Massaud's unique design approach is as much about the perils of opulence and extravagance as it is about beauty and innovation. His extended use of new premium materials like bamboo creates a sustainable yet desirable, and more humanistic, alternative to industry traditions.

855. HYBRID/24 ELECTRIC BICYCLE
Transport, 2014

Smooth, secure and stable, the A2B Hybrid/24 provides everything for the modern commuter. The in-built technology seamlessly integrates pedal power with that of the motor to deliver a range of over forty miles on a single four-hour charge. Perhaps uniquely, its silhouette is simple enough to give the impression that it is a bicycle 'that happens to be electric', rather than the other way around.

856. IFMOVE BICYCLE
Transport, 2014

The IFmove commuter bicycle folds more easily and faster than any other folding bike. It transforms into a convenient package in less than two seconds, and weighs no more than 12kg. Usability is the cycle's highest priority: the bike rides, folds and travels fast and instinctively, without compromising performance or handling. It is more than just a folding bike, though: it provides a user-friendly solution for the urban environment.

857. E-GO SINGLE-SEATER AIRCRAFT
Transport, 2014

The e-Go's unique appearance is reminiscent of the glory days of British aviation, and it is the first aircraft manufactured solely with British-made parts since the Harrier Jump Jet. The result of cutting-edge design and material innovation, it has an airframe designed by Giotto Castelli, an aeronautical engineer who helped design the Airbus A340, that benefits from techniques used to produce the monocoques common to Formula One racing cars.

858. BMW i8 CAR
Transport, 2015

The BMW i8 is a sports car with the consumption and emission values of a compact vehicle. It is made from the lightest, strongest materials using the most advanced techniques that BMW could apply, and it is driven by a revolutionary petrol-electric plug-in hybrid, all-wheel drive powertrain. Dihedral door-opening adds a touch of theatre, and the materials and finishes present the car as an object of the future.

859. TESLA MODEL S ELECTRIC CAR
Transport, 2015

Tesla has come closest to making electric cars a feasible, everyday reality. The Model S is not hair-shirted or austere; it is impressively refined in its details, shape and luxurious interior. The company is all about change in an industry that was stagnating: it has redefined automobile manufacturing, repurposing energy-conscious concerns into something that works.

860. LOOPWHEELS
Transport, 2015

Smaller wheels on bicycles have many advantages: compactness, weight and low inertia. However, they have a big disadvantage – comfort. The technically advanced twenty-inch Loopwheel puts suspension in the wheel – an old idea, but never successfully achieved before. The carbon-fibre springing, derived from bows used in archery, is light, rigid and does not require parts moving against each other. Furthermore, complexity in the frame is reduced by integrating braking and gears.

861. GOOGLE SELF-DRIVING CAR
Transport, 2015

The Google self-driving car concept is significant mainly because it is the first hint of what will be a culture-changing technology: owning your own car makes little sense when you can command a robotic vehicle with your smartphone to come and pick you up. We can read a book or catch up on emails when on public transport, but not while driving. On congested public roads, this is 'dead time' for drivers – a perfect scenario for automation, which can potentially provide a safer experience too.

862. D-AIR STREET BAG SAFETY EQUIPMENT
Transport, 2015

Dainese have reconfigured the in-car airbag for motorcyclists. They have managed this by measuring exact vehicle behaviour. An impact is the simplest case, because then accelerometers can detect a truly abnormal situation. The Dainese suits recognise impacts but, amazingly, also detect loss of traction when the bike is sliding out from under the rider, and in that case arrange a slower triggering sequence.

863. MOTIV.E CITY CAR
Transport, 2015

The MOTIV.e City Car is as much a proof of concept as an actual car. Electrically powered, the car is made using iStream, a radical rethink of the manufacturing process. Body panels are 'married' to the completed chassis near the end of the assembly process, allowing the chassis to be scaled for different products, with each new design requiring only low-cost tooling and software changes.

864. OKO E-BIKE
Transport, 2016
Aimed at commuters who want to arrive free of sweat, the OKO e-bike includes an electric-assist motor to help when riding up hills and covering longer distances. The electric power bank is located in the central crossbar to ensure weight is evenly distributed, which makes riding OKO feel more like travelling on a conventional bike. The internal routing of cables, as well as integrated mudguards, helps maintain the bike's clean, modern lines.

865. LUMOS HELMET
Transport, 2016
The Lumos Helmet addresses some cyclists' safety fears. A bright white light on the front ensures the cyclist can see and be seen by other road-users, while at the rear the helmet integrates a red brake light in the shape of a warning triangle (activated automatically when a cyclist slows). Yellow indicators on either side to communicate the cyclist's turning or lane-changing intentions. The hope is that it will encourage cyclists and motorists to cooperate easily and effectively.

866. TESLA MODEL 3
Transport, 2016
With the Models X and S, Tesla showed that it was possible to design beautiful and desirable vehicles that happened to be electric. With the Tesla Model 3, however, there was a huge waiting list before the final design was even unveiled. Elon Musk has designed not only a covetable car, but also – with the Nevada-based Gigafactory to produce it – a manufacturing process that is environmentally friendly on a breathtakingly audacious scale.

867. TX: THE ELECTRIC TAXI
Transport, 2016
A familiar sight on London's streets for over a century, it is fitting that the re-design of the black cab should capture the spirit of past models. Its design builds on existing features, such as the headlights, grille and strong roof lines, while still paying attention to passenger and driver comfort. The rear-hinged door, removed in previous iterations, returns as a means of improving passenger access.

868. GOGORO SMARTSCOOTER AND GOSTATION
Transport, 2016
The Smartscooter is the world's first high-performance electric scooter. The numbers are impressive (0-50kph in 4.2 seconds, 95kph top speed), but the Smartscooter really stands out through its revolutionary energy-saving

system. Combining smart technology, tools for analysing big data and the unique battery-swapping/refuelling GoStation, the Smartscooter silently monitors and controls how energy is used during each journey and while recharging.

869. BEELINE – SMART NAVIGATION FOR BIKES
Transport, 2016
Simplicity of use is the guiding principle for the Beeline navigator, a handlebar-mounted device that helps users find their way around on two wheels without having to consult a difficult-to-read map display. Controlled by the GPS of your smartphone, it reduces navigation to the bare basics by providing a general indicator of direction of travel rather than prescriptive commands.

870. AUTONOMOUS-RAIL RAPID TRANSIT (ART)
Transport, 2017
The Autonomous-Rail Rapid Transit system is a self-driving electric vehicle that is guided not by tracks, but a double-dashed line painted on the street. Its seductiveness lies in its promise of providing all the benefits of light rail without the costs and other drawbacks of the rails themselves. Instead, it runs on sensors and rubber wheels, making it something of a cross between a train, bus and urban Roomba (those little robotic vacuum cleaners).

871. OLLI
Transport, 2017
Olli embraces autonomous vehicle technology to offer flexible urban transport to the public. The electric vehicle, designed for up to twelve passengers, provides last-mile connectivity as part of a multimodal urban transport system. Significantly, Olli is produced with 3D-printing technology, which radically reduces the time required to design, manufacture, test, mass produce and deliver vehicles, while also supporting decentralised, local fabrication.

872. GITA
Transport, 2017
Piaggio's Gita will follow you politely as you swan around at the airport, fancy free. Since control technology is getting so cheap, why depend on a few multifunctional robots when any number of appliances could take on autonomous tasks? The Gita team didn't get carried away with the usual futurist vernacular, and instead created something that already feels quite approachable.

873. MAHJOUBA INITIATIVE
Transport, 2017
Eric van Hove's Mahjouba Initiative is a social and entrepreneurial undertaking, centred on making art. In 2015, van Hove created a prototype indigenous motorbike, Mahjouba 1, which borrows

its basic design concept from cheap Moroccan mopeds. It is ninety per cent handcrafted from locally sourced materials and powered by an electric engine. The project plugs local artisans into the formal industrial economy, offering them a path to financial stability.

874. SEABUBBLES
Transport, 2017
Seabubbles are emission-free, noiseless and electric-powered water taxis that can be rented using a transportation-sharing app like Uber. Built with lightweight fibreglass and high-density foam, the vessel has four foils attached to the hull to reduce any drag. When it reaches 12kph (7.5mph), it hovers above the water, avoiding contact with waves for a smoother ride.

875. HONDA MOTO RIDING ASSIST
Transport, 2017
Honda's Silicon Valley engineers have created a robotic motorbike that won't fall over. The aim is to greatly reduce accidents, particularly at low speeds, as well as improve the riding experience. The technology disengages the handlebars from the front forks at speeds of three miles per hour or less. The front wheel is then controlled by the computer, which senses the bike leaning and makes tiny adjustments to counteract any tipping.

876. LIGHT TRAFFIC
Transport, 2017
As the reality of self-driving vehicles draws nearer, other elements of our road-based infrastructure require a wholesale reinvention. For this smart traffic-light system, the researchers have developed slot-based intersections that could significantly reduce queues and delays. The idea is based on a scenario in which sensor-equipped vehicles are allocated a crossing slot when approaching an intersection, with their speed adjusted before they pass through. At all times the vehicles' relative proximity is communicated, so that they remain at a safe distance from each other.

877. SCEWO
Transport, 2017
Scewo is a stair-climbing mobility device developed by a group of students at the Swiss Federal Institute of Technology. Using a retractable set of rubber tracks, the wheelchair can safely and smoothly travel both up and down stairs. An extra pair of wheels at the rear allows users to raise the chair so that they can engage with others at eye level. It is heart-warming to see this brilliant wheelchair giving users a hitherto unreachable level of independence.

ARCHITECTURE

6a architects: p.40, 104; Adrià Goula: p.141; Aggrey Magonga: p.118; Al Borde: p.107; Alan Karchmer: p.145; Allison Hu: p.54; Amiaga: p.83; Andrés García Lachner: p.57; Andrés Jaque / Office for Political Innovation: p.80; Andy Stagg: p.19; Anja Schlamann p.55; Anthony Charlton / ODA: p.73; Are Carlsen: p.137; Arne Maasik: p.16; Arturo Vittori: p.139; Arup: p.135; Assemble: p.70, 122; Bas Princen / Fondazione Prada: p.123; Benjamin Healley: p.47; BIG / TOPOTEK / SUPERFLEX: p.86; Bill Timmerman: p.109; CaixaForum Madrid / Maximo Garcia: p.24; Charles Hosea: p.91; Chris Martin: p.78; Christian Richters: p.84; CIO / John Gichigi: p.15; Concrete Canvas: p.61; Daniel Malhão / DMF: p.92; Daria Scagliola / Jeroen Musch: p.76; Daria Scagliola & Stijn Brakke: p.111; David Grandorge: p.69; Dean Kaufman: p.17, 89; Delfino Sisto Legnani / OMA: p.138; Dennis Gilbert / VIEW Pictures: p.116; Donn Holohan / The University of Hong Kong: p.146; Duccio Malagamba: p.18; Edmund Sumner: p.49, 50, 56; Eduardo Arroyo / NO.MAD: p.21; Elemental: p.45; Filip Dujardin: p.58; Frédéric Druot Architecture: p.79; Gareth Gardner: p.77; Gerald Zugmann: p.33; Gilbert McCarragher: p.100; Grainne Hassett: p.148; Hélène Binet: p.53, 144; Hemingway Design: p.127; Hiroyuki Oki: p.108; Hufton + Crow: p.71, 88, 132; Hufton & Crow / Fondazione MAXXI: p.43; Ioana Marinescu: p.101; Iwan Baan: p.30, 38, 39, 48, 51, 60, 64, 65, 74, 75, 85, 98–99, 114, 130, 131, 134, 136; Jakob + MacFarlane / Nicolas Borel: p.106; James Morris: p.142; Jonas Nyström: p.128; Jonathan Lovekin: p.46; Jorge Hernandez Fernandez: p.32; Junya.ishigami+associates: p.31; Kida Katsushida / Fototeca: p.95; Luis Ros / Cloud 9: p.63; Lyndon Douglas: p.22; Lyndon Douglas: p.35; Marlon Blackwell Architects: p.41; Nacása & Partners: p.82; Naoya Hatakeyama / Japan Foundation: p.81; Nelson Kon: p.102; Nic Lehoux: p.133; Nico Saieh: p.119; Nicola Betts / Waterfront Toronto: p.28; Nigel Young / Foster + Partners: p.72; NLÉ: p.97; Numen / For Use: p.52; OMA / Philippe Ruault: p.68; Paramodern / Shuhei Endo: p.29; Paul Riddle: p.105; Paul Rivera: p.14; People's Architecture Office / Gao Tianxia: p.147; Peter Cook: p.42; Pezo von Ellrichshausen: p.125; Philip Vile: p.87; Philppe Raultc: p.96; Pietro Savorelli: p.12; Public Domain: p.44; Rafael Gamo: p.103; Rasmus Hjortshøj / COAST: p.113; RBANUS Architecture & Design: p.143; Refik Anadol / The Innocence Foundation: p.90; RO&AD Architecten: p.66; S27 / Fred Moseley: p.140; Sergio Grazia: p.94; Shu He: p.20, 36; Simon Menges: p.93, 115; Simon Wood / Ateliers Jean Nouvel: p.112; SOM / Nick Merrick / Hedrich Blessing: p.59; SPK / David Chipperfield Architects / Jörg von Bruchhausen: p.37; Su Shengliang: p.117, 121; Suberquitectura: p.34; Tatiana Bilbao Studio: p.124; Thomas Mayer: p.120; Tim Crocker: p.26; Tim Soar: p.27, 126; Tim Soar / Benedetti Architects: p.23; Tirol Advertising / Kathrein Verena: p.13; View Pictures / Getty Images: p.67; Vitra / Julien Lanoo: p.62; Wieland Gleich / ARCHIGRAPHY: p.26.

DIGITAL

11 bit studios: p.255; Adrian Westaway: p.234; AeroSee: p.232; Alexandra Daisy Ginsberg & James King / Osa Johannesson: p.196; Amazon Inc.: p.182; Area/Code: p.155; ART+COM Studios: p.165; Arturo Castro / Kyle McDonald: p.211; Bare Conductive: p.209; BBC User Experience & Design Team: p.208; BBC: p.180, Bloom / Opal Limited: p.178; British Airways: p.162; Bruce Bell / Phi-Hong Ha: p.160; Citymapper: p.236; Condé Nast: p.195; Daici Ano: p.175; Dave Hakkens: p.257; Dentsu London: p.206; Diego Trujillo: p.215; Diller Scofidio + Renfro: p.269; Dirk Jan-Visser: p.249; DixonBaxi: p. 262; Ekene Ijeoma / Hyperakt: p.240; Erik Douglas: p.197; Erwin Zwart: p.241; Evan Roth: p.176; EyeWriter project: p.177; Fernanda Viégas / Martin Wattenberg: p.218; Flipboard Inc.: p.153; Forensic Architecture / Amnesty International: p.266; Galactic Cafe: p.203; Golan Levin (F.A.T. Lab) / Shawn Sims (Sy-Lab): p.214; Government Digital Service / Guy Moorhouse: p.224–5; Greyworld: p.187; Guardian: p.199; Hal Watts: p.256; Hamish Dinsdale / YCN: p.183; Harmonix Music Systems Inc.: p.190; Hayeon Yoo: p.169; Hello-Enzo: p.247; Homeplus: p.207; Hufton+Crow: p.243; Ipogeo / Joe Wentworth / Artemide: p.174; James Frost: p.164; James Medcraft: p.201; Jasmine Cox / BBC R&D: p.239; Jason Bruges Studio: p.184, 198, 209; Jeff Warren: p.231; John Adrian: p.152; Johnny Cash Project: p.188; Jump Studios: p.204; Jouke Schoorl: p.253; Klaus Obermaier / Ars Electronica Futurelab: p.156; LittleBigPlanet: p.168; Loren Schmidt / Katie Rose Pipkin: p.259; Luckybite: p.170; Lytro Inc.: p.227; MakeMagazine: p.171; Marek Z. Jeziorek / Google Inc.: p.263; Marion Ferrec: p.244; Marshmallow Laser Feast: p.254; McCann Australia: p.235; Microsoft: p.205, 223; MIT / Christophe Guberan / Steelcase: p.267; MTV: p.250; mySociety: p.154; Niantic: p.260; Nippon Design Center Inc.: p.226; Oculus VR: p.228; Onedotzero: p.186; OpenFrameworks: p.179; OTHR: p.268; Pachube: p.181; Pan Studio: p.237; Patrick Bergel: p.219; Paul Beech / The Raspberry Pi Foundation: p.222; Peek: p.233; Pier Vona: p.258; Poke: p.161; Post-Spectacular: p.167; rAndom International: p.216; Reactable Systems: p.191; Refugee Text: p.265; Ross Atkin: p.246; Ross Phillips / Showstudio: p.153; Rovio: p.194; Samuel Pious: p.238; Sidekick Creatives: p.230; Six to Start / Naomi Alderman: p.220; Stamen Design: p.157; Stamen Design: p.212; The Guardian Design / Mark Porter Associates: p.202; The Incidental / From No One: p.185; The Rumpusroom: p.166; TheGreenEyl: p.163; Theodore Gray / Touch Press Inc.: p.189; Tim Moore: p.210; Toby Farrow: p.248; Tom Vack / map Maurer GmbH: p.217; Tomo Kihara: p.251; Transport Accident Commission: p.264; Troika: p.172–3; Trussardi: p.158; Unanico Group: p.213; Unfold: p.245; Unicode Emoji / Google Inc.: p.261; Uniform: p.221; United Visual Artist: p.200; Usman Haque: p.159; ustwogames: p.242; WALLPAPER* / Kin Design: p.192; Wellcome Collection: p.252; Will Ragozzino: p.269.

FASHION

A magazine / Nicolas Ouchenir / Stephen Jones: p.341; Adam Katz Sinding: p.338; Agência Fotosite: p.342; Aitor Throup: p. 305; Alexander McQueen: p.301; Amy Gwatkin: p.359; Anastasia Garcia: p.354; Axel Hoedt: p.353; Balmain: p.304; Basso & Brooke: p.290; Brompton Bicycle: p.328; Céline: p.320; Chloe Mukai / Ethical Fashion Initiative: p.322; Chris Moore / Catwalking. com: p.279, 285, 299, 324, 327; Chris Yates: p.356; Christian Dior: p.279; Comme des Garçons: p.300, 337; Comme des Garçons / Trading Museum: p.309; Craig Green: p.329; Dan&Corina Lecca: p. 316; Daniel Dent: p.363; Danielle Scutt: p.275; David Sims / Uniqlo: p.315; Diana Vreeland Estate: p.335; Dior: p.344; DONDA: p.365; Duckie Brown / Platon: p. 292; E. Smith-Leverock: p.330; Ecoalf: p.361; Evans: p.303; Filippo Fior: p.349; firstView: p.277; Focus Features: p.334; Gareth Pugh: p.313; Gavin Bush: p.345; Giles Deacon/ Catwalking.com: p.332; Illuminati II: p.274; Isidora Bojovic: p.340; Issey Miyake: p.321; J.W. Anderson: p.352; Jeremy Sutton-Hibbert / Getty Images: p.287; Jil Sander: p.276; Johannes Helje: p.312; Kristian Lövenborg: p.346; Lanvin: p.295, 310; Linda Grant / Virago: p.291; Louis Vuitton Malletier / Stéphane Murdet: p.331; Louise Goldin: p.294; Luke Stephenson: p.355; Maison Martin Margiela / Giovanni Giannoni: p.289; Margaret Howell Plus: p. 317; Melissa: p.326; Michael Howells / V&A: p.306; Mitchel Sams: p.282; Neil Bedford: p.364; Nick Knight / SHOWstudio: p. 284, 298; Nike: p.360; Ohne Titel: p.311; Onna Harvilahti: p.348; Patrick Gries: p.307; Pierre Hardy: p.286; Platform 13 Ltd / Boudicca: p.302; Prada: p.288, 333, 339; Prada / James Lima / James Jean: p.296; Proenza Schouler / Monica Feudi: p.336; Pussyhat Project: p.362; Raf Simons: p.351; Raquel Azvari: p.314; Rodarte: p.350; Ruth Hogben: p.318; S. Piano / Galliera / Roger-Viollet: p.308; Sadie Williams: p.343; Selve Sundsbø / Art + Commerce: p.319; Steven Meisel / Condé Nast: p.293; SUNO: p.323; Thomas Tait: p.347; Viktor & Rolf / Siebe Tettero / Artist Bar Gallery: p.297; WENN Ltd / Alamy: p.325; Xinhua / Alamy: p.280; Yokamoto: p. 358; Yolanda Dominguez: p.357; Yves Saint Laurent: p.281; Zhou Mi: p.283.

GRAPHICS

Adam Thirlwell / Visual Editions: p.453; Aidan Brown: p.432; Alejandro Magallanes: p.502; Alex Delfanne / Artwise Curators: p.400; Alexandra Daisy Ginsberg: p.482; André Morin: p.467; Andrea Pohancenik: p.433; Angela Luna / Adiff: p.507; Angela Moore: p.477; Animography: p.487; Anomaly / Unit9: p.440; Anthony Burrill: p.460; APFEL / Book Works: p.409; APFEL: p.382, 452; Apple / TBWA Media Arts Lab: p.493; Aram Han Sifuentes: p.515; Baghdad Calling / Geert van Kesteren: p.402; Barnbrook: p.495; Ben Terrett: p.413; Birkhäuser Basel: p.392; Bloomberg Businessweek: p.444; Brave New World: p.470; Buero Bauer: p.498; Cardon Webb: p.463; Carl Kleiner: p.429; Carlos Alejandro: p.435; Channel 4: p.499; Chris Ware / The New Yorker / Condé Nast: p.410; Chris Ware: p.419; Christien Meindertsma / Thomas Eyck / Mathijs Labadie: p.494; Christien Meindertsma: p.423; Colophon Foundry: p.475; Commonwealth of Australia: p.462; Dalton Maag: p.447; Daniel Eatock: p.396; David Lane / Marina Tweed: p.476; Davy Jones: p.390; Dianna Snape: p.393; Eiler Forsius: p.448; Engine Service Design: p.397; Experimental Jetset / Whitney's in-house Graphic Design Dept.: p.472; Farrow: p.417; Francis Ware: p.443; FUEL Design and Publishing: p.414; Gerrit Serne: p.442; Gestaltung Manuela Pfrunder: p.386; Giorgia Lupi / Stefanie Posavec: p.501; Gordon Young / Why Not Associates: p.439; Gordon Young: p.422; Gorilla: p.421; GRUPA: p.503; Guang Yu: p.383; Guardian: p.401; Haraldur Jónasson:

the Design Museum
224-238 Kensington High Street
London W8 6AG

designmuseum.org

First published in 2017
© 2017 the Design Museum

ISBN 978 1 8720 0538 6

Publishing Manager: Mark Cortes Favis
Editors: Tom Wilson and Mark Cortes Favis
Picture Researcher: Anabel Navarro Llorens
Editorial Assistant: Giulia Morale
Designers: Fernando Gutiérrez and
Michael Curia at Studio Fernando Gutiérrez

The Design Museum is proud to partner
with Beazley and greatly appreciates their
support of *Beazley Designs of the Year*.

The publishing team would like to
thank Simon Coppock, Lisa Footitt
and Jessica Read for their editorial
contributions; the exhibition curators,
jurors, nominators and nominees without
whom this book would not be possible;
Fernando Gutiérrez and Michael Curia
for their patience, creativity and enthusiasm;
and to our many colleagues at the
Design Museum for their support
and encouragement.

Printed in Italy by VeronaLibri